Computers and Telecommunications Networks

MICHAEL PURSER
Department of Computer Science
Trinity College
Dublin

BLACKWELL SCIENTIFIC PUBLICATIONS

OXFORD LONDON EDINBURGH

BOSTON PALO ALTO MELBOURNE

© 1987 by
Blackwell Scientific Publications
Editorial offices:
Osney Mead, Oxford, OX2 0EL
(*Orders:* Tel. (0865) 240201
8 John Street, London, WC1N 2ES
23 Ainslie Place, Edinburgh, EH3 6AJ
52 Beacon Street, Boston
  Massachusetts 02108, USA
667 Lytton Avenue, Palo Alto
  California 94301, USA
107 Barry Street, Carlton
  Victoria 3053, Australia

First published 1987

Photoset by Enset (Photosetting),
Midsomer Norton, Bath, Avon.
Printed and bound in Great Britain
by Billing & Sons Limited, Worcester.

Coc.B 36980 /18.50. 6.88

DISTRIBUTORS

USA and Canada
  Blackwell Scientific Publications Inc
  PO Box 50009, Palo Alto
  California 94303
  (*Orders:* Tel. (415) 965–4081)

Australia
  Blackwell Scientific Publications
  (Australia) Pty Ltd
  107 Barry Street,
  Carlton, Victoria 3053
  (*Orders:* Tel. (03) 347 0300)

British Library
Cataloguing in Publication Data

Purser, Michael
  Computers and telecommunications
  networks.
  1. Computer networks   2. Telecommunication
  I. Title
  621.38′0413   TK5105.5

████████████████████████
████████████████████████

Library of Congress
Cataloging-in-Publication Data

Purser, Michael, 1937–
  Computers and telecommunications
  networks.

  Bibliography: p.
  Includes index.
  1. Telecommunication systems.
  2. Data transmission systems.
  3. Computer networks. I. Title.
  TK5102.5.P87 1987   004.6   86-31727

ISBN 0-632-01647-7
ISBN 0-632-01648-5 (pbk.)

Contents

Preface

This book addresses the topic of the 'convergence' between data processing and telecommunications. It is written largely from the standpoint of the computer person who finds himself more and more concerned with telecommunication systems, as the means of linking terminals in general and computers in particular, and as subjects of control and management by computers.

Telecommunication engineers have often been considered to be slow to grasp the implications of computers and the power and flexibility of control by software. However, this charge can hardly be levelled against them today, although it may well have been true in the past. On the contrary, it is the computer expert who is likely to be almost totally ignorant of well-established disciplines such as traffic theory; and who has very little appreciation of the complexity, sheer high speed and large-scale parallel processing which characterize, for example, digital switches. The book attempts to remedy this situation, by presenting networks of many sorts in a form comprehensible to computer people.

In Chapter 1 basic network concepts and traffic theory are presented. In Chapters 2 and 3 circuit-switched and store-and-forward (SAF) data networks are reviewed, respectively. The aim of these two chapters is to review and clarify basic switching techniques. Chapter 4 looks at network design and routing techniques. Chapter 5 specifically considers the area of convergence between data and other network services. The role of PBXs and LANs in interfacing to networks is reviewed, and Integrated Services Digital Networks (ISDNs) are introduced. Chapter 6 discusses the Open Systems Interconnection Reference Model (OSI/RM). It is presented late in the book so that the need for such an architectural framework (however defective) can be appreciated. It was felt that an earlier introduction might be tedious and incomprehensible. Chapter 6 terminates by discussing telematic and Message Handling Systems in the OSI/RM context. Finally, Chapter 7 looks towards future Integrated Broadband Communication Networks (IBCNs) and other developments such as the provision of security in networks.

Where reference is made to international standards, those of CCITT have been used preferentially. This is not to minimize the importance of ISO, ECMA and other standardization bodies. However, it is felt that in the real world of telecommunications, wherever the inspiration may come from, it is the CCITT standard which nearly always prevails. (A glossary is provided explaining the meaning of 'CCITT' 'OSI/RM' and other abbreviations, as well as several standard technical terms.)

The book presupposes a familiarity with basic data communication topics such as synchronous transmission and line procedures, but a detailed knowledge of such subjects is not necessary. It also presumes a certain command of mathematics in one or two places, but the reader who finds this disconcerting may skip them without significant loss.

It should also be pointed out that the book is concerned with 'active' switching performed by 'intelligent' networks which consciously route traffic. 'Passive' switching as used in many Local Area Networks (LANs) is assumed to be familiar to readers and is not described in detail.

Finally, it is my pleasure to be able to record the support and encouragement I have received whilst writing this book both from my wife and family and from students in Trinity College, Dublin. The book was typed by Helen Smith, to whom I owe a great debt for her efficiency, patience and good nature.

Michael Purser
Trinity College, Dublin
1987

Chapter 1
Computers and Networks

1.1 WHAT IS A NETWORK ?

A computer network can be defined in various ways. One approach is to consider the network to be simply the 'physical network'. The physical network may be said to consist of all internal switching nodes,* their interconnecting links and the links leading to externally connected devices. The external devices themselves, computers and terminals collectively referred to as Data Terminal Equipment (DTE), are then considered as attached to, rather than forming part of, the physical network (Fig. 1.1).

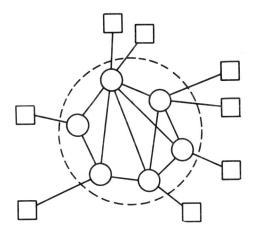

Fig. 1.1   A 'physical network' with switching nodes.

This minimal definition is convenient when we consider the typical control of a network, in which the physical network is operated by a Telecommunication Administration (TA, or more commonly 'PTT'), while the DTEs belong to users or subscribers.

*We call the points where links unite and traffic is switched 'Nodes' or 'Exchanges'. When the switching function is to be emphasized a Node is sometimes referred to as a 'Switch'.

1

Another, wider view would hold that the network consists not only of the physical network plus all attached DTEs, but of all the services available 'on' it—including those provided on attached DTEs. What is the network but the totality of all services that can be reached from any particular DTE?

Without considering further possible definitions, it is worth pointing out some of the problems with the above ones. For example, is a system for interconnecting many computers which contains no *switching* nodes a valid physical network? In such a system a sending DTE broadcasts a message, in which the selected destinations are identified over a common medium linking all DTEs; only the selected DTEs are supposed to receive it (Fig. 1.2). A minimal network of this type might connect only two DTEs. Again, is a 'star network' in which there is no switching, but all traffic is to or from one central DTE (Fig. 1.3) a valid physical network? In this book we shall not consider these networks which do not have switches, except superficially. However, they are generally regarded as valid networks, since many local area networks [1] and satellite-based networks use the broadcast-and-selected-destination technique; while the meshless (or netless) star network is one of the most familiar configurations for computer systems.

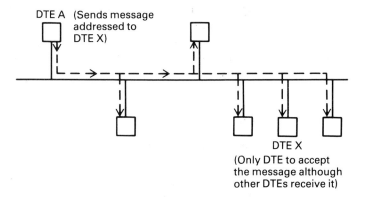

Fig. 1.2 A network without switching.

But, if we take the wide view that any system of interconnected computers and services is a network, then many networks apparently have no identifiable boundaries. They stretch worldwide; since from one

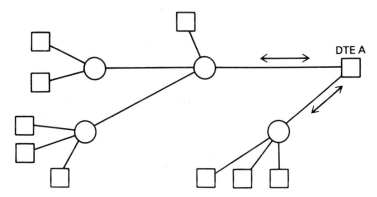

Fig. 1.3   A star network. All traffic in network is to/from DTE A.

terminal you can probably access literally millions of machines and services on the combined interconnected data, telephone, telex and other networks of the earth.

To avoid these problems we shall not attempt a precise definition of the term 'network'. However, the user should envisage a network being generally composed of the nodes and transmission links under the control of a single administration, using a more or less homogeneous technology; plus the DTEs immediately connected to it. When we wish to confine remarks to the switching and transmission portion we shall call it the physical or 'bearer' network; since it carries or bears the traffic, but is not, in general, a source or sink of traffic. When we want to emphasize the services (other than pure transmission and switching) available on or via the network, we shall explicitly use the term 'network services'.

1.1.1 Computers in networks

When the term 'computer network' is used, the common interpretation is that a network, in which the DTEs are computers, is meant. But in almost every network today the switching nodes are, if not computers, then largely controlled by computers. For the purposes of this book we regard these computer-based switches as comprising as important a subject of discussion as the attached DTEs.

Moreover, most services supplied 'on' the network, i.e. supplied by the administration operating the physical networks, are also based on computers. These computer-based services may be built into the nodes in software, or perhaps provided on an attached computer which is in every way like a DTE, except that it is owned and operated by the administration of the physical network and not by a subscriber (Fig. 1.4).

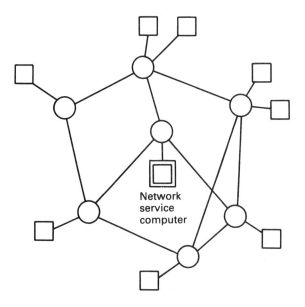

Fig. 1.4   A service 'on' the network provided on a special computer.

Yet another instance of computers which are not DTEs in networks is provided by the 'gateway'. A gateway is an interface between two distinct networks, in which some sort of conversion or mapping between the formats and functions of data valid for each of the two networks takes place (Fig. 1.5). The gateway enables traffic to travel usefully between the two distinct networks.

This book aims to discuss the use of computers in networks, with particular emphasis on networks used to carry data traffic, wherever those computers may be—inside or outside the physical network.

1.1.2 Different switching techniques

It has been stated that we are concerned with *switched* networks. A switched network is one in which traffic arriving on some link at a switching node is routed out on another (or possibly the same) link,

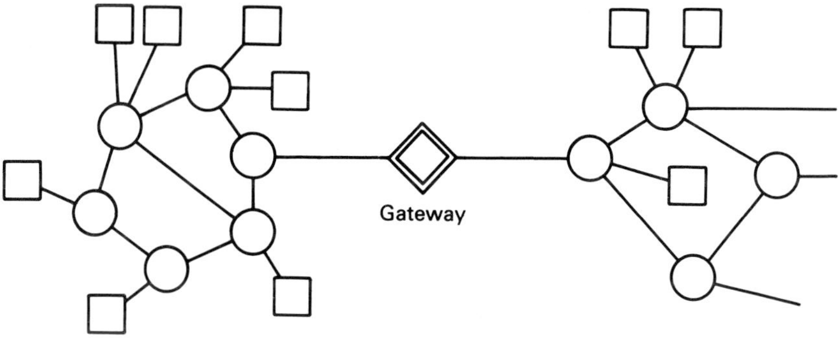

Fig. 1.5 A gateway between two networks.

under the active control of the node. If we consider a data-switching node, it makes the decision as to how to route the traffic on the basis of information normally carried in the traffic data. That information may be included in each data unit which has to be switched, like the address on the envelope of a letter in the post. Alternatively, the information may be supplied at the start of a data exchange across the network, usually in the form of special data units or commands to establish a 'call', in a manner analogous to the telephone network. Once established, a call is a conceptual pipeline through the node, through which all traffic associated with the call is routed. The call must, of course, be cleared sometime.

These two distinct ways of switching go by different names in different circumstances, but may be broadly classified as 'message-switching' (like a letter) or 'call-switching' (like a telephone call).

The ways in which data are handled (as opposed to routed) on passing through a switch also separate into two broad categories. In one technique, called 'circuit-switching', there is effectively no buffering in the node, incoming data are routed out directly. Since there is no buffering, if continuous data streams are to be handled successfully, the rate of input and the rate of output must be the same. Circuit-switching is usually a subclass of call-switching, since it is hardly feasible to dispense with buffering if each data unit has to be examined and routed independently, as it would be if message-switching were used. There is in effect a direct correspondence between the circuit (the physical pipeline) and the call (the conceptual pipeline). Alternatively, the 'store-and-forward' technique may be used for handling data traffic. In this case, a data unit is stored in the node before being forwarded. Queues of such stored data units can build up in the node, depending on the availability of an outgoing link for forwarding. The store-and-forward technique can be used with call-switching, notably in the case of virtual call packet-switched data networks. It is almost always used with message-switching.

Store-and-forward is the technique which most obviously suggests itself to those familiar with computers. It does however present an immediate problem. How much buffering capacity should be provided in a node and what is to be done if it threatens to become exhausted? This problem does not exist with circuit-switching, but instead a question of efficiency arises. The capacity of the circuit, the physical pipeline, is wasted if the user does not maintain a continuous flow of data.

A compromise switching technique is that of packet-switching. Packets are small blocks of data, usually of a fixed maximum size (e.g. 128 octets). If a real message is larger than this size it is divided into the requisite number of packets. The packets are handled by the store-and-foward technique. If message-switching is used (each packet is self-contained) we refer to a packet as a 'datagram'. If call-switching is used, we have a conceptual pipeline named a 'virtual call' (VC). By placing restrictions on the maximum packet-size the buffering problems associated with store-and-forward are somewhat eased. By choosing store-and-forward rather than circuit-switching the waste of capacity when handling 'bursty' non-continuous data flows is obviated.

VC packet-switched data networks (PSDNs) are favoured by PTTs, for reasons we shall discuss later, for public PSDNs. Datagram PSDNs are more acceptable to academics and researchers for their greater flexibility, and for whom the concept of a 'call' is not relevant to the bearer network, but only to the users involved in the communication.

Circuit-switching is discussed in Chapter 2, store-and-forward switching in Chapter 3. In Chapter 4 some topics applicable to both techniques are presented, and in Chapter 5 new types of networks are discussed, in particular Integrated Services Digital Networks.

1.1.3 Interfacing to networks

A switching network exists in its own right. It is not 'transparent' to users. If we consider the star network of Fig. 1.3 we can see that such a network can be largely transparent since control is vested in the central computer. All other DTEs should be compatible with it and its physical extensions, such as communication links. However, Fig. 1.2 shows that when there is no single central control, if arbitrary DTEs are to be able to exchange data meaningfully, then some standards (which may be usefully called 'network standards') should exist. Such standards would at least define how to connect physically to the network, and how destination addresses are to be represented in messages so that all potential recipients can recognize them.

Thus even a 'passive' network, such as that of Fig. 1.2, will require standards, defining the interface to the network, which are not necessarily those normally used by the individual DTEs in the absence of a network.

In the case of networks with active switching the need for network interfacing standards is even greater. This is because the network is no longer transparent to users, except at a considerably higher level of communication. To establish contact with a DTE *across* the network an originating DTE must talk *to* the network itself. Specifically the originating DTE must send information to the nodes themselves, so that they may actively route the data.

Thus the existence of a switched network implies the existence of interfacing standards for it. All computers or other DTEs requiring connection to such a network must be adapted, by suitable hardware and software means, to be compatible with those standards.

Among such interfacing standards are to be included the well-known X.25 [2] and ISDN [3] recommendations. They are international standards, recommended by CCITT for use with specific types of networks throughout the world. The need for an interfacing standard for a given network has been made clear, but why have an *international* standard for all networks of that type? The answer is based on economics. Since DTEs require special hardware and software to interface to a given network, there are capital costs incurred by network users, as well as current costs for transmitting or receiving data across the network. It is obviously advantageous to users and manufacturers of DTEs alike if those capital costs can be kept as low as possible, by ensuring that the interfacing hardware and software are as widely applicable as possible.

1.1.4 Internal and internetwork standards

Just as it is clear that interfacing standards are required for a given network, it is also clear that there must be internal standards. It would be ludicrous to have to define a different procedure for the exchange of data between each pair of interconnected nodes in a network. Some internal standards must apply to the use of links and to the construction and behaviour of the nodes or switches themselves. It is not clear, however, that these internal standards should be applicable to other networks besides the one under consideration.

Nevertheless, if distinct networks are to be interconnected usefully (Fig. 1.5), it is desirable that their internal standards should not be too dissimilar; otherwise the gateway becomes unnecessarily complicated. After all, seen from the outside, a collection of interconnected networks is just a single large network. The commands given by a DTE to this network (in accordance with the interfacing standards) have somehow to be amenable for interpretation by *all* the nodes which might receive them. This will certainly be facilitated if such commands are forwarded internally in the network in some relatively standardized form. Examples of functions needing such standardization are addressing and routing, which are relevant to the combined networks.

In practice, although international standards do not exist for all aspects of internodal communication, standards do exist for multiplexing, signalling and addressing. More specifically, there are international standards, such as X.75 [4], for the interconnection of networks belonging to different administrations.

1.1.5 End-to-end communication

The aim of the network is to make the interconnection of DTEs possible. This is pointless if the DTEs which have been connected are incapable of understanding the messages received from each other. There is a need for the standardization of end-to-end messages (that is, messages between DTEs) across the network. At this 'higher' level we are in a sense back to the situation discussed earlier in which a transparent network is available, provided that the lower level interfacing standards have been obeyed.

Firstly, these higher-level, end-to-end standards must address the problem of concealing or masking any residual problems not taken care of by the network. Such problems might include loss of messages by the network. The end-to-end standards should define means for the detection of, and recovery from, such network errors. Secondly, agreement must be reached on the method for establishing communication between 'entities' or 'processes' within the corresponding DTEs; not merely between the DTEs themselves. A remote user at a terminal may wish to access a particular service in a computer across the network. How is that service selected? Does he have to use a different mechanism for all such services in different computers, or is there an (internationally) standardized procedure?

Between corresponding processes there must then exist agreement on the format and the meaning of end-to-end messages. This stipulation is anything but trivial, if one considers the very wide range of messages one could envisage sending between computers. For example, one might send a job file to be run on one remote computer; or one might receive a colour display for a graphics terminal from another such computer.

This requirement for end-to-end standardization has been addressed by the International Standards Organisation (ISO), among others. It is discussed in the general framework of the Open Systems Interconnection Reference Model (OSI/RM) [5] in Chapter 6.

1.1.6 Services and applications

The mention of the need for standardization on the format and meaning of end-to-end messages leads naturally to the topic of services and applications. After all, end-to-end communication is not an end in itself; it exists to enable services to be used or applications to be performed. It could be argued that networks are only incidental to services or applications, but this is a simplification. For example, an application which involves many simultaneous participants, such as a real-time teleconference, presupposes some sort of networking infrastructure. More importantly, the boundaries between the bearer network and the services supplied by means of it are not always clear. To see this one need only consider the Telex network, where the DTEs are usually integrally supplied by the TA.

A more up-to-date example of services closely allied to the supporting network is provided by that of Electronic Mail in which documents, in coded electronic form, are exchanged or shared between users via a network. The Message Handling Systems (MHS) of the X.400 [6] recommendation are a concrete case. The end-to-end service enabling documents coded in facsimile, teletex or other formats, to be exchanged is associated with explicit functions built into the supporting network, such as the 'holding' of traffic for users who are not on-line.

Moreover, purely end-to-end applications, such as the transfer of files between two communicating computers, are affected by the nature of the intervening network. Some network technologies are suitable for some applications and other technologies for other applications. A classic example is that of packet-switching: admirable for bursty interactive traffic; inefficient (and usually very expensive) for bulk data transfers.

Thus although it may be possible to discuss networks without discussing the applications running 'on top' of them, it would give only an incomplete view of the subject. This subject of services and applications is also discussed in Chapter 6.

1.1.7 An overview

The foregoing sections, under the general heading of 'The nature of a network', have touched on some of the topics to be covered in later chapters. It will be noted that standards (for interfacing, for internetworking and for end-to-end communication) form a central theme. But no less important is the underlying technology, which provides the infrastructure of the network. It has to be chosen, designed or dimensioned to be able to support the traffic which the users and applications generate.

Accordingly, the remainder of this chapter is devoted to a brief introduction to traffic and network theory, which can then be applied to dimensioning and analysing the performance of networks discussed in later sections.

1.2 SOME BASIC TRAFFIC THEORY [7]

A general requirement in designing the elements of a network, be they switches or multiplexed transmission circuits, is to be able to state what traffic they will support.

All networks *concentrate*. No network, except possibly a very small and specialized one, is designed to handle all the traffic that could arise at the same time. The basic assumption is that traffic arises from each particular source with a certain probability. The network is built to support the sum of all such traffic up to a certain level, the network's capacity. Associated with that capacity is a 'Grade of Service' which is the probability of the offered traffic exceeding that capacity. For example a Grade of Service of 0.1% means, in approximate language, that there is a chance of 1 in 1000 that the network will become overloaded because the offered traffic exceeds the capacity. The dimensioning of a network is thus a complex exercise, in which one starts from assumptions (hopefully well justified) about the traffic offered by users; and proceeds to design the network to provide capacity where needed at minimum cost, subject to Grade of Service constraints.

To further our discussion it is necessary to define 'traffic'.

We shall define traffic in terms of 'calls', such as ordinary telephone calls, but traffic theory, which is merely a branch of queue theory, is of more general application, as will be shown. The amount of traffic, carried by a system in time T is defined as

$$\sum_i n_i h_i$$

where n_i = the number of calls originating from terminal i in time T, h_i = the average holding time of the calls from terminal i, and the sum is over all terminals, $i = 1$ to N.

The traffic flow is defined as

$$A = \sum n_i h_i / T.$$

If the traffic characteristics for all terminals are the same, then

$$A = (n/T)hN.$$

In other words, the traffic flow is the call rate per terminal multiplied by the average hold time, multiplied by the number of terminals. It is easily seen that A is the average number of simultaneous calls, as follows: If P_k is the probability of k simultaneous calls then

$$P_k = \left(\frac{nh}{T}\right)^k \left(1 - \frac{nh}{T}\right)^{N-k} N!/k!(N-k)!$$

since (nh/T) is the probability of a given terminal being busy with a call and there are $N!/k!(N-k)!$ ways in which k terminals can be busy.

Therefore

$$P_k = \left(\frac{A}{N}\right)^k \left(1 - \frac{A}{N}\right)^{N-k} N!/k!(N-k)! \tag{1.1}$$

The expected number of simultaneous calls is then

$$\sum_{k=1}^{N} kP_k = N \cdot \frac{A}{N} \sum_{k=1}^{N} \left(\frac{A}{N} \right)^{k-1} \left(1 - \frac{A}{N} \right)^{N-1-(k-1)}$$

$$(N-1)!/(k-1)!(N-1-(k-1))!$$

$$= A \sum_{k=0}^{N-1} \left(\frac{A}{N} \right)^{k} \left(1 - \frac{A}{N} \right)^{N-1-k} (N-1)!/k!(N-1-k)!$$

$$= A$$

since the summation is unity. Therefore traffic flow is the average number of simultaneous calls. It can also be shown that A is the average number of calls arising in the average hold time, h.

The (dimensionless) unit in which A is measured is the Erlang, in honour of the principal founder of traffic theory. It will be seen that, for example, six 10-minute calls (or three 20-minute calls) in an hour represents a traffic flow of one Erlang. Another unit sometimes used to measure traffic flow is that of hundred-call-seconds per hour (ccs/hour). Since there are thirty-six 100-seconds in an hour, 1 Erlang = 36 ccs/h.

It is well known that Equation (1.1), the binomial distribution, tends to the Poisson distribution as $N \to \infty$, assuming A remains finite. Thus for large N

$$P_k = \frac{A^k}{k!} \exp(-A).$$

If only M simultaneous calls can be supported by the system, then the probability that it is fully (or over-) loaded is

$$\sum_{k=M}^{\infty} P_k = \sum_{k=M}^{\infty} \frac{A}{k!} \exp(-A). \tag{1.2}$$

This is the Molina equation for obtaining a Grade of Service. The formula suffers from two limitations:

(1) It assumes that calls, over and above the M which can be supported simultaneously, actually exist. This is the 'blocked-calls-held' supposition. In practice most networks reject such calls, so the offered traffic is in fact limited by the system's capacity. There are no such surplus calls, with associated holding times present.

(2) If we take Equation (1.2) as a measure of the probability of system

congestion, it assumes that congestion exists when all *M* supportable calls exist. This is called 'time-congestion', the probability of the system being fully loaded. It is not the same as 'call-congestion' which is the probability of a call being rejected, i.e. an $(M+1)$st call arising.

The difference between time-congestion and call-congestion is small and can be ignored and since time-congestion is more easily computed, we shall use it. However, the 'blocked-calls-held' assumption (involving holding times) does make a material difference, so we shall recalculate the time-congestion using different assumptions.

Let us assume that when there are *k* calls present the probability of a new call arriving in time d*t* is $(\lambda_k \, \mathrm{d}t)$ and the probability of a call terminating is $(\mu_k \, \mathrm{d}t)$. Then

$$P_k(t+\mathrm{d}t) = \text{the probability of } k \text{ simultaneous calls being present}$$
$$\text{at time } (t+\mathrm{d}t)$$
$$= P_k(t)(1-\lambda_k \, \mathrm{d}t-\mu_k \, \mathrm{d}t)+P_{k-1}(t)\lambda_{k-1} \, \mathrm{d}t+P_{k+1}(t)\mu_{k+1} \, \mathrm{d}t$$

or

$$\frac{\mathrm{d}P_k}{\mathrm{d}t} = -(\lambda_k+\mu_k)P_k+\lambda_{k-1}P_{k-1}+\mu_{k+1}P_{k+1}.$$

In the steady state the probability P_k can be assumed to be constant, so

$$(\lambda_k+\mu_k)P_k = \lambda_{k-1}P_{k-1}+\mu_{k+1}P_{k+1}. \tag{1.3}$$

If we assume $\mu_0 = 0$, so that a call cannot end if none exists, and $\lambda_M = 0$, so that a call cannot arise if *M* already exists, we have limiting equations

$$\lambda_0 P_0 = \mu_1 P_1 \qquad (\lambda_{-1} \text{ is also zero}) \tag{1.4}$$

and

$$\mu_M P_M = \lambda_{M-1}P_{M-1} \qquad (\mu_{M+1} \text{ is also zero}) \tag{1.5}$$

The solution to equations (1.3), (1.4) and (1.5) is

$$P_k = \left(\prod_{i=0}^{k-1} \lambda_i \Big/ \prod_{i=1}^{k} \mu_i\right)P_0 \qquad k = 1 \text{ to } M \tag{1.6}$$

and

$$P_k = 0 \qquad k > M,$$

where Π is the symbol for the product. Now the sum of all the probabilities P_k, $k = 0$ to M must be unity, which thus determines P_0

$$1 = P_0 + P_0 \sum_{k=1}^{M} \left(\prod_{i=0}^{k-1} \lambda_i \bigg/ \prod_{i=1}^{k} \mu_i \right). \tag{1.7}$$

We now make two further assumptions

(1) We assume $\lambda_k(k = 0$ to $(M - 1))$ is constant, λ. This means that we assume we are dealing with a large number of terminals, so that the fact that some are already busy does not materially affect the probability of arrival of new calls.

(2) We assume $\mu_k = k\mu$. This effectively means that we assume each call's duration has an exponential distribution [8] and that in time dt it has probability $\mu\,dt$ of terminating, given that it has not already terminated. k independent calls then give a probability of $k\mu\,dt$ for any one terminating in time dt. The average call duration is also $h = 1/\mu$. Substituting in equation (1.6) we have

$$P_k - = P_0(\lambda h)^k / k! = P_0(A^k / k!) \tag{1.8}$$

and from (1.5):

$$1 = P_0 \left(1 + \sum_{k=1}^{M} A^k / k! \right),$$

giving

$$P_0 = 1 \bigg/ \sum_{k=0}^{M} A^k / k! \tag{1.9}$$

Substituting Equation (1.9) in (1.8) gives the Erlang-B Formula for the probability of k simultaneous calls

$$P_k = \frac{A^k / k!}{\displaystyle\sum_{i=0}^{M} A^i / i!}. \tag{1.10}$$

From this we can calculate the time-congestion $E(M, A)$,

$$E(M, A) = \frac{A^M / M!}{\displaystyle\sum_{i=0}^{M} A^i / i!}. \tag{1.11}$$

$E(M, A)$ is the probability of a system capable of supporting M simultaneous calls being fully occupied, given that the offered traffic flow is A and assuming that any calls in excess of M are rejected—the 'blocked-calls-lost' assumption.

1.2.1 Applications of the Theory

Suppose 1000 terminals each generate 0.1 Erlang in the busy hour and they are connected to a switch capable of handling 123 simultaneous calls. Then $A = 100$, $M = 123$, and the Grade of Service (the probability of full loading) is

$$E(123,100) = 0.01 \text{ or } 1\%.$$

If 1% of the traffic is lost, then 99 Erlang is the average traffic flow supported by the 123 internal links in the switch, so each link has a load factor of $99/123 = 0.80$, or 80%.

Again, if 10 terminals each generate 0.1 Erlang, and the switch can support two simultaneous calls, then $A = 1$, $M = 2$ and the Grade of Service $E(2,1) = \frac{1}{3}$, or 33%. Nevertheless, the load factor is only 33%. This shows that equation (1.11) is highly non-linear; and that low traffic flows require much more capacity to handle them in proportion to high traffic flows; and that the former systems must be lightly loaded to maintain a Grade of Service. Conversely, if the offered traffic does increase, systems handling large traffic flows (being more heavily loaded already) are more susceptible to total overload.

In practice, of course, in most systems the required Grade of Service $E(A, M)$ and the offered traffic A are given. The objective is to calculate M. Figure 1.6 is a graph of M against A for given Grades of Service. The curves can be approximated by straight lines for large A, for example

$$M = 5.5 + 1.17A \qquad \text{for } E(M, A) = 1\%, \qquad (1.12)$$

$$M = 7.8 + 1.28A \qquad \text{for } E(M, A) = 0.1\%. \qquad (1.13)$$

The above examples might apply to circuit-switched exchanges. An example more relevant to data traffic is shown in Fig. 1.7. Here a population of 80 terminal users each generating 0.2 Erlang can dial in via the telephone network to a communications multiplexor, offering M channels on a trunk link to a computer. For 1% Grade of Service we can calculate that 25 channels should be provided, since $A = 16$. Equation (1.12) is used.

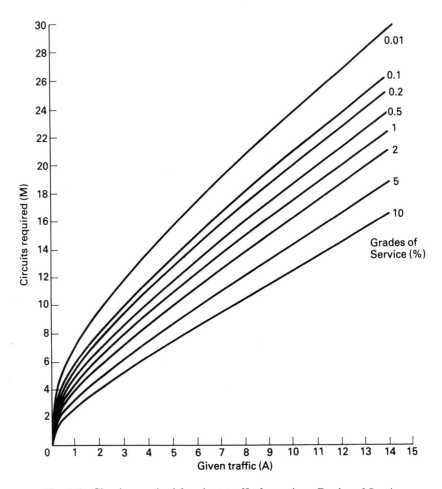

Fig. 1.6 Circuits required for given traffic for various Grades of Service.

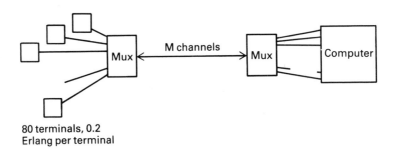

80 terminals, 0.2
Erlang per terminal

Fig. 1.7 M multiplexed channels shared by 80 terminals.

But traffic theory is not necessarily restricted to the notion of a 'call'. Suppose, in a message-switching system, each message spends on average 100 ms in a switch and the average message rate is 60 per second. Then on average there are six messages in the switch at any time, and for 0.1% Grade of Service, using Equation (1.13), we should provide 16 message buffers.

In this instance one might question the validity of the assumption that $\mu_k = k\mu$, which is the one which implies that each message remains a standard average time in the switch. In practice when more than a certain number of messages are present, say n, then the probability of some message finally leaving the switch ceases to rise with k. Essentially this is because all n output channels are occupied. Assuming $M > n$ we would have

$$\lambda_k = \lambda \ 0 \leq k \leq M-1, \ \mu_k = k\mu \qquad 1 \leq k \leq n-1$$

$$\lambda_k = 0 \ M \leq k \qquad , \ \mu_k = n\mu \qquad n \leq k \leq M$$

and from Equation (1.6) we can find

$$P_k = P_0 A^k/k! \qquad 1 \leq k \leq n-1$$

$$= P_0(A/n)^k n^n/n! \qquad n \leq k \leq M$$

with

$$P_0 = 1 \bigg/ \left(\sum_{k=0}^{n-1} A^k/k! + (n^n/n!) \cdot ((A/n)^n - (A/n)^{M+1})/(1-A/n) \right) \ (1.14)$$

If we take $M = 16$ for $A(= \lambda/\mu) = 6$, which gave us a Grade of Service of 0.1% previously, but now we put $n = 1$, we find that P_M, the probability of all buffers being occupied, has risen to about 0.2%. The moral is that one should check one's assumption when applying these formulae for traffic handling.

The time congestion, the probability of all output channels being occupied, is nearly 9.5%. It is given by

$$\sum_{k=n}^{M} P_k = P_0(n^n/n!)(A/n)^n(1-(A/n)^{M-n})/(1-A/n) \qquad (1.15)$$

This is the Erlang-C formula.

1.3 SOME BASIC NETWORK THEORY

Just as the designer of a network is concerned with the traffic carrying capacity of the elements of the network, so he is concerned with that of the network as a whole. How many separate channels can be established between A and B across a network? What is the maximum number of internodal links over all the shortest paths joining such source-destination pairs? These topics are discussed more fully in a later chapter, but some of the basic concepts are reviewed here.

A network, for example that of Fig. 1.8, can be represented by a connectivity matrix, C, in which the elements C_{ij} are unity where node i is directly connected to node j, and zero otherwise. In the figure we have not included attached terminals as nodes in the network. If, in multiplying matrices, we take addition to be a logical 'OR' and multiplication to be a logical 'AND', we can see that the elements of C^2, $(C^2)_{ij}$, show whether nodes i and j are connected by a path, of length

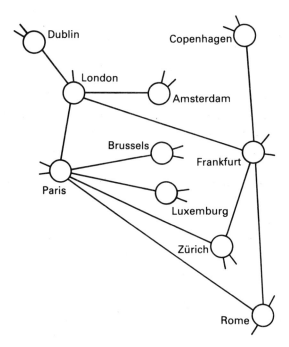

Fig. 1.8 An example of a network (Euronet c. 1982).

two internodal links, or not. $D_2 = C + C^2$ shows all those nodes connected by paths of length two or less. Following this procedure, if $D_n = C + C^2 \ldots + C^n$ is the first matrix in the series with no zero elements, then the *diameter* of the network is n. No two nodes are more than n links apart. In the case of Fig. 1.8 we have

	A	B	D	F	K	L	P	R	X	Z
A	0	0	0	0	0	1	0	0	0	0
B	0	0	0	0	0	0	1	0	0	0
D	0	0	0	0	0	1	0	0	0	0
F	0	0	0	0	1	1	0	1	0	1
K	0	0	0	1	0	0	0	0	0	0
L	1	0	1	1	0	0	1	0	0	0
P	0	1	0	0	0	1	0	1	1	1
R	0	0	0	1	0	0	1	0	0	0
X	0	0	0	0	0	0	1	0	0	0
Z	0	0	0	1	0	0	1	0	0	0

$C =$ (above)

$C^4 =$

```
1 0 1 1 0 0 1 0 0 0
0 1 0 0 1 1 0 1 1 1
1 0 1 1 0 0 1 0 0 0
1 0 1 1 0 0 1 0 0 0
0 1 0 0 1 1 0 1 1 1
0 1 0 0 1 1 0 1 1 1
1 0 1 1 0 0 1 0 0 0
0 1 0 0 1 1 0 1 1 1
0 1 0 0 1 1 0 1 1 1
0 1 0 0 1 1 0 1 1 1
```

$C^2 =$

```
1 0 1 1 0 0 1 0 0 0
0 1 0 0 0 1 0 1 1 1
1 0 1 1 0 0 1 0 0 0
1 0 1 1 0 0 1 0 0 0
0 0 0 0 1 1 0 1 0 1
0 1 0 0 1 1 0 1 1 1
1 0 1 1 0 0 1 0 0 0
0 1 0 0 1 1 0 1 1 1
0 1 0 0 0 1 0 1 1 1
0 1 0 0 1 1 0 1 1 1
```

$D_2 =$

```
1 0 1 1 0 1 1 0 0 0
0 1 0 0 0 1 1 1 1 1
1 0 1 1 0 1 1 0 0 0
1 0 1 1 1 1 1 1 0 1
0 0 0 1 1 1 0 1 0 1
1 1 1 1 1 1 1 1 1 1
1 1 1 1 0 1 1 1 1 1
0 1 0 1 1 1 1 1 1 1
0 1 0 0 0 1 1 1 1 1
0 1 0 1 1 1 1 1 1 1
```

$C^3 =$

```
0 1 0 0 1 1 0 1 1 1
1 0 1 1 0 0 1 0 0 0
0 1 0 0 1 1 0 1 1 1
0 1 0 0 1 1 0 1 1 1
1 0 1 1 0 0 1 0 0 0
1 0 1 1 0 0 1 0 0 0
0 1 0 0 1 1 0 1 1 1
1 0 1 1 0 0 1 0 0 0
1 0 1 1 0 0 1 0 0 0
1 0 1 1 0 0 1 0 0 0
```

$D_3 =$

```
1 1 1 1 1 1 1 1 1 1
1 1 1 1 0 1 1 1 1 1
1 1 1 1 1 1 1 1 1 1
1 1 1 1 1 1 1 1 1 1
1 0 1 1 1 1 1 1 0 1
1 1 1 1 1 1 1 1 1 1
1 1 1 1 1 1 1 1 1 1
1 1 1 1 1 1 1 1 1 1
1 1 1 1 0 1 1 1 1 1
1 1 1 1 1 1 1 1 1 1
```

$D_4 =$ All elements are unity

The network is actually Euronet [9], as it was about 1982, and it can be seen that its diameter was 4, that London was no further than two links from any node, while Luxembourg and Brussels were both four links from Copenhagen (see the zero elements in D_3).

The calculations suffer from three defects:

(1) Bogus connections are included. For example from C^2 the Dublin-to-Dublin distance is 2. In short, paths which double back are included.

(2) The *number* of paths of length n between two nodes is not counted. If we did real addition and multiplication, instead of ORs and ANDs, the elements of C^n would give these numbers; subject to the first defect of counting bogus paths.

(3) The capacities of the links—for example the number of channels each link will support—are not taken into account.

Rather than refine the calculating procedure to remedy these defects (which is done in Chapter 4 and where the Ford–Fulkerson algorithm for calculating flow capacities between pairs of nodes is also presented), we prefer to point out that the procedure is only one of many algorithms which can be applied to the network as a whole. This particular algorithm can serve to identify the minimal number of internodal links between any pair of nodes; the maximum minimum giving the diameter. Refined, it can give the maximum flow capacity (or simultaneous channels) linking any pair of nodes. But such results may be of limited use in isolation.

REFERENCES

1 Local Area Networks are considered in many texts. See for example: *Introduction to Local Area Networks,* Digital Equipment Corporation, 1982; *Networking with Microcomputers* by P.H. Jesty, Blackwell Scientific Publications, 1985; *Data Communications for Programmers* by M. Purser, Addison-Wesley, 1986.

2 *Recommendation X.25,* CCITT Red Book **VIII. 3,** Geneva, 1985.

3 *I-Series Recommendations,* CCITT Red Book **III. 5,** Geneva, 1985.

4 *Recommendation X.75,* CCITT Red Book **VIII. 4,** Geneva, 1985.

5 ISO 7498, International Standards Organization.

6 *X.400 Series Recommendations*, CCITT Red Book **VIII. 7,** Geneva, 1985.

7 Many books discuss Traffic Theory. Two useful references are: *Telecommunication System Engineering* by Roger L. Freeman, John Wiley & Sons, New York, 1980; and *Telecommunications Switching Principles* by M.T. Hills, George Allen & Unwin, London, 1979.

8 Exponentially distributed holding times are discussed in most books on Queuing Theory, for example: *Queues* by D.R. Cox and Walter L. Smith, Chapman & Hall, London, 1961.

9 For a discussion of Euronet see 'The Euronet Diane Network for Information Retrieval' by M. Purser, *Information Technology: Research and Development* (1982) 1, 197–216.

Chapter 2
Circuit-Switched Data Networks

2.1 THE CONCEPT OF CIRCUIT-SWITCHING

In Chapter 1 circuit-switching has been presented as 'switching without buffering', so that two communicating DTEs have effectively a continuous path between them—the circuit—over which information is transmitted at a given speed, which is the same for all the links in the path. The circuit is established at the start of the 'call' and cleared at the end.

A familiar circuit-switching network is the public Telex network, handling characters coded according to international alphabet No. 2, using a start-stop envelope and running at 50 bps. An even more familiar circuit-switched network is the telephone network. This however, traditionally carries analogue, voice frequency signals, although there is a rapid conversion to the use of digitized voice (PCM) taking place in most of the world's telephone networks (see Section 2.2).

To understand more fully the concept of switching in general and circuit-switching in particular, it may be useful to return to first principles. Figure 2.1 illustrates a network in which each of N DTEs can connect

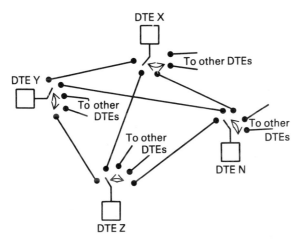

Fig. 2.1 N DTEs each with $(N-1)$-way switch.

to any other DTE, by means of N local switches and $N.(N-1)/2$ links.
To make a connection from X to Y the following sequence must occur
(1) X drives its local switch to pick the output to Y.
(2) At Y some signal must be generated as a result of X's action, which indicates to Y there is an incoming call.
(3) If Y is free to accept the call it must drive its local switch to pick the input from X.
(4) At X some signal must be generated as a result of Y's action, which indicates to X that the circuit is established.
(5) If Y did not respond to the incoming call (engaged, out of order) then X could either be informed explicitly by some error signal from Y, or could deduce the error by timing out.

The points to be made are
(i) That switches must be driven by commands to make the appropriate connections.
(ii) That signals must be sent across the network to indicate the progress of a call, for example that a selected destination has or has not responded to an incoming call.

Important questions are: How are these routing, call progress and other control signals transmitted? Are separate channels required for them, or can they be sent along the same channels as are used for the real traffic (e.g. data or voice)? In the latter case we have what is sometimes called 'in-band signalling'. With in-band signalling it is essential that clear conventions are established so that switches can distinguish traffic, which they should handle transparently, from control signals to which they should respond.

Figure 2.1 is obviously inefficient for any large system. Figure 2.2 replaces it with a centralized switch. One immediate saving is that there are now N, rather than $N(N-1)/2$, links. Other savings are achieved by using common control logic to drive the switches and to generate and respond to the signals; by using common power supplies; by having a single site to maintain, etc. An immediate complication is that the switch is *remotely controlled* by the DTEs.

One central switch can clearly serve a certain geographical area, for example a small town. Several such switches could be interconnected by 'trunk' links, so that any one could access any other in a manner similar to that of Fig. 2.1 (with the 'DTEs' now becoming central switches). But the same reasoning which gave rise to Fig. 2.2 again applies: a centralized 'primary' trunk switch interconnecting the 'local'

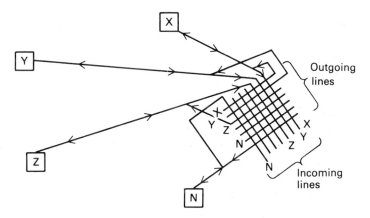

Fig. 2.2 The switch centralized and remotely controlled.

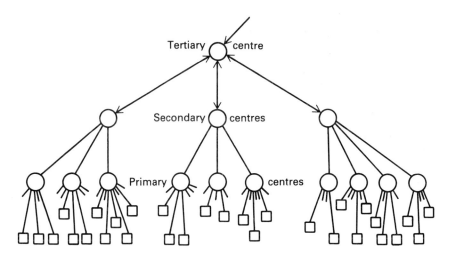

Fig. 2.3 Hierarchy of switching nodes.

switches is more economical. The result is the hierarchical structure of Fig. 2.3.

This reasoning can be extended further, to three, four, or even five levels of switching in the hierarchy. Moreover, in certain circumstances it may be convenient to break the strictly hierarchical structure, allowing some switches at a given level to interconnect directly (not necessarily via a higher level); or to permit cross connections between distinct branches of the hierarchy, or between two non-adjacent levels.

In this manner traditional circuit-switching networks are constructed, in particular the telephone network. The amount of remote control involved in a call which goes through several layers of the hierarchy will be appreciated. The complexity of deciding when, where and how to add new switches and circuits in response to changing traffic patterns will also be appreciated. Finally, it may be noted that most *data* networks are not hierarchical, but employ switches which indifferently handle trunk links to other switches and local links to DTEs at a single level. The reason for this is, probably, that data traffic patterns are not sufficiently well established and understood to justify the traditional hierarchical design.

2.1.1 Concentration of Traffic

It has been stated (Chapter 1) that switches concentrate and that it is not necessary to be able to support all possible simultaneous calls, but rather all probable ones (with a certain Grade of Service). This means that the main portion of a switch can be reduced in size and hence in cost. The size and cost are roughly proportional to the number of possible cross-connections, or crosspoints, in the switch. For example in Fig. 2.2 there are $N(N-1)$ crosspoints (or N^2 if we allow a DTE to call itself).

In Fig. 2.4 the switch has been decomposed into two switches
(1) An $N \times M$ Access Switch (AS) which concentrates traffic enabling only M simultaneous calls to be supported.
(2) An $M \times N$ Main Switch (MS) enabling a call accepted by the access switch to reach any of the N destinations.

From Section 1.2 we can see that if we require 1% Grade of Service and the offered traffic per terminal is 0.1 Erlang ($A = 0.1N$) then

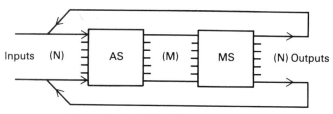

Fig. 2.4 A switch with concentration.

$M = 5.5+0.117N$. Suppose $N = 10000$, then $M = 1175$; and the number of crosspoints is reduced from 10^8 to 2.35×10^7 (a factor of 4).

It should be noted that the natures of the two switches, AS and MS, are somewhat different. The function of AS is to allow a specific input (the calling DTE) to be connected to *any* free input to MS. The function of MS is to connect that specific input to another specific output (the called DTE).

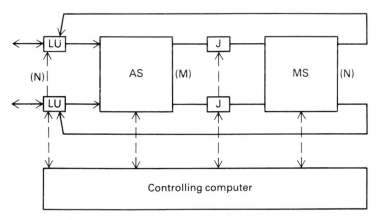

Fig. 2.5 SPC control of concentrator and switch. J = junctor; LU = line unit.

Figure 2.5 is Fig. 2.4 with some more detail. We suppose it illustrates a typical computer-controlled switch, in which the control logic is very largely software or Stored Program Control (SPC) and the switches themselves are electro-mechanical, for example composed of reed relays. Many SPC telephone exchanges are of this type. Each incoming line has an associated Line Unit (LU). Each link between the AS and MS has an associated 'junctor' (J). The purpose and behaviour of the units in Fig. 2.5 are best explained by illustrating the progress of a typical call

(i) The calling DTE sends a 'seize' signal showing that it wishes to make a call (telephone analogy: pick-up handset).

(ii) The LU detects the 'seize' signal and requests the control unit (the computer) to attach the LU to a junctor via the AS.

(iii) If the LU is successfully attached to the junctor it sends an 'Accept' signal to the calling DTE (telephone analogy: dialling tone). If no junctor is available another signal is sent to the calling DTE which is then supposed to abandon the call, or 'clear' it.

(iv) On hearing dialling tone, the calling DTE selects the required destination number (i.e. 'dials').

(v) The junctor receives this number and requests the control (the computer) to operate MS to connect the junctor to the called line (LU).

(vi) If the connection can be made through MS, the called LU is commanded by the control to send an incoming call signal to the called DTE. Simultaneously a call progress signal 'calling taking place' may be sent to the calling DTE (telephone analogy: ringing tone). If the connection cannot be made (called number engaged, non-existent, out-of-order, or possibly the MS is overloaded) then the control will release the junctor and the connection through AS and command the calling LU to send the appropriate signal (or tone) to the calling DTE, who should then clear the call (telephone analogy: engaged tone, number unobtainable tone).

(vii) When the called DTE responds, the called LU signals the control which starts monitoring the call for billing purposes. A through path now exists over which calling and called DTEs can communicate.

(viii) The call may be cleared by either end. For simplicity we assume only the calling DTE can clear it. The calling DTE's LU detects the clear command and signals the control. The control releases the AS and MS connections and the junctor. It signals the called LU, which signals the called DTE in turn that the call is cleared. The called DTE acknowledges this (telephone analogy: replacing the handset).

The above procedure can obviously be represented by a flow diagram, and indeed by a state diagram, in which the call progresses through various 'states' (idle, waiting for selection, etc.). We shall see similar state diagrams when we consider X.25 [1].

It is worth pointing out that certain functions, such as receiving the selection (dial) commands, analysing and using them to drive MS (routing) only occupy a small fraction of the total duration of the call. In old-fashioned electro-mechanical exchanges this information for 'selection' was held in special registers of relative complexity and expense. To reduce this expense a further level of concentration was applied between the junctors and the registers, with a Register Access Switch (RAS) connecting M junctors to R registers ($R \ll M$). Where selection information is held in the memory of a large SPC computer this kind of economy is no longer justified.

It should also be noted that, before control was centralized in computers, each LU and each junctor would have its own in-built control functions. For example, an LU could 'hunt' for a free junctor, or a junctor could 'find' a calling LU. Although technology has changed, such terms as 'hunting' and 'line-finding' are still used and the concepts may still be valid depending on circumstances.

For example, Fig. 2.6 illustrates a rather different SPC Telex switch [16]. Here the traffic is in the form of coded characters. The LUs are built into 'scanners' which effectively scan for incoming calls (they are 'line finders'). An incoming call is signalled by a voltage transition on the line; followed by coded digits giving the destination address in response to a signal from the scanner to the terminal. The receiving scanner sends these up to the controlling computer which in turn commands the scanner containing the requisite outgoing LU to contact the called terminal. When the terminal responds, the control delegates the sending and receiving of characters to the two scanners which pass the characters directly between them on their way between calling and called terminals. The capacity of the scanners to handle simultaneous

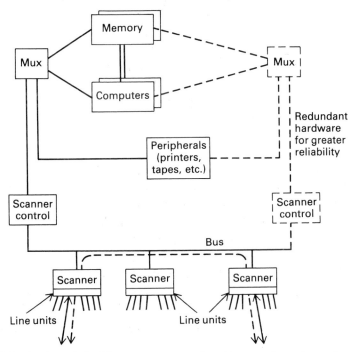

Fig. 2.6 A telex switch. (Characters are transferred between incoming and outgoing lines via the bus.)

calls will again be less than the total of all possible simultaneous calls; concentration applies.

Finally, in Fig. 2.7, a trunk line interface has been added to Fig. 2.5. MS has been renamed TS (Trunk Switch). It supports incoming and outgoing trunk calls as well as local calls. Because trunk signalling is different from local line signalling the trunk lines have special junctors (TJs). Because the traffic on trunk lines is much higher than on local lines it is not concentrated on input. The TS, for outgoing trunk calls, need not pick a specific trunk line, but one of many going towards the required destination.

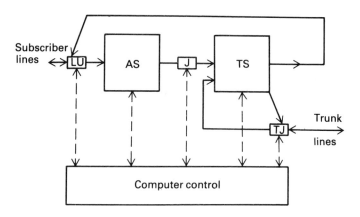

Fig. 2.7   Handling trunks as well as subscriber lines.

2.1.2 Switches and Internal Blocking

If, for the moment, we leave aside further discussion of the establishing and clearing of calls, there are still questions to ask about the nature of the switches themselves. The traditional 'Space-division' (S) switch, so-called because it employs physical connections in space, is illustrated in Fig. 2.7. (Figure 2.2 is also an S switch.) To connect an input to an output circuit a crosspoint is 'made', e.g. by closing the appropriate relay. Note that a circuit will usually consist of more than one wire, so that several relay contacts are closed at the crosspoint. Note also that the mechanism for making the crosspoint could be solid-state rather than relay switching, or it could be the more old-fashioned 'crossbar' mechanism, or even Strowger. Obviously the mechanism must be such that the crosspoint remains made until the call is cleared; and it should also be unaffected by the making or breaking of other crosspoints in the switch, as other calls are set up or cleared.

By contrast with space switching we have 'Time-division' (T) switching. In this case, supposing that the switch can handle N simultaneous calls, in each time interval of t seconds 'information' from each of N inputs is transferred to the appropriate output serially (i.e. one after the other). Each input is attended to during t/N seconds, once every t seconds (see Fig. 2.8). For the Telex switch of Fig. 2.6, which is a T switch, the interval t could be 150 ms, corresponding to one 7½ bit character (5 data bits plus 1 start plus 1½ stop bits) at 50 bps. In this case each input and output line would be equipped with a one-character buffer, so that characters could enter and leave the switch on those lines while other lines were being attended to. If this technique were used for analogue (e.g. voice) switching, assuming it is not practicable to buffer an analogue signal, the information transferred would be a 'sample' of the analogue signal, once every t seconds. It is well known that if speech is sampled 8000 times per second, all analogue frequencies up to 4 KHz are faithfully transmitted. Thus a T switch for voice might have $t = 125$ μs, and the width of the sample would be 625 ns if, say, N were 200.

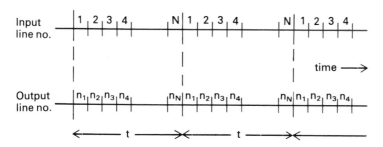

Fig. 2.8 Handling inputs and outputs in a Time-division switch.

Space-division switching is clearly more 'old-fashioned' than time-division switching, which relies on high speed, carefully synchronized, logic; but both are relevant to circuit-switching, as the discussion of the time-space-time (TST) switch in Section 2.2 will show. Accordingly, we shall continue to examine S switching, since, additionally, some of the concepts involved are also illuminating.

If the cost of an S switch is roughly proportional to the number of crosspoints, it is desirable to reduce that number. We have seen how this can be done by concentration; but now let us, for simplicity, leave concentration temporarily aside and consider how the number of crosspoints in a 'square' $M \times M$ switch may be reduced, always maintaining 'full availability' (the ability of any input to reach any output). Suppose $M = 100$. The basic square switch has 10000 crosspoints. By subdividing the switch into two stages, A and B, each made up of ten 10×10 switches, the number of crosspoints can be reduced to 2000 (Fig. 2.9).

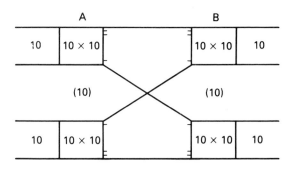

Fig. 2.9   A two-stage (100×100) switch.

In Fig. 2.9 all internal connections are not shown explicitly, but are only indicated. For example, the ten outputs from the first (10×10) switch of A go to the *first* inputs of each of the ten (10×10) switches of B; the ten outputs of the second (10×10) switch of A (not drawn) go to the *second* inputs of each of the ten (10×10) switches of B, etc.; the ten outputs of the tenth and last (10×10) switch of A go to the tenth and last inputs of each of the ten (10×10) switches of B.

Figure 2.10 illustrates this method of subdivision applied to a system with $M = 1000$; and the number of crosspoints has been reduced from 10^6 to 3×10^4. In general if $M = 10^k$ then there are k stages and $k \times 10^{(k+1)}$ crosspoints instead of 10^{2k}. The number of crosspoints per input is $k \times 10^{(k+1)}/10^k = 10k$. (It is easily shown that, if we ignore other costs, the elementary switch size which gives least crosspoints for a given number of inputs is $(n \times n)$, not (10×10), where $n = e$, the base of natural logarithms.)

Unfortunately, the switches of Figs. 2.9 and 2.10 suffer from a serious drawback: 'internal blocking'. Internal blocking is said to arise when it is possible that the desired input to and output from a switch are free,

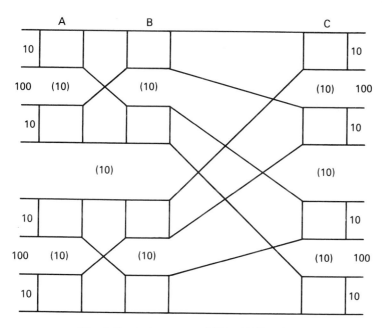

Fig. 2.10 A three-stage (1000×1000) switch.

but there is no path to be found between them because of the presence of other calls. For example, in Fig. 2.9, all calls between the first ten inputs of A and the first ten outputs of B must use a *single* link between the corresponding first elementary (10×10) switches of each of them. If one such call exists no other such calls can be established.

If the traffic per input is A, since there are as many links between each stage of the switch as there are inputs and if calls are randomly distributed over these links, the probability of a link being free is $(1-A)$. There is a unique path through the switch for a given input-output pair, involving $(k-1)$ links. The probability that all these links are free is $(1-A)^{k-1}$, so the blocking probability, the probability they are not free, is $(1-(1-A)^{k-1})$. If $A = 0.5$, remembering that after concentration traffic can be high, and $k = 3$ (Fig. 2.10), the probability of blocking is 75%! Even with $A = 0.1$ it is 19%.

There are various methods available for reducing the probability of internal blocking. For example, one might have three or four links between each pair of elementary switches in adjacent stages, instead of one. Another method is to introduce a 'mixing' stage into the existing 'distribution' stages, as in Fig. 2.11. Here, the last stage D is a mixing

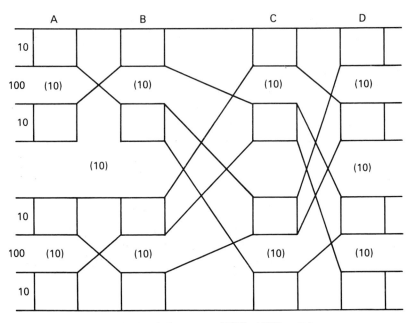

Fig. 2.11   A four-stage (1000×1000) switch.

stage, giving as a result ten parallel paths between any pair of elementary switches selected from A and D. The probability of all ten paths being in use is $(1-(1-A)^{k-1})^{10}$; which even for $A = 0.5$, $k = 4$, now gives 25%, instead of 75%.

Figure 2.12a shows the interconnection scheme simplified; with the three distribution stages labelled 'D' and the mixing stage labelled 'M'. Between any input point and output point there are parallel connecting paths of the form of Fig. 2.12b (drawn for the third input, second output). Such a 'channel graph' shows the topology of the connections for this

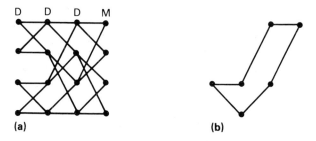

Fig. 2.12   Channel graphs for Fig. 2.11.

DDDM configuration. Other configurations are possible, with more than one mixing stage differently located and we could draw and analyse the channel graphs of these configurations.

Returning to the topic of concentration, which any real S switch will employ, we again consider the switch of Fig. 2.4, with 10000 inputs (N = 10000) and a 10:1 concentration, so M = 1000. We take the traffic as A = 0.05 Erlang per input before concentration, or 0.5 Erlang per link after concentration. The Grade of Service associated with concentration is thus well below 0.1%. Following the principle of subdivision, AS and MS could be composed of ten (1000×100) switches each; with ten parallel links between each corresponding pair of (1000×100) switches of AS and MS (Fig. 2.13). The number of crosspoints is 2×10^6 (instead of 2×10^7 without subdivision, but with concentration) and the probability of internal blocking is $(10A)^{10}$ = 0.1%. This is not very satisfactory in terms of number of crosspoints, 200 per input or 4000 per Erlang, although very good with respect to internal blocking.

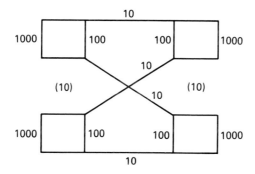

Fig. 2.13   Concentration with multiple paths between stages.

Figure 2.14 shows the switch of Fig. 2.11 redesigned to have five stages. The number of crosspoints is now only 230000 and there is a lower probability of internal blocking (approximately 6% as compared with 25% for four stages) as is to be expected from the DDDMM meshed channel graph (Fig. 2.15). The theoretical calculation of blocking probabilities can be quite complex for larger switches and simulation techniques are usually used to estimate them. The number of crosspoints per input is 23 and the number of crosspoints per Erlang of offered traffic (500) is 460.

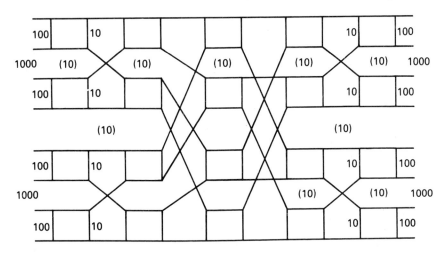

Fig. 2.14 Concentration with five stages (two mixers).

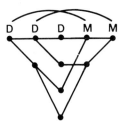

Fig. 2.15 Channel graph for Fig. 2.14.

A further technique, not previously mentioned, for reducing crosspoints while minimizing blocking is to dispense with full availability of access to trunk circuits; since an input need not have access to all but only a subset of trunks to a given neighbouring node.

We do not pursue this subject further [2] but simply draw attention to the fact that internal blocking is a potential problem and that techniques exist for analysing the problem and reducing its impact.

2.2 A DIGITAL CIRCUIT-SWITCH

In the preceding section typical space-division switches have been presented, as exist in many SPC exchanges. The switch is controlled by computer and is well suited to handling analogue traffic such a voice telephony.

But modern voice transmission systems are heavily based on digital (PCM) technology. A typical transmission link operates at 2048 Kbps; although much higher speeds, suitable for optical fibres, are available. At 2048 Kbps, 30 voice channels are carried on the link, in the form of a frame of 32 octets. Thirty octets of the frame represent 8-bit digitized voice samples, made 8000 times per second; while the remaining two octets are used for frame synchronization, signalling and control. Thus each voice channel represents a 64 Kbps stream; and since the frame rate must also be 8000 frames per second, and there are 256 bits per frame, the aggregate rate is 2048 Kbps.

It will be appreciated that since 30 voice channels are multiplexed on a single link, and their associated conversations do not all have the same source and destination exchanges, switching must consist of extracting the octet from, say, 'slot' 5 of an incoming frame on one link and inserting it into, say, slot 7 of an outgoing frame on another link; and similarly for all the other incoming slots. In principle all incoming slots, or voice samples, must be switched to different slots on distinct physical links. In addition, we must bear in mind that full-duplex channels are supported on the full-duplex links, so that reverse traffic belonging to the same conversation must be switched simultaneously. How is this achieved?

The illustration presented is taken from the Group Switching Subsystem (GSS) of a well-known commercially available digital switch [3]. It uses time-division switching for extracting the voice samples from the slots; space-division switching for interconnecting different links; and time-division switching for loading the voice samples into the outgoing slots. This results in a time-space-time (TST) switch. The switch is designed, of course, for voice, but since it handles the digital voice samples transparently as 8-bit octets, it can equally well switch data.

The basic switch handles the equivalent of 32 links each carrying 512-octet frames (formed by multiplexing sixteen 32-channel PCM frames) at a rate of 8000 frames per second. The 32 links are space-division switched in parallel, so the time-division switching is at a rate of $512 \times 8000 = 4.096$ million times per second. (The two control octets in the PCM frame can be switched in addition to the 30 speech octets, if required. See Fig. 2.16.) For each link, carrying a 512-octet frame, there is a 512-octet input speech store (ISS) into which the speech samples,

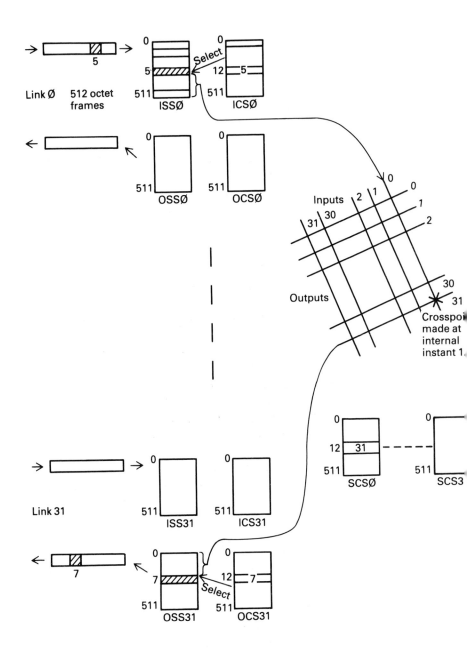

Fig. 2.16 A time-space-time switch.

the contents of the slots, are written cyclically. The contents of slot 0 in the frame goes to ISS location 0; slot 1 to ISS location 1, etc.

Switching is performed in accordance with an *internal* clock or slot-counting mechanism. This is used to index into an input control store (ICS) of 512 locations. If the contents of ICS location 12 is, say, '5', this means that at internal slot count 12 the speech sample is ISS location 5 is to be routed into the space switch on the line corresponding to the link in question (link 0, say). Thus the ICS arranges that the speech samples in ISS are read out and fed to the S switch in a different order, but at the same frequency as that in which they arrived on the link. This is the first T switch.

The S switch is also controlled by the internal clock. It has a switch control store (SCS) per input link (0 to 31) each with 512 locations. The contents of each location identifies which crosspoint is to be made, i.e. which of the 32 outgoing links is to be connected to that input link, during that internal time-slot. For example, if our input on link 0 is to be output to link 31 at internal time-slot 12, then location 12 of link 0's SCS contains the number 31.

The T switch output is the same as the input, but in reverse. That is, there is per link an output store (OCS) of 512 locations, corresponding to the internal time slots, and an output speech store (OSS) of 512 locations corresponding to the external slots in the 512-octet frame on the link. In our example, for link 31, OCS location 12 would contain '7'. This means that, at internal time-slot 12, the octet output from the space switch towards link 31 is to be written into OSS location 7. From there it will automatically go into slot 7 of the frame on the link.

The reverse full-duplex path is set up out of phase by 256 internal time-slots. Thus if the reverse path is from incoming slot 7 of link 31 to outgoing slot 5 of link 0, then: Link 31's ICS location 268 (256+12) will contain '7'; link 0's OCS location 268 will contain '5'; and link 31's SCS location 268 will contain 0.

By adopting this policy for handling the reverse path, it is clear that the control stores in fact contain redundant information. This allows them to be simplified. In fact, ICS and OCS for a given line are one single control store, but for simplicity they are shown as distinct.

It is of interest to ask how the control stores are set up when a new call arises. In our example, an internal time-slot had to be chosen to connect link 0 to link 31 (and vice versa). The procedure is to select the first empty slot in link 0's SCS, say number 12, provided that slot 12 in no other SCS contains the number 31 (i.e. no other link is outputting to link 31 then). If the phase shift of 256 internal slots for the reverse paths is rigidly adhered to, there is no need to check slot 268 of link 31's SCS: it will automatically be empty. Can internal blocking occur in the space-division switch (which is a single square matrix)? If it occurs it can only be because there are vacant slots in both the input and output links' SCS, but it is not possible to write the corresponding link numbers in these slots, because corresponding slots in other SCSs already contain them (the link is already engaged in a call at that time interval). The SCSs could reach such a state after several calls have been set up and cleared, but it appears that reorganizing their contents, if this can be done without upsetting extant calls, will always solve the problem. It is not clear how this situation is handled in practice; nevertheless the manufacturers claim a probability of internal blocking of 10^{-6} with 0.8 Erlangs per input to the switch—which is very good.

The setting up of calls, i.e. the loading of the control stores, is of course done by controlling computers. The space switch can be expanded to (128×128) links supporting $128 \times 16 \times 32 = 65\,536$ channels.

The GSS is normally front-ended by a Subscriber Switching Sub-system (SSS) (Fig. 2.17). SSS can act as a concentrator, which in its minimum configuration supports 16 line switch modules (LSM). Each LSM concentrates 128 subscriber lines down to one PCM 2 Mbps line, 16 of which are multiplexed together on entry to the time-division switch as explained previously. These 2048 subscriber lines can carry an average traffic flow of 0.2 Erlang per line.

The SSS can also act as a part locally and part remotely controlled local switch, using time-division switching between the 2048 subscriber lines.

From the figures above it is clear that this circuit-switching system can handle (before concentration) up to $4 \times 65\,536 = 262\,144$ voice (or 64 Kbps) channels, at 0.2 Erlang per channel.

A Trunk and Signalling Subsystem (TSS) is also usually associated with the GSS (see Fig. 2.17). TSS is responsible for the control of the trunk circuits, and for signalling between exchanges (see Section 2.4).

2.3 INTERFACES TO CIRCUIT-SWITCHED DATA NETWORKS

In this section we firstly consider digital interfaces to PCM equipment (CCITT G.703, G.732) [4]. Digital PCM circuits are often used to provide

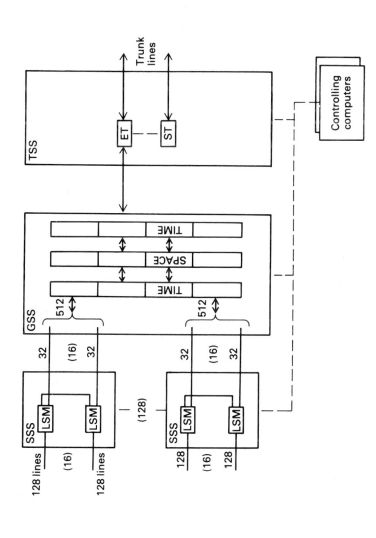

Fig. 2.17 Line and trunk handling on the TST switch. ET = exchange terminal; ST = signalling terminal.

higher speed (64 Kbps or higher) channels for data because of their ready availability in many countries. The channel provided will usually be a point-to-point permanent (i.e. not switched) connection—the equivalent of a leased line.

However, proper circuit-switched data networks, in which the subscriber can establish a switched connection by appropriate commands on the interface, require a different interface; these networks must have switches capable of responding to the commands on the interface. Such interfaces are defined by the CCITT X.24, X.20, X.21 and X.22 Recommendations [5], discussed subsequently.

2.3.1 The G.703 Interface

The G.703 Recommendation defines the physical, functional and electrical characteristics of digital interfaces operating at 64, 1544, 6312, 32 064, 44 736, 2048, 8488, 34 368 and 139 264 Kbps. It should be noted that the last four speeds are commonly used in Europe, the previous four speeds in the USA, while 64 Kbps is used world-wide. The interfaces are for the interconnection of digital network components, such as line sections, multiplex equipment and exchanges; and, strictly speaking, have nothing to do with *data* networks or switching. However, since data networks frequently use such digital links, for example for interconnecting circuit-switching nodes, the G.703 Recommendation is discussed briefly.

The purpose of the interface is to carry digital information simultaneously in both directions between two pieces of equipment, together with timing information to enable a receiver to identify the bits. At 64 Kbps three possibilities exist for the source of the timing

(1) Codirectional. Each sender provides timing for its data. The timing is encoded in the data stream, using a 3-level code. The 64 Kbps bit period (a 'block') is divided into four unit intervals. A binary one is encoded as 1100, a binary zero as 1010. The polarity of blocks is alternated between (0, +1 volt) and (0, −1 volt). Every 8th block this alternation is violated, enabling the 8th binary bit to be identified (see Fig. 2.18). The transmission medium in each direction is a symmetric pair, and the specification defines the pulse shape and characteristics.

(2) Centralized Clock Interface. The timing, in the form of two 'bits' (10) per binary data bit, is supplied to each piece of equipment from a central source, on separate symmetric pairs. The timing signal is 3-level, of different polarity for alternating data bits and with a polarity violation

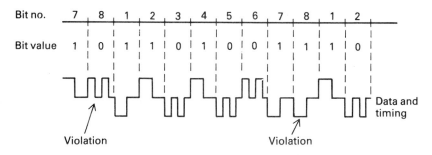

Fig. 2.18 G.703 64 Kbps coding (codirectional).

every 8th bit. The data bits are also encoded in three levels, on separate pairs, using Alternate Mark Inversion (AMI). In AMI a binary 1 is a Mark (1 volt), a binary 0 a Space (0 volt). Alternate Marks are inverted (i.e. -1 volt) (see Fig. 2.19).

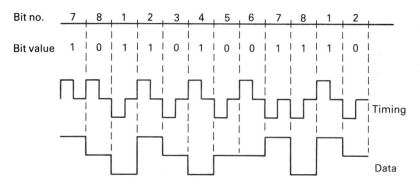

Fig. 2.19 G.703 AMI coding for 64 Kbps centralized clock.

(3) Contradirectional. The timing (encoded as for the centralized clock interface) is taken from only *one* side of the interface, on separate symmetric pairs. AMI encoding is used for the data on the two other pairs.

The G.703 interfaces at 1544, 6312, 32 064, 44 736 Kbps are all bipolar (3-level) using, for example, a scrambled AMI code. The higher speed ones use coaxial pairs rather than symmetric pairs in each direction. Separate timing is not provided, as the coding enables it to be extracted from the data.

The interface at 2048 Kbps is, after the 64 Kbps interface, that most likely to be of interest to data users. It operates either over one coaxial or one symmetric pair in each direction. Coding is HDB3, with three states denoted B_+, B_- and 0. Marks (binary 1s) are alternately B_+ and B_-. Spaces (binary 0) are 0, but a string of four spaces is coded in a special manner, which involves using Marks (to preserve timing), and polarity inversions to distinguish such Marks from binary 1s and to avoid any DC component. An alternative form of the interface is allowed.

The 8488 and 34 368 Kbps interfaces also use HDB3 and one coaxial pair in each direction, while the 139 264 Kbps interface uses a 2-level AMI code.

2.3.2 The G.732 Specification

This specification is not for an interface, but rather defines the 30-channel multiplexing scheme for PCM at 2048 Kbps, already mentioned. The total of thirty-two 64 Kbps channels are numbered 0 to 31. Each channel is represented by an 8-bit slot in the 32-slot frame. Slot 0 is used for frame alignment. Alternating slots 0 either contain the frame alignment signal X0011011 (X is reserved for international use) or other information (e.g. alarms). Slot 16 in the frame is either used as a 'transparent' 64 Kbps channel for Common Channel Signalling (CCS) (see Section 2.4); or is used for explicit signalling (e.g. call set-up and clearing) for each of the 30 voice channels over a 16-frame 'multiframe'. In this 'multiframe' slot 16 of frame 0 is used for special purposes, slot 16 of frame 1 for

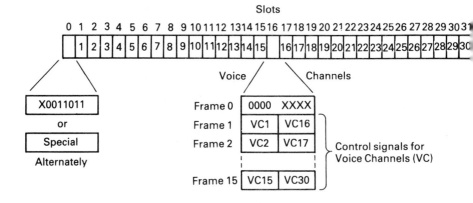

Fig. 2.20 G.732 frame and multi-frame structure.

'voice' channels 1 and 16, slot 16 of frame 2 for voice channels 2 and 17, etc. (Note: 'voice channel 16' = slot 17, etc.). See Fig. 2.20.

The relevance of the G.732 specification is that the data user of a 2048 Kbps PCM link should be aware of the special role of Channels 0 and 16. It may be that the (digital) switches along the path he uses can switch transparently all 32 channels as a unit, and slots 0 and 16 can then hold data. It may be that the user must avoid these slots, or put explicit bit patterns into them; so that only 30 channels are available for data.

(It should be noted that there is a similar specification, G.733 [4], for PCM multiplexing at 1544 Kbps.)

2.3.3 The X.24, X.20, X.21 and X.22 Interfaces [5]

As has been explained, the G.703 Recommendations define interfaces to PCM digital circuits, which the builder of a data network might use, for example, as leased bearer circuits between his data nodes. The X.24, X.20, X.21 and X.22 interfaces are the real user interfaces (see Fig. 2.21). In particular they provide the user with facilities for *selection* ('dialling') as an integral part of the interface, so that a call can readily be established by a computer, for example.

The circuit-switched data network may be regarded as superimposed on a leased-line bearer network which could itself be digital (e.g. PCM), or indeed analogue (e.g. group-band according to Recommendation H.14) [6] with suitable modems (e.g. V.36 at 64 Kbps) [7].

(i) *X.24.* The basic structure of the user interface to a data network (not necessarily a circuit-switched data network) is defined in Recommendation X.24. It applies to the interface between DTE and DCE, as does the famous V.24 interface, but here the DCE is not a modem but rather a special 'circuit-terminating' equipment. Seven 'interchange' circuits are supported on the X.24 interface, together with earth returns depending on the electrical characteristics used (e.g. V.28, X.26 (V.10), X.27 (V.11)) [8]. The seven circuits are

    T   Transmit. DTE to DCE.
    R   Receive. DCE to DTE.
    C   Control. DTE to DCE.
    I   Indication. DCE to DTE.
    S   Signal element timing. DCE to DTE.

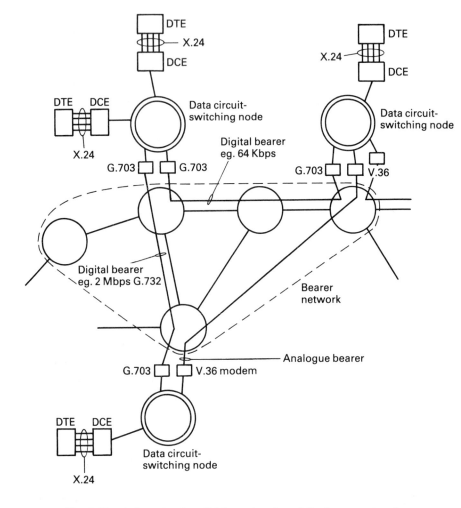

Fig. 2.21 A data circuit-switching network and the bearer network.

B   Byte (octet) timing. DCE to DTE.
F   Frame start identification. DCE to DTE.

The procedures for the *use* of these circuits are defined in the appropriate recommendations (e.g. X.20, X.21).

(ii) *X.20*. The X.20 Recommendation states how the X.24 interface will be used for start-stop ('asynchronous') terminals [9]. Circuit F is not used. Circuits S and B are not required for start-stop use since timing is deduced from the start-stop envelope. Circuits C and I are not used because signalling associated with the start and finish of a call can be carried on circuits T and R. (This is because in asynchronous start-stop communication the normal state of these lines during data transfer is logical 1 (Mark); so logical 0 (space) can only exist for the length of a character at most. Longer 'spaces' can therefore be used for control purposes.)

Figure 2.22 illustrates call set-up and clearing at both the calling and called DTEs. It will be noted that
— The idle state of T and R is 0. A new call is indicated by the transition of one of these to 1, the other changing to 1 by way of a response.
— Selection (i.e. 'dialling') signals are coded characters on the calling DTE's T circuit.
— Provision is made for sending the identification of the DTE at the other end of the circuit as coded characters on circuit R.
— The successful establishment of the call is signified by an ACK character from the DCE.
— Data transfer is full-duplex.
— The call is cleared by returning the T and R circuits to 0.
X.20 is used for stop-start DTEs at various speeds up to 300 bps.
(iii) *X.21.* The X.21 Recommendation states how the X.24 interface will be used for continuous isochronous (popularly 'synchronous') communications [9]. Since the T and R circuits cannot be relied upon to be normally '1' during data transfer, C and I are also used. Circuit S is required for isochronous timing; the use of circuit B is optional. Circuit F is not used.

Figure 2.23 illustrates call set-up and clearing at both the calling and called DTEs. It will be noted that
— The idle state of circuits C and I is OFF. An outgoing/incoming call is indicated by C/I switching to ON, and its acceptance by I/C switching to ON.
— Selection, line identification, call progress signals, etc. are sent as coded characters on circuits T or R.
— Data transfer is full-duplex.
— The call is cleared by circuits C and I returning to OFF.
X.21 is used for isochronous transmission at various speeds from 600 to 64 000 bps.
(iv) *X.22.* The X.22 Recommendation provides for time-division multiplexing several 'X.21-like' interfaces onto a single 48 Kbps link. All

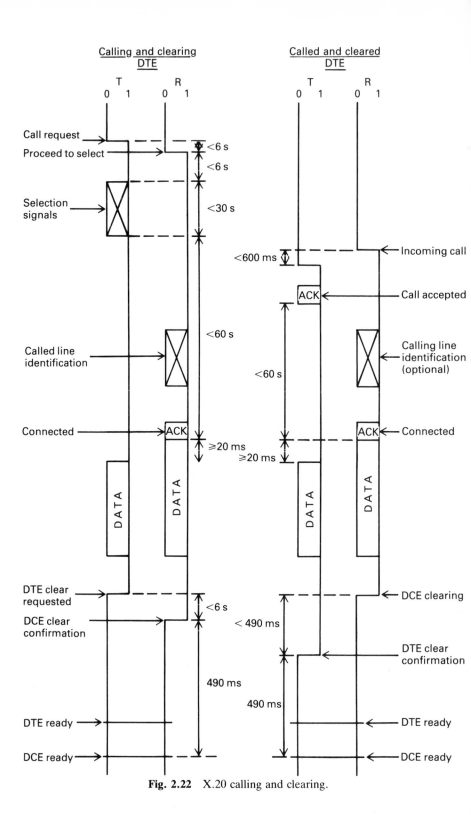

Fig. 2.22 X.20 calling and clearing.

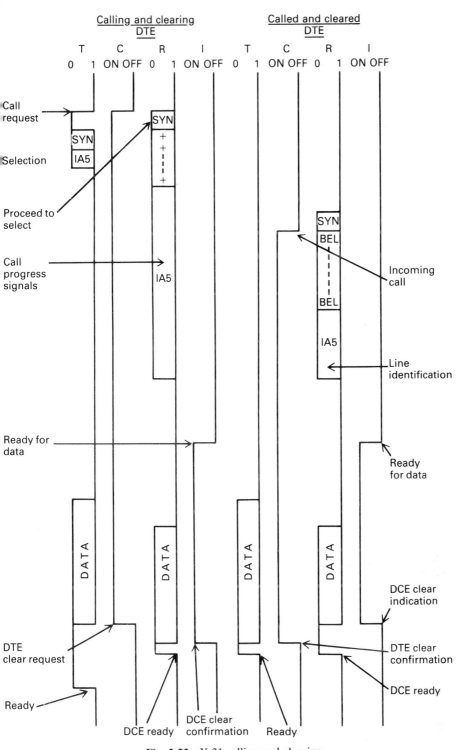

Fig. 2.23 X.21 calling and clearing.

seven circuits are used, a pulse on circuit F signifying the start of a new multiplexing frame. Individual X.21 channels should all be of the same bit rate (600, 2400, 4800 or 9600 bps). For example, if there are five 9600 bps channels, using 8-bit octets for data, each channel will be allocated eight time intervals on the 48 000 Kbps bearer. Those eight time intervals are allocated simultaneously to circuits T, R, C, I of the channel; so T and R can convey an octet, while C and I reflect the state of those circuits for that channel. The next eight bearer time intervals are allocated to the next X.21 channel, etc. After five channels a new frame begins, marked by an F pulse equal to one bearer time interval (approximately 21 μs).

2.4 INTERNAL STANDARDS FOR CIRCUIT-SWITCHED DATA NETWORKS

In the preceding Section 2.3 various interfacing standards, recommended by CCITT, which apply to digital and to data networks have been discussed. The need for an interfacing standard for any particular network is clear and the requirement that such standards should be international rather than national or local has also been argued.

It is not, however, immediately clear that data networks need any internationally agreed internal standards, since the internal conventions of the network concern nobody other than its manufacturer and its operator. However, if networks are to be interconnected at the international level, then they must have a certain degree of compatibility; and this international compatibility is very much the domain of CCITT. Moreover, if internetwork standards exist, it is not only desirable that internal network conventions should be similar to them (to minimize the complexities of mapping internal to international standards); it is also possible that the internetwork standards can be directly applied to internal connections.

Three areas of internetwork, and hence possibly internal, standardization can be identified

(1) The bearer channels used to carry the data between nodes. These could be voice analogue or group analogue circuits with suitable modems, or PCM channels as previously discussed.

(2) Multiplexing techniques used to merge several data channels on to a single bearer channel. (We shall only consider time-division multiplexing, or TDM, techniques).

(3) Signalling techniques for the exchange of call control information between nodes. This is by far the most complex area, since signalling covers a very wide range of functions from call establishment and clearing, through metering (for charging), to alarm and fault signalling.

2.4.1 Standards for Bearer Channels

For lower speed, start-stop DTEs, the bearer channels are typically provided by voice grade circuits, meeting for example the H.12 [6], M.1020, or M.1025 [10] specifications; with suitable modems such as V.26 (2400 bps), V.27 (4800 bps), V.29 (9600 bps) [11]. All these recommendations are well-known standards in conventional data communications [9]. The low speed data channels will be multiplexed (see below) on to these bearer channels.

For both higher speed start-stop and continuous isochronous DTEs, 64 Kbps is the standard rate for a bearer channel. It is provided either by a V.36 modem over a group link (60 to 108 KHz analogue H.14 channel), or by a PCM slot in a G.732 frame. The higher speed data channels will also be multiplexed on to these bearer channels.

2.4.2 Standards for Multiplexing Data Channels on to Bearer Channels

We do not discuss the Frequency Division Multiplexing (FDM) techniques for multiplexing start-stop DTEs on to an analogue channel. They are covered by Recommendations R.35, R.37 and R.38 [12].

Two TDM techniques are recommended for multiplexing *start-stop* channels on to a synchronous bearer operating at speeds up to 64 Kbps. The R.101 [12] Recommendation handles forty-six 50-baud channels on a 2400 bps bearer. By contrast, the R.111 [12] Recommendation is independent of the code and speed of the channels handled. Essentially, the 240 bits of a 256-bit frame contain bit-interleaved samples of the start-stop channels which can then be recreated by demultiplexing. Provided the sampling rate is high in comparison to the bit rate on the individual channels, the distortion introduced by the technique is acceptable. In both the R.101 and R.111 techniques start and stop bits are transmitted, not discarded. (Note that, because the bearer is synchronous, the multiplexed bit stream produced by the R.101 or R.111 TDM can itself be multiplexed further using the X.50 or X.51 technique, below.)

The CCITT X.50 and X.51 Recommendations [13] are for multiplexing *synchronous* (e.g. X.21) channels on to a 64 Kbps bearer. With each channel two extra bits per 'character' on a channel are required to carry framing and control information. X.50 assumes 6-bit characters, resulting in a 6+2 = 8-bit envelope. X.51 uses 8-bit characters and an 8+2 = 10-bit envelope. X.50 also makes provision for 8-bit characters by grouping four 8-bit envelopes to carry three 8-bit characters plus 4×2 = 8 extra control and framing bits.

According to X.50, the basic TDM framing mechanism supports eighty 8-bit envelopes per frame. Suppose a multiplexed channel is at 9600 bps. The 6+2 expansion gives rise to a 12.8 Kbps channel, which can be accommodated in every 5th envelope slot of the frame on the 64 Kbps bearer. Other channel rates such as 4800, 2400 and 600 bps are handled similarly. The two extra bits per envelope are an F (Frame) bit and an S (Status) bit. The 80 F bits in the frame carry a framing pattern. The S bits carry call control information.

The X.51 TDM mechanism uses 2560 bits per frame, of which 160 are padding and 2400 support two hundred and forty 10-bit envelopes at an effective aggregate rate of 60 Kbps. If we again consider a 9600 bps multiplexed channel, it expands (8+2) to 12 Kbps; and five slots per frame accommodate it. The extra two bits (called S and A) per envelope carry call control and envelope alignment information. Framing information is left in the padding bits.

It is clear that, in principle, these two schemes for TDM can interwork since the channels they carry have compatible data rates. Their *use* is

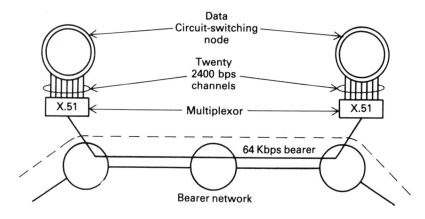

Fig. 2.24   Multiplexing data channels with X.51.

illustrated in Fig. 2.24, in which an X.51-compatible TDM is used to multiplex twenty 2400 bps data channels onto a single 64 Kbps bearer between two data circuit-switching nodes. In Fig. 2.23 it is conceivable that the multiplexing at one or at both nodes could be done *within* the node, rather than by an externally connected multiplexor.

2.4.3 Standards for Signalling Between Nodes (Exchanges) in Circuit-Switched Data Networks

The subject of signalling is large and complex. The general requirement is that for each call, control information must be transmitted in both directions along the route of the call between nodes (and, of course, between the DTEs and their local nodes also). Examples of such control information are

(i) The request to establish the call from DTE A to DTE B.

(ii) The acceptance by DTE B of the call.

(iii) The clearing of the call by either end at any moment. (For example DTE A might choose to clear the call *before* it is successfully established. All nodes along the selected route must be informed and respond.)

(iv) Requests for special facilities (e.g. reverse charging) on setting up the call.

(v) Alarms associated with the call, etc.

There are essentially two aspects to signalling

(1) The method whereby the signalling information is carried along the route of the call.

(2) The format and significance of the signalling information.

Let us consider firstly the method of carrying the signalling information. In traditional networks the signalling information was carried on the same channel as the user information. Thus opening or closing a DC path on a telephone circuit could be used to convey signals. Special control characters on a Telex circuit could convey signals (e.g. destination address), etc. This is in-band signalling. In-band signalling is obviously an inflexible approach as it must impose certain restrictions on the user information if false signals are not to be generated. It is also liable to the errors that may occur on the user's channel. Ideally, the signalling controlling a user channel should be more secure than the channel itself, so if the user's channel 'fails' in some way it can be cleared in an orderly fashion. The complexities associated with in-band signalling become more acute when a channel on one network (e.g. a PCM channel with its own signalling) is used as a bearer to carry channels of another network (e.g. multiplexed data channels of a circuit-switching data network).

Thus the requirement for special general-purpose signalling channels, independent of the user channels being controlled, has become apparent. Such channels are high capacity and one such Common Channel Signalling (CCS) channel can carry signalling information for *many* user channels. Because of its high bit rate (typically 64 Kbps), a CCS channel also allows faster call set-up than if the lower speed user channel were employed for signalling. CCS channels in effect form a parallel network to the user channels, and signalling information for a given user call can follow a different route through the network from that used by the user channel itself—provided, of course, the signalling information can reach all the necessary nodes on the user channel's route (see Fig. 2.25).

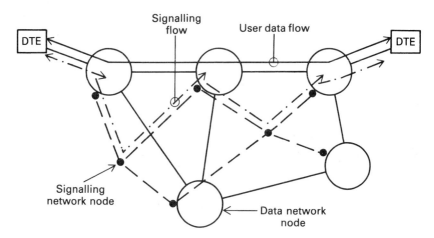

Fig. 2.25   User data network and associated signalling network.

CCITT has developed Signalling System No. 7 in an extensive series of Recommendations (Q.701 to Q.795) for CCS [14]. Signalling System No. 7 is intended to replace, in the long term, all other signalling systems.

Not only can CCS permit many user channels to be controlled via a common signalling channel; it also allows heterogeneous user channels to be so controlled. A single CCS channel might carry signalling information for both voice and data channels. Additionally, a CCS channel can carry information not directly associated with user calls at all. It can be used to carry *network* monitoring and control signals; for example for reporting on the state of nodes, or for exchanging billing information, etc.

The idea of CCS arises directly from SPC of switches by computers. The computers exchange call control and general supervisory information between themselves via CCS channels. The switches they control are linked by the circuits used to carry the user channels.

Returning to circuit-switched data networks we discuss briefly three signalling standards.

(1) X.70 signalling for start-stop data traffic.

(2) X.71 signalling for synchronous data traffic.

(3) X.61/Q.741 for CCS signalling for synchronous data traffic [13].

(1) *X.70.* The X.70 recommendation is for signalling on anisochronous data networks—networks carrying start-stop traffic such as that generated by X.20 terminals. The signalling procedure between nodes may be regarded as a logical extension of the signalling procedure on the DTE/DCE interface (see Fig. 2.22). The signalling associated with each channel is 'in-band', the nodes involved examining the state of each channel separately.

The signals are formed either by polarity changes of the transmit (T) and receive (R) lines of the channel or by coded characters sent on them. Any multiplexing equipment used on the internodal link may be regarded as completely transparent, as far as signalling is concerned, since the R.101 and R.111 TDMs do not drop start and stop bits, break characters, etc.

Considering a path between two exchanges X and Y, in which X to Y is the forward direction (calling to called DTE), a sample of the signals is

(i) Free line. X and Y each maintain a logical 0 (Space) on their transmit lines to each other.

(ii) Calling signal. X changes to 1 and sends selection signals. Selection signals include: characters specifying the class-of-traffic (for example indicating what further characters follow, if alternative routing is allowed, etc.); the user class (for example the bps rate of the caller's DTE); the identification of the called network; the identification of the called terminal.

(iii) Reception-confirmation signal. Y changes to 1.

(iv) Network identification signals. Y sends the identification of its network as coded characters if it belongs to a different network from X.

(Used for apportioning bills on international calls, etc.).

(v) Call-connected signal. Y sends a special character.

(vi) Terminating through-connection signal. Y sends another special character to show a through-connection to the destination DTE exists.

(vii) Originating through-connection signal. X sends the ACK character.

(viii) Clearing signal. Either X or Y sends 0.

(ix) Clear confirmation signal. X or Y responds to a received clearing signal by sending 0.

Other signals exist, notably various call progress signals from Y, and also call progress signals with clearing, with characters showing why the attempted call has failed, followed by a return to 0.

(2) *X.71.* X.71 in-band signalling applies to *synchronous* data networks supporting DTEs using, for example, X.21 (see Fig. 2.23). The signalling information is carried either in the S bit of the multiplexing envelope (see above), which corresponds to the state of the C or I lines on the X.21 interface; or in coded characters in the data stream itself, corresponding to the T and R lines. In each direction S = 1 when the call has been established, otherwise S = 0. The signalling functions are similar to that of the X.70 interface, but the characters used and the relative timing of the signals are distinct.

(3) *X.61/Q.741* (formerly X.60). X.61 and Q.741 are the same recommendation for CCS for *synchronous* data networks, but appearing in different CCITT volumes. The general concept of CCS has been presented above. It is based on various functional layers (see Fig. 2.26).

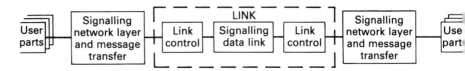

Fig. 2.26   CCS architecture.

The first functional layer of Signalling System No. 7 is the link layer. Its function is to ensure that all signalling traffic is safely delivered, error-free, across an internodal link. It specifies a signalling frame structure, redundant check bits and a link procedure to ensure this (Q.703).

The next layer is the signalling network and message layer. A signalling message may have to be routed through some transit node on the signalling network, to get to the node where it will be used to control the user's channel. Moreover, since CCS can be used to control heterogeneous traffic, signalling messages have to carry information identifying the traffic to which they refer (e.g. data or voice). The Q.704 Recommendation specifies the concepts, formats and procedures used at the network and message layer.

The third layer is that of the user part, which defines the contents and use of the signal messages by the nodes controlling the end-user's call. Different user parts (here 'user' means the signalling procedure using the signalling link and network layers) apply to different types of end-user traffic. For example there is a user part for telephony, and a user part for data (the 'data user part') which concerns us here, and is defined by X.61.

X.61 is a lengthy specification which can only be treated very superficially here. It defines the signalling messages used for CCS control of synchronous circuit-switched data networks; their formats; and the associated control procedures (when are the messages generated? What is done on their reception?). A special point to bear in mind when considering CCS is that, since the signalling is on channels independent from the channels of the user traffic, the signalling procedures must include tests that the user channel which has theoretically been established has actually been established—i.e. that a real through-connection exists between user DTEs. X.61 defines the following signal messages
(i) Address messages, sent in the forward direction (calling to called DTE) containing address information (network, DTE), class of service information (terminal bit rate, etc.) and additional information relating to user and network facilities (e.g. closed user group, reverse charging).
(ii) Calling line identity message. Sent in the forward direction.
(iii) Response message. Sent in the backward direction containing an indication of the called DTE's or called network's condition (engaged, unobtainable, etc.), information relating to user facilities, possibly an address or identification.
(iv) Clear message. Sent in either direction containing either a call-released signal or confirming a call-released signal.

The coding of the messages is in a 40-bit field. The coding reflects among other things the state of and characters transmitted on the X.21 T and R lines, and the state of the X.21 C and I lines.

The procedures for using the signalling messages are similar to those for call establishment and clearing that we have already seen (see X.71), plus special checks that the controlled circuit really has been established successfully, together with many additional procedures for the support of user facilities.

The reader is referred to the X.61 specification for further details.

2.5 CIRCUIT-SWITCHED DATA NETWORKS— A REVIEW AND ADDITIONAL COMMENTS

Circuit-switched data networks enable switched connections, in the form of unbuffered continuous circuits, to be established between compatible DTEs.

The techniques of switching were reviewed in Section 2.1 (space- and time-division switching) and Section 2.2 (TST-switching).

The interfaces for start-stop DTEs (X.20) and for synchronous DTEs (X.21) were considered in Section 2.3; together with the G.703 interface to digital bearer channels, applicable to internodal trunks and special leased (non-switched) digital circuits.

The multiplexing techniques for carrying many circuit-switched data channels on a single synchronous bearer channel were presented in Section 2.4. R.101 and R.111 apply to start-stop traffic, X.50 and X.51 to synchronous traffic.

Also in Section 2.4, the standards for signalling between the nodes of the circuit-switched data network were considered: X.70 for start-stop traffic, X.71 and X.61 (CCS) for synchronous traffic. The overall scheme is illustrated in Fig. 2.27.

However, before leaving the subject of circuit-switching, four additional topics should be addressed.

(1) Interworking between different traffic types and signalling methods.
(2) The quality of the circuits provided.
(3) Timing in synchronized networks.
(4) The architecture of the SPC nodes.

There are of course many other relevant topics (such as user facilities, or routing) but since these apply to all types of data networks they are relegated to later chapters.

2.5.1 Interworking

CCITT defines (in Recommendation X.1) [15] different classes of service for public circuit-switched data networks. Two categories exist
(1) Start-stop (Class 1 = 300 bps, Class 2 = 50–200 bps).

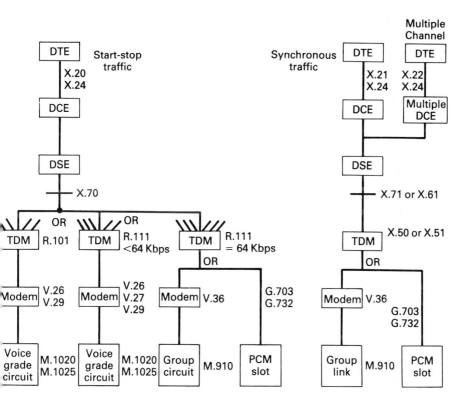

Fig. 2.27 Circuit-switched data network standards (simplified).

(2) Synchronous (Classes 3–7 are 600, 2400, 4800, 9600 and 48000 bps respectively).

Because of the direct connection between DTEs across the network, with no buffering, it is not really possible to interconnect two terminals belonging to a different class, although of course code conversions could be performed if their transmission rates were compatible. Thus a circuit-switched data network may be viewed as a collection of subnetworks, each one of which shares the same internodal trunks, the same switches and the same computers controlling the nodes, but only interconnects DTEs belonging to one class.

However, it is possible to carry start-stop traffic on synchronous links and it is possible to interwork the signalling systems, e.g. X.71 with X.61 for synchronous traffic.

This relatively inflexible situation should be compared with store-and-forward switching, in which DTEs of different characteristics and working at different rates can be interconnected.

2.5.2 Circuit Quality

Start-stop traffic can be distorted in a network both on transmission links and by multiplexing equipment such as the R.111 TDM which samples the bit stream. By distortion is meant the stretching or compression of the width of a bit. Recommendation R.121 [12] specifies acceptable limits to the distortion. In general, in any node which uses time-division switching, signals are regenerated, thereby limiting distortion. A pure space switch may not do this.

CCITT also has a recommendation (X.130) [13] for call set-up and clear-down times.

A topic not properly addressed by CCITT, however, is that of bit error rates experienced by the end-users of circuit-switched data networks. Such errors can certainly occur on, for example, analogue bearer circuits using group-band modems; or indeed on PCM circuits when slippage occurs (see below). A subscriber to a circuit-switched data network should try to find out from the operating administration what bit error rates can occur, so as to determine whether or not he should employ his own end-to-end error correction procedures.

2.5.3 Timing in Synchronous Networks

If traffic between two DTEs is synchronous and there is no buffering on the path through the network, then they must operate at exactly the same speed. On the X.21 interfaces, circuit S provides a clock from the DCEs, presumably originally from their local nodes; but how are the two nodes synchronized? This problem also occurs with traffic through a node. One node may send data to another node at a rate marginally faster or slower than the rate at which the second node passes it on further.

Various synchronizing schemes exist for digital networks. For example one can use

(i) Plesiochronous timing. Here each network (which could be a single node) of a group of networks has its own clock used to control the rate of transmission from it. All clocks are high precision so the networks are almost exactly synchronized. On the input lines from another network a few bits of buffering may permit small discrepancies over a period of time. However, if, over a long period of time, input is consistently marginally faster than output, then input traffic must be thrown away and the receiver must resynchronize with whatever incoming frame structure is in use. This is known as a 'controlled slip'. For example CCITT Recommendation G.811 [4] states that controlled slips on PCM links between international networks should occur less than once every 70 days.

(ii) Despotic synchronization. Here a master clock source controls the timing in slave nodes, who take their clocking from the incoming links from the master. This is suitable for a star-network, with the master clock at the hub.

(iii) Mutual synchronization. In this case each node adjusts its own clock towards some weighted average of the frequencies it receives from its neighbours. This supposes that a node's clock is adjustable. It is a technique suitable for highly meshed networks.

In practice, a mixture of these techniques is often used in a network. A typical approach is illustrated in Fig. 2.28. Here a master clock (plesiochronous with respect to other networks) controls despotically the timing of some major network nodes, which use mutual synchronization

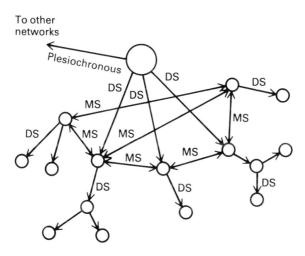

Fig. 2.28 Synchronizing a network. DS = despotic synchronization; MS = mutual synchronization.

between themselves and other meshed nodes. The nodes receiving the master signal give it added weight. Should the master clock fail, the network can still operate. The major nodes in turn control subsidiary networks using the master-slave approach.

2.5.4 The Architecture of a Node

Each manufacturer of circuit-switched data exchanges or nodes will have his own approach to designing the hardware and software of the system. The architecture employed will naturally reflect not only the subjective views of the designers, but also the volume of traffic the node is designed to handle and its overall flexibility. Is it a special purpose system, or is it a component in a range of equipment which can be extended to support a wide range of traffic and services? However, certain general principles apply to all such nodes

(i) It will be modular in both hardware and software, with clearly defined interfaces between modules. These systems are too complex to design and maintain if the design is not modular. Identifiable hardware sub-systems could be

— Subscriber line interfaces and concentration
— Trunk line interfaces
— The central switch
— The main computer(s) supporting the higher level programs controlling switching, charging, subscriber services, maintenance, etc.
— The peripheral devices such as magnetic tapes, disks, etc.
— Possibly a man-machine interface subsystem allowing an operator to observe and control the system via graphic displays or other devices.

Software subsystems could be

— Routing and switch control
— Signalling (subscriber and trunk lines)
— Charging
— Subscriber special services (e.g. support of multi-destination calls, closed user groups, etc.)
— Operational maintenance (e.g. attachment of new subscribers)
— Hardware monitoring and control (e.g. logging of faults).

(ii) The system will be redundant in its equipment. Computers will be duplicated to enable recovery from failure to take place. One favoured technique is to have two (or three) computers operating in exact synchronism on the same data and traffic, so that if one fails another can take over at once, with no hiatus.

(iii) Processing power will be distributed. In real-time systems such as SPC nodes the computing load is heavy. It is normal that subscriber and trunk lines should be grouped together under the control of one or two microprocessors. The same approach applies to other hardware sub-systems such as the main switch, or the peripherals. The main computers will handle the less time-critical tasks, such as charging, maintenance, updating routing tables, etc. The low-level hardware is controlled by a hierarchy of computers in each node, with microprocessors at the bottom of the hierarchy.

(iv) It will be designed to be maintainable. The operators of networks do not rely on external maintenance by the manufacturer. They maintain the system themselves. This means that subsystems, subassemblies, cards, power supplies, etc. must be easily accessible and can be removed in favour of a replacement in a few minutes. Powerful diagnostic functions are required, operating in real-time, to identify and locate malfunctions.

In summary, the nodes of data networks are high-performance, high-reliability, specialized real-time multi-processor computer systems, with all that this implies for hardware and software design.

REFERENCES

1 *Recommendation X.25* CCITT Red Book, **VIII. 3**, Geneva, 1985.
2 See Reference 7 of Chapter 1.
3 The TST example is taken from L.M. Ericsson's AXE-10 SPC switching system. See *AXE-10—System Survey* Telefonaktiebolaget L.M. Ericsson, S-12625, Stockholm, Sweden.
4 *Recommendations G.703, G.732, G.733, G.811* CCITT Red Book, **III. 3**, Geneva, 1985.
5 *Recommendations X.20, X.21, X.22, X.24* CCITT Red Book, **VIII. 3**, Geneva, 1985.
6 *Recommendations H.12, H.14* CCITT Red Book, **III. 4**, Geneva, 1985.
7 *Recommendation V.36* CCITT Red Book, **VIII. 1**, Geneva, 1985.
8 *Recommendations V.10, V.11, V.28* CCITT Red Book, **VIII. 1**, Geneva, 1985.
9 See the second and third references in Reference 1 of Chapter 1 for introductions to basic data communications.
10 *Recommendations M.1020, M.1025* CCITT Red Book, **IV. 2**, Geneva, 1985.
11 *Recommendations V.26, V.27, V.29* CCITT Red Book, **VIII. 1**, Geneva, 1985.
12 *Recommendations R.35, R.37, R.38, R.191, R.111, R.121* CCITT Red Book, **VII. 1**, Geneva, 1985.

13 *Recommendations X.50, X.51, X.61, X.70, X.71, X.130* CCITT Red Book, **VIII. 4,** Geneva, 1985.
14 *Q Series Recommendations* CCITT Red Book, **VI. 1–VI. 9,** Geneva, 1985.
15 *Recommendation X.1* CCITT Red Book, **VIII. 2,** Geneva, 1985.
16 The example of a Telex switch is taken from the Hasler AG T.200 system, Bern, Switzerland.

Chapter 3
Store-and-Forward Data Networks

3.1 THE CONCEPT OF STORE-AND-FORWARD SWITCHING

In Chapter 1 the basic concept of store-and-forward (SAF) switching was presented. Information is transmitted in the form of messages of finite size, although the length of messages may vary considerably between different 'conversations', and indeed within a conversation. When a message begins to arrive at a node in the network on an incoming link it is accumulated—i.e. it is assembled into a storage area—until it is completely received. The control function of the node then examines the message and decides on which outgoing link it is to be forwarded; and proceeds to start sending it out on that link.

Since links are of finite capacity, that is they have a maximum rate at which they can carry information, it takes a finite time for a node to receive or transmit a message. In the absence of errors on the link this is the baud rate, or signalling rate; or a multiple of the baud rate, e.g. 2, 3 or 4, if several information bits can be encoded as a single signal (as is possible with higher-speed modems operating over telephone circuits). In the presence of errors on the link, Shannon's famous theorem [1] shows that there still exists a (smaller) finite capacity at which information can be carried by the link with arbitrarily small probability of residual error. In effect, redundant information can be included in the message to enable errors to be detected and corrected with an arbitrarily large probability of success. Some of the 'raw' capacity of the channel is used up by the redundant information.

3.1.1 Multiplexing Traffic on a Channel

In general a *single* channel unites a pair of nodes, or a node and a DTE. The channel could be, for example, a 64 Kbps channel on a 2048 Kbps PCM circuit; or it could be a physical 4-wire telephone circuit with suitable modems. (In certain cases multiple parallel channels may exist between nodes, or between a node and a DTE, but for the moment we ignore this possibility.) But this channel is not reserved for the messages of a single 'conversation', supposing the concept of a 'conversation' is defined. Messages belonging to different conversations are interleaved on the channel, and indeed there will be periods when no message is travelling on the channel (see Fig. 3.1). Thus access to the channel is multiplexed between its different users. This multiplexing applies not only to internodal 'trunk' links, but also to DTE-node links, assuming that the DTE itself can handle several simultaneous users. If the DTE is a computer it can obviously, if suitably programmed, handle such simultaneous users. If it is a simple terminal it probably will not do so.

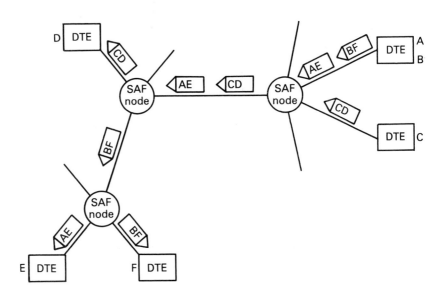

Fig. 3.1 Interleaving of messages. ◁XY = Message travelling from DTE X to DTE Y.

The multiplexed use of a channel is *dynamic,* so that the capacity of the channel is allocated to the messages of different conversations as they need it, although certain restrictions may still apply. For example, if the concept of a conversation or a 'call' is recognized by the network, there may be restrictions on the number of simultaneous calls using the channel, and/or the number of messages per second per call.

3.1.2 Flow Control

There is no reason why the capacity of all the links used by the messages traversing the network between a pair of DTEs should be the same. It is normal that the capacity of individual trunk links is higher than that of individual DTE-node links; and it is also normal that the combined capacity of trunk links out of a node is less than the combined capacity of DTE-node links into it. The node, once again, concentrates traffic, on the assumption that all DTE-node links will be working at full capacity simultaneously with only a very small probability.

A particular case of links having different capacities arises when two DTEs exchanging messages each have links to their local nodes of different capacities. Provided that the *average* rate of messages between the two DTEs is less than the lower capacity of the two DTE-node links, no problem will arise. If necessary, this can be enforced by control procedures known as flow-control. Since the SAF nodes contain buffering, short-term deviations from the average message rate can be accommodated by holding messages, which cannot go out on the next temporarily fully loaded link, in the buffers.

Flow control in SAF networks exists not only to avoid overloading of DTE-node links. In general flow control is used to protect against overload of

(i) DTE-node channels

(ii) Internodal trunks

(iii) The nodes themselves (which will have a finite capacity for processing and switching messages)

(iv) The DTEs themselves (which will also have a finite capacity for processing messages).

In the latter case, protecting the DTEs against overload, we speak of 'end-to-end' flow control if the mechanism operates directly between the two communicating DTEs, transparently to the intervening network.

Another way of looking at flow control is to state that it exists to ensure that the buffers used to hold messages in the nodes and DTEs do not become exhausted. Each node on a path across the network can be represented as having two buffer queues: one for messages arriving at the node and awaiting switching or other processing, a processing queue or PQ; and one for messages waiting to go out on a channel, a channel queue or CQ. A sending DTE has a CQ; a receiving DTE has a PQ (see Fig. 3.2).

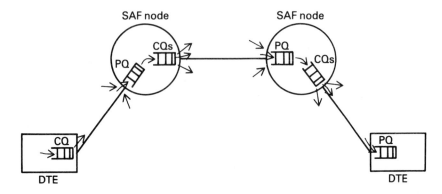

Fig. 3.2 Typical queues in SAF networks.

3.1.3 Error Control

We have seen that in circuit-switched data networks the corruption of data in transit is in theory held to an acceptable level by the quality of the channels used, pulse regeneration, etc. However, if data are corrupted then it is essentially regarded as a user problem. Control of errors by the network is preventive rather than corrective.

In SAF data networks it is generally accepted that the operator of the network is responsible for correcting as well as preventing errors, at least to provide a low residual bit error rate (BER) such as 1 bit in 10^9 (BER = 10^{-9}). The reason for this is that, due to the SAF technique, it is *possible* to correct errors. Redundant error control bits can be introduced into the forward traffic on a channel, for error correction on reception at the end of the channel. Alternatively, the receiver can use the extra bits to detect errors and request a retransmission, in the manner familiar in ordinary data communications, e.g. using the BSC [19] or HDLC [4] protocols. The dynamic use of the channel permits the insertion of retransmission requests and retransmitted messages into the backward and forward data streams respectively.

Error control may go further than correcting corrupted messages. In many pure message-switching networks messages are systematically allocated sequence numbers and archived by the network. Not only can the loss of messages be detected and recovery effected automatically; it is also possible for users to recover messages, perhaps two or three days old, from the archive.

3.1.4 Network Protocols

Standards, procedures and conventions are required for establishing communication between DTEs across an SAF network, just as we have seen that they are needed in a circuit-switched network. If the concept of a 'call', recognized by the SAF network, exists; then there must exist call set-up and call-clearing procedures.

However, unlike circuit-switched data networks whose data transfer phase is very simple, in SAF networks additional procedures are required for flow control and error control during data transfer. Such procedures are generally referred to as 'protocols', and an SAF network will have associated interfacing, internodal, internetwork and possibly end-to-end protocols to control the setting-up and clearing-down of connections (if applicable) and the data transfer itself.

Such protocols are discussed at some length later in this chapter.

3.1.5 Some Other Characteristics of SAF Networks

Most data traffic is asymmetric; more data travels from DTE A to DTE B than from DTE B to DTE A. It is only necessary to consider interactive use of a computer, with the user typing in short messages and receiving long ones in reply, to realize this. A more extreme example is a file transfer. In circuit-switching, a two-way circuit is established for the duration of the call. The use made of the circuit is of little interest to the network designer. In SAF-switching, use of channels and nodes is dynamic. The capacity of nodes and channels should be designed to handle the traffic; but if traffic flows are not symmetric the design problem is more difficult. On average, perhaps, internodal trunks carry the same traffic in each direction; but on DTE-node channels this is almost certainly not the case.

Another important difference between circuit-switched and SAF data networks is that transit times are almost constant (for a given connection) in the former, and can vary significantly in the latter. An SAF network can be regarded as a queueing system (see Fig. 3.2), and the service time (the transit time) is dependent on the load or occupancy of the network, in a very non-linear fashion. For this reason SAF networks are not suitable for real-time data such as voice or video unless special precautions are taken either to control variable transit delays, or to mask them by very substantial buffering at the receiver.

Finally, if the SAF network supports the 'call' concept, call set-up and clearing times are also variable. However, this is not so very different from the situation which pertains with circuit-switching when CCS is used over a signalling network (which is often SAF); except that the signalling is not further delayed by data in CCS, whereas it is in most SAF networks.

3.2 CAPACITY, LOADING AND PERFORMANCE IN STORE-AND-FORWARD DATA NETWORKS

In circuit-switched data networks, when a new call arises, the situation is clear: either a circuit can be made available to it, or it cannot; and in Chapter 2 the probability of finding a suitable circuit on internodal links and through a switch was discussed. Assuming that a circuit can be found, then it is of known fixed capacity and interconnects DTEs operating at the same data rate.

In SAF networks the situation is much less 'black-or-white'. If call-switching is employed, as in virtual circuit (VC) packet-switching networks, then the decision to allocate or not to allocate a VC to a new call is, to a certain degree, arbitrary. Since the existing calls do not use a fixed fraction of the total capacity available, the network might elect to allow a new call depending not only on the number of existing calls, but also on their associated activity or data rate. In practice it is normal, although perhaps not wholly logical, for virtual-call networks to pre-allocate a maximum number of VCs to each subscriber's DTE interface. The subscriber is then free to take up this number, but not more, at any time, irrespective of the use he makes of each VC. Of course, once the VC has been allocated to the call, there is no hard guarantee of the performance the user will obtain from it—it depends on the current load on those parts of the network used by the VC. However, some notional 'Grade-of-Service' may apply; for example that transnetwork delays will be less than a certain number of ms for 90% of all messages sent.

If VCs do not exist, and the network is a pure message-switching or datagram packet-switching network, then there may be no attempt to guarantee performance. Alternatively, if strict flow control is exercised at the DTE interface so that new incoming messages are not accepted unless there is a reasonable probability that they can be transferred across the network within an acceptable delay, then some suitable 'Grade-of-Service' may also be offered to the subscriber.

In the following sections we consider the loading of circuits and nodes in SAF networks, so that the effect on performance can at least be estimated, if not rigorously calculated.

3.2.1 Capacity and Loading of Channels

If the raw capacity of a channel is N bps and the average message size sent on it is n bits (including redundant bits for error-correction and control bits for routing, message delimitation, etc.), then the channel capacity is $\mu = N/n$ messages per second. If we accept the model of Fig. 3.2, in which there is a CQ per channel, conventional queuing theory [2] (random arrival rate of λ messages per second and exponential service time μ^{-1}) tells us that the number of messages in the system, i.e. in CQ and being transmitted on the channel, is $\rho/(1-\rho)$, with $\rho = \lambda/\mu$.* The average time for a message to get from one node to another is given by $1/(\mu-\lambda)$. To achieve acceptable delays, and remembering that large variances are associated with these queuing distributions, it is really necessary that ρ should be small; $\rho < 0.5$, say, and certainly ρ should always be less than 0.7.

For example, if the message length is 256 octets plus 24 extra octets, so that $n = 8\times(256+24) = 2240$ bits and the average message rate $\lambda = 4$ messages per second, for $\rho = 0.5$ we require $N = n\mu = n\lambda/\rho = 2240\times4\times2 = 17\,920$ bps. A 19.2 Kbps channel is indicated.

In practice, channels will be full-duplex and there will be messages flowing in the other direction. Due to the existence of protocols, associated with each data message in either direction, there will usually be a (smaller) acknowledgement or flow control message in the reverse direction. These reverse messages are generally of higher priority than the forward messages, preempting them in CQ. One way of modelling this situation is to suppose that if the reverse message size is n' bits and its frequency is λ', then the capacity is reduced from N to $(N-n'\lambda')$, so

---

*This model for CQ can be derived from the Erlang-C formula (1.15) of Chapter 1 by putting $n = 1$ (a single output line) and letting $M \to \infty$. The assumption that service time has an exponential distribution, rather than being of fixed duration, is not easily justified. However, if message lengths are exponentially distributed, so then are service times.

$\mu = (N-n'\lambda')/n$. If we introduce this into our previous example we require

$$N = n\mu+n'\lambda' = \frac{n\lambda}{\rho}+n'\lambda' = 17\,920+n'\lambda' \text{ bps.}$$

Typically we might have $n' = 80$, $\lambda' = \lambda = 4$, so the 19.2 Kbps channel is still adequate.

Suppose now that VCs apply on the channel and that the offered traffic in one direction is A Erlang, with, as usual

$$A = \lambda hN$$

where h = the average call duration or hold-time; N = the number of subscribers or computer processes capable of originating calls and λ = the average rate at which a subscriber makes calls.

We can use the Erlang-B formulae of Section 1.2.1 to estimate the maximum number of VCs, M, that should be supported on the channel for a given Grade of Service $E(M, A)$.

In the case when a channel linking a DTE to a node is under consideration, the number of processes, N, in the DTE capable of making calls is probably limited and it might be better to use the Engset rather than the Erlang-B distribution. The Engset equations may be derived as follows.

We refer back to Equation (1.6) of Section 1.2.1 and take $\mu_k = k\mu = k/h$ (as in the case of Erlang-B), but now take $\lambda_k = (N-k)\lambda$, where λ is the average call rate of an *idle* originator (or process). This assumption means that the more calls which exist the smaller the probability of a new one arising. It is easily shown that the probability of k simultaneous calls is now

$$P_k = \left(\frac{\lambda}{\mu}\right)^k \frac{N!}{k!(N-k)!}P_0 \qquad k = 0 \text{ to } M$$

Now if A is the total traffic, the average rate of calls per originator is $A/Nh = A\mu/N$. This must be equal to $(1-A/N)\lambda$, since the expression in parentheses is the probability of the originator being idle, and λ the call rate when idle. Thus

$$\lambda = A\mu/N(1-A/N)$$

or $\dfrac{\lambda}{\mu} = A/(N-A)$

The time congestion for the Engset distribution is thus

$$E(M, A) = P_M = \left(\frac{A}{N-A}\right)^M \frac{N!}{M!(N-M)!} P_0 \tag{3.1}$$

$$\text{with } P_0^{-1} = \sum_{k=0}^{M} \left(\frac{A}{N-A}\right)^k \frac{N!}{k!(N-k)!}$$

For a given Grade of Service $E(M, A)$ we could use the Engset Equation (3.1) to calculate M, the number of VCs to be supported on the channel given an offered traffic A, rather than using the Erlang-B formulae. The resultant value for M would be smaller.

A more serious objection to the above method of estimating the number of VCs to be supported on a channel is that, in most SAF networks, the VCs have to be shared between calls in *both* directions. Two separate groups of VCs are *not* reserved for outgoing and incoming calls. The situation is analogous to that pertaining in circuit-switching networks where a number of trunks link two nodes, either of which might seize a trunk to originate a call to the other. To minimize the number of 'collisions' (a new outgoing call being attempted simultaneously with a new incoming one on the same circuit, real or virtual), it is normal that, if the VCs are numbered 1 to M, outgoing calls 'hunt' for free VCs in the sequence 1 to M, incoming ones in the sequence M to 1.

Suppose the total traffic offered in the forward direction is A, that the traffic offered to VC number n, VC(n), is A_n, and the traffic carried by it is A_n^*, then we have

$$A_1 = A$$

$$A_n = A \cdot E(n-1, \bar{A}_{n-1}) \tag{3.2}$$

$$A - A_n = \sum_{i=1}^{n-1} A_i^* \tag{3.3}$$

$$A_n^* = A(1 - E(n, \bar{A}_n)) - \sum_{i=1}^{n-1} A_i^* \tag{3.4}$$

where $\bar{A}_n$ is the *total* traffic offered to VC(1) to VC(n), including traffic from other sources (e.g. the opposite direction).

Equation (3.2) states that the forward traffic offered to VC(n) is the overflow of A from VC(1) to VC ($n-1$). Equation (3.3) states the same in another way. Equation (3.4) states that the forward traffic carried by VC(n) is A, less the forward traffic carried by VC(1) to VC($n-1$), less the overflow to VC($n+1$).

The equations combine to give

$$A_n^* = A(E(n-1, \bar{A}_{n-1}) - E(n, \bar{A}_n)). \tag{3.5}$$

If we ignore the backward traffic, $\bar{A}_n = A$ for all n. As a practical example, suppose $M = 8$ (VCs), $A = 2$ Erlang, then the traffic (in the forward direction) carried by each VC is given in Table 3.1.

Table 3.1 Forward traffic carried per VC for $A = 2$ (no backward traffic)

VC No. (n)	Traffic carried (A_n^*)
1	0.667
2	0.534
3	0.380
4	0.230
5	0.116
6	0.048
7	0.017
8	0.006
	1.998

If the backward traffic is also considered, $\bar{A}_n$ is no longer equal to A. For simplicity we assume the total offered backward traffic is the same as the offered forward traffic, A. Then

$$\bar{A}_n = A + A - \sum_{k=n+1}^{M} A_k^* \text{ (backward)} \tag{3.6}$$

$$= 2A - \sum_{k=1}^{M-n} A_k^* \text{ (forward)} \tag{3.7}$$

Equation (3.6) states that the total traffic offered to VC(1) to VC(n) is A (forward) plus A (backward) less the backward traffic carried by VC(M) to VC($n+1$). Assuming the solution to the traffic flows is symmetric, Equation (3.7) can replace Equation (3.6). Thus, for equal offered traffic A in each direction, Equation (3.5) becomes

$$A_n^* = A\left\{ E\left(n-1,\, 2A - \sum_{k=1}^{M+1-n} A_k^*\right) - E\left(n,\, 2A - \sum_{k=1}^{M-n} A_k^*\right)\right\} \quad (3.8)$$

This Equation (3.8) may be solved iteratively, taking the solutions to Equation (3.5) with $\bar{A}_n = A$ as starting values for A_n^*.

If, for example, we do this for the previous example, the new results obtained for carried traffic are as shown in Table 3.2.

Table 3.2 Forward traffic carried per VC for $A = 2$ (with backward traffic)

VC No. (n)	Traffic carried (A_n^*)
1	0.652
2	0.522
3	0.366
4	0.218
5	0.108
6	0.048
7	0.018
8	0.008
	1.940

If we add backward and forward traffic the result is as shown in Table 3.3.

From the results of this analysis we see that, for 4 Erlang offered, 0.12 Erlang are lost, so the Grade of Service (GOS) is 3%. We could repeat the analysis with another trial value of M, the number of VCs required, to obtain a better GOS, although in practice we could just as well solve

$$E(M,\, A) = \text{Required GOS}$$

for M, given $A = $ the total (forward plus backward) offered traffic, if the only subject of interest is M. The point of the above example is that

Table 3.3 Total traffic carried per VC for $A = 2+2 = 4$

VC No. (n)	Total traffic carried
1	0.660
2	0.540
3	0.414
4	0.326
5	0.326
6	0.414
7	0.540
8	0.660
	3.880

it shows how to calculate the traffic carried on each individual VC.

It will be noted that the middle VCs, which are the ones where collision is likely to occur, are carrying nearly half as much traffic as the end VCs. Given the time-window, during call set-up, in which collisions can occur, it is possible to calculate the probability of a collision on each channel. However, we do not pursue the matter further; but merely emphasize that there exist criteria for analysing the traffic carried by VCs on a shared link when the 'hunting' technique, described above, is used.

Finally, it should be noted that the actual message rate on a given VC may be very variable and that the channel capacity in bps should be dimensioned to handle the aggregate message rate of the traffic carried (average number of simultaneous VCs). Message rates on a VC in practice range from perhaps 1 message every 3 seconds for interactive traffic, to the capacity of the channel for bulk transfers, unless individual flow control per VC restricts this.

3.2.2 Capacity and Loading of SAF Nodes

SAF-switching nodes can become loaded with traffic in two ways
(1) Loading of the processor(s). Loading of the processor(s) occurs because the messages or packets in transit require a certain amount of processing as they pass through the node, such as obeying protocols (acknowledgement, issuing of flow control commands, etc.) or routing

(examining destination addresses or logical channel numbers and posting the messages to the queue for the chosen output link). Typically, nodes handle between 10 and 10^3 messages per second, depending on their design. A node in which all processing is performed by a single processor, with, say, DMA input/output to help it, might handle 50 to 100 messages per second. A multiprocessor node with microprocessors dedicated to links to obey the protocols would handle more. Whatever the processing capacity of the node in messages per second, as the arrival rate of messages rises towards that capacity, queues of messages awaiting processing will build up. The messages in the queue require buffer space to hold them.

(2) Loading of the internodal links. It takes time to output a message on a link, a time essentially (but not strictly) proportional to the message length and inversely proportional to the speed of the link. If the arrival rate of messages for output on a given link rises towards that link's output rate, then output queues will build up. Again, buffers are required to hold the queued messages.

Thus, if the service rates μ_p (for processing) and μ_i (for communication on link i) are given in messages per second and the arrival rates of messages into the node are known, it should be possible to calculate the buffering requirements of the various queues to achieve a target Buffer Grade of Service, here defined as

> Buffer Grade of Service of an SAF node =
> Probability of exhausting the buffers provided.

Before attempting this task for an example node some remarks are in order.

The Grade of Service of interest to a user of an SAF network is probably definable in terms of throughput (how many messages per second can be sent across the network?) and transnetwork delays (how long does it take a message to cross the network?). It is in the nature of SAF systems, which are based on queuing, that as a user's throughput increases towards the capacity available, the associated transnetwork delay tends to infinity. Thus high throughput and small delay are somewhat incompatible. They can only be achieved by very high values of μ_p and μ_i, implying, normally, much surplus capacity. The network designer will obviously select nodes with processing power, and links with bit rates which will give some acceptable Grade of Service to the forecast traffic without squandering capacity uneconomically.

Once the designer has chosen these parameters he can then calculate buffering requirements to meet the 'Buffer Grade of Service' we defined above. Of course, computer memory for buffering is not as expensive as it once was, but this does not invalidate the exercise of calculating a Buffer Grade of Service. On the contrary, this is one of the principal indicators of the node's performance as seen by the user. If, to meet a Buffer Grade of Service, a very large number of buffers is required, it shows at once that the server (processor or link) is too slow. As always, a shortage of time shows itself in an excess of space for queuing. Thus the analysis of buffering requirements is not only useful for its ostensible purpose, but also as a direct check on the correctness of the speed of the servers involved.

The queuing model of an SAF node which follows supposes that the node can be represented as containing a single processor. Buffering is required at four stages in a message's transfer through the node, as follows

(1) On input a buffer is required into which the message arriving on a given line can be accumulated.

(2) Buffers are then required to hold messages queued for processing.

(3) Processed messages are next queued for output.

(4) Output messages are held in buffers until their receipt by a remote node or DTE is acknowledged, i.e. the message is held awaiting possible retransmission (e.g. in X.25 Level 2 [3] or HDLC [4]).

To simplify the calculations, the assumption is made that all lines are, on average, equally loaded. This implies that if the arrival rate for line i is λ_i, and the service rate is μ_i, then $A_i = \lambda_i/\mu_i = A_c$ for all i. This assumption essentially supposes that the network is well designed, with capacities proportional to the traffic to be carried.

A further general assumption is that messages for which there is no buffer available are lost, i.e. thrown away. In practice they will be recovered by the communication protocols, but from our point of view the input rate is *reduced* as a result of buffer shortage, whether by causing retransmissions or by flow control is immaterial. The assumption is equivalent to the 'blocked-calls-lost' assumption of circuit-switching. Finally, although messages can be considered as copied between buffers when moving from one stage to the next of the four stages supposed, we can equally well assume that the same buffer moves from stage to stage. Under this assumption, loss of a message for want of a buffer will only occur on input, but the number of buffers to be provided will be calculated assuming possible loss at each stage. The number will give a conservative estimate, since it will not account for the marginal advantages of full dynamic allocation of buffers.

The buffers required at stages (1) to (4) to meet a Grade of Service G_i for stage (1) can now be calculated. n input and n output links are assumed.

(1) Input. The Engset formula is used since the number of links is finite. The number of buffers, M_i, is given by solving

$$G_1 = P_0\left(\frac{A}{n-A}\right)^{M_1} \frac{n!}{M_1!(n-M_1)!} \quad \text{for } M_1, \tag{3.9}$$

with

$$P_0^{-1} = \sum_{k=0}^{n}\left(\frac{A}{n-A}\right)^k \frac{n!}{k!(n-k)!}$$

and

$$A = nA_c$$

(2) Processing. The usual equation for a finite single-server queue is used (Erlang-C with one server). The number of buffers, M_2, is given by solving

$$G_2 = \frac{A_p^{M_2}(1-A_p)}{(1-A_p^{M_2+1})} \quad \text{for } M_2, \tag{3.10}$$

with

$$A_p = \sum_{i=1}^{n}\lambda_i/\mu_p = \lambda/\mu_p$$

(3) Output. The question is: What is the probability of k buffers in use in n output queues? We tackle this approximately, as follows. It is easily seen that if k messages are distributed among n links, then on average the number of links without a message is $nk/(n+k-1)$; assuming that the probability of a link having a message is equal (A_c) over all links. We can then take the probability of a message buffer becoming free in time dt, given that k are in use, as

$$dt.\mu_k = dt.\mu_c nk/(n+k-1) \quad k = 1 \text{ to } M_3,$$

where

$$\mu_c = \sum_{i=1}^{n} \mu_i/n, \text{ the average service rate per link.}$$

Substituting this μ_k in Equation (1.6) of Chapter 1, with $\lambda_k = \lambda$ for $0 \leqslant k < M_3$, we get a new distribution for the number, k, of buffers in use

$$P_k = P_0(A_c)^k \frac{(n+k-1)!}{k!(n-1)!}$$

with

$$P_0^{-1} = \sum_{k=0}^{M_3} (A_c)^k \frac{(n+k-1)!}{k!(n-1)!}$$

(The same result can be obtained by considering the distribution of

$$k = \sum_{i=1}^{n} k_i$$

where k_i is the number of items in output queue i, and a geometric distribution for k_i is assumed.)

The required number of buffers, M_3, is then given by solving

$$G_3 = P_0(A_c)^{M_3} \frac{(n+M_3-1)!}{M_3!(n-1)!} \qquad \text{for } M_3. \tag{3.11}$$

(4) Retransmission. The Erlang-B formula is used to give the probability of a total of M_4 retransmission buffers being occupied. The service time for line i is taken to be x/μ_i, where x is a factor depending on the protocol and the probability of line errors. If $x = 2$, it means that a message is held in a retransmission buffer on average for the duration of two further message outputs. Typically $1 \leqslant x \leqslant 2$.

The required number of buffers, M_4, is given by solving

$$G_4 = P_0(xnA_c)^{M_4}/M_4! \qquad \text{for } M4, \tag{3.12}$$

with

$$P_0^{-1} = \sum_{k=0}^{M_4} (xnA_c)^k/k!.$$

The overall Grade of Service from Equations (3.9) to (3.12) is given by

Buffer Grade of Service $= G_1+G_2+G_3+G_4$.

As an example, suppose the required Buffer Grade of Service is 0.4%, and we take $G_1 = G_2 = G_3 = G_4 = 0.1\%$; and suppose there are 8 lines ($n = 8$), $\mu_p = 64$ messages per second, $\lambda = 16$ messages per second (arriving), and $A_c = 1/3$ (all lines 33% loaded), then we find

$$M_1 = 8; M_2 = 5; M_3 = 13; M_4 = 10 \ (x = 1) \text{ or } 16 \ (x = 2).$$

If we take $x = 1$, the conclusion is that 36 message buffers should be provided in this switch for an overall 0.4% Buffer Grade of Service.

The above calculations serve as an illustration. A given SAF switch may require a different model. It may be simpler to fix M_1 and M_4 at their known maximum values (e.g. $M_1 = n$; $M_4 = Wn$, if W is the size of the node's transmit window in the absence of acknowledgements), and concentrate attention on M_2 and M_3. In fact in our example $M_1 = n(8)$ as a result of the calculations.

Such a simpler approach is illustrated in Fig. 3.2, where the SAF node is modelled by a single processing queue, PQ; and a communications circuit queue, CQ. It may help to consider some cases, with this model, heuristically rather than analytically.

(i) *A1.* ($\mu_p > n\mu_c$). There will be no PQ of significance, since processing speed exceeds the input and output rate. There will also be no CQs of significance if the message arrival rate $\lambda \ll n\mu_c$. When λ begins to rise towards $n\mu_c$ the number of items in the output queues is theoretically given by Equation (3.11). In practice this often does not happen, because the traffic ceases to be random as the input rate rises to a fixed maximum value. Input and output tend to become synchronized at the rate $n\mu_c$ and the node begins to operate like a time-division circuit-switch. As an indication of what figures may occur in practice, for a single 9600 bps channel and 128-octet messages (plus extra control octets) $\mu_c = 8$ messages per second approximately. It requires several tens of such channels to produce an aggregate μ_c which exceeds the μ_p typical of most SAF switches.

(ii) *A2.* ($\mu_p < n\mu_c$, single processor used.) In this case the nature of processing should be looked at more closely. In practice we may take

$$\mu_p^{-1} = 2\mu_{PIO}^{-1}+\mu_{PSW}^{-1}$$

where μ_{PIO} is the input or output processing rate and μ_{PSW} is the switching processing rate. Input and output processing will be given a higher priority to switching in a single processor, as assumed, so that, as λ approaches μ_p, PQ will start to grow; and when λ exceeds μ_p, PQ will grow very rapidly since processor power is dedicated to input/output. CQ will generally not grow. If λ continues to grow to exceed μ_{PIO} then input traffic is simply dropped—the processor is not fast enough to handle it. A critical figure is the ratio of μ_{PIO} to μ_{PSW}. If it is small, as it often is, so that input/output processing dominates performance, then the danger interval ($\mu_p < \lambda < \mu_{PIO}$) is small.

(iii) *A3*. ($\mu_p < n\mu_c$, separate I/O processors used). In this case there are effectively three queues: input processing, switching and output processing; and μ_P is the lesser of μ_{PIO} and μ_{PSW}. If λ exceeds μ_p and $\mu_{PIO} < \mu_{PSW}$ traffic is dropped on input; otherwise PQ (the queue for switching) will grow significantly. In neither case will CQ grow.

Now suppose explicit concentration is taking place in a node, as might occur when it supports subscribers as well as trunks. We have an aggregate capacity μ_{CIP} for input channels and μ_{COP} for output channels, with $\mu_{CIP} > \mu_{COP}$. Three cases arise

(1) B1. ($\mu_{CIP} < \mu_p$). Only CQ will grow significantly when λ approaches μ_{COP}.

(2) B2. ($\mu_{CIP} > \mu_p > \mu_{COP}$). Behaviour is as for cases A2 or A3, except that CQ will also grow, since the output channels cannot keep up with the message rate from the switch.

(3) B3. ($\mu_{CIP} > \mu_{COP} > \mu_p$). The processor(s) will overload as λ rises above μ_p as in A2 or A3. CQ will not grow.

A few general observations are in order

—It is desirable that μ_p exceeds μ_c; if not, it should at least be well in excess of the average message rate, λ. This avoids all *processing* queuing problems, and a simple situation exists (A1 or B1) which can be analysed.

—If λ can approach μ_p only simulation or modelling techniques can really predict performance. In particular, the internal (probably multi-processor) structure of the node and the routing of traffic should be taken into account.

—A good general approach to handling 'space-loading' is simply *not* to provide many buffers. If they are needed there is already a problem, and it is probably better dealt with by discarding traffic on input, leaving it to the low-level internode or DTE-node protocols to recover from this situation [5].

Finally, it should be noted that, since the capacity of channels is likely to rise in the next few years faster than that of processors, the problems of overloaded SAF nodal processors is likely to become more acute. Parallel processing of switching as well as of input/output will be necessary (it is often available already) and the resultant high frequency access to *shared* storage areas (message buffers, tables, etc.) will have to be made more efficient, if that is not to become a 'bottleneck' in turn. We return to the topic of fast packet-switching in Chapter 7.

3.3 MESSAGE-SWITCHING NETWORKS

In the previous section some aspects of the performance of SAF networks were examined. A particular class of SAF networks is message-switching networks. Insofar as it is possible to distinguish clearly between a message-switching and any other SAF network it may be said, generally, that

(i) Message-switching networks recognize the existence of user messages. They do not handle user data transparently, as do, for example, packet-switched networks. A packet in a packet-switched network may contain an entire message or, more usually, only a fragment of such a message; and the network receives and delivers packets. It is left to the users of a packet-switched network to fragment and reassemble messages. By contrast, a message-switching network will take responsibility for transferring complete messages; reassembling them, if necessary, at each node through which they pass; ensuring that the selected destinations receive complete messages; and recording the message delivery at least internally, if not also confirming it directly to the sender. Thus message formats must be standardized so that the network can recognize the messages. In short, message-switching networks are concerned with aspects of the user's application, rather than acting as a transparent infrastructure.

(ii) Because message-switching networks handle complete messages the nodes require significantly more storage than straight forward in-and-out packet-switching nodes. Messages are buffered on disk, rather than in direct access memory. If, as is usual, some sort of longer-term storage or archiving, for later retrieval of messages, is supported, then the disk requirements are non-trivial. Since messages are buffered on disk, the discussions of performance in the previous section are only partially relevant. The processing time per message in a node is relatively long, because disk accesses are involved. Transnetwork delays are measured in terms of several seconds, if not minutes or even hours.

(iii) Message-switching networks offer high integrity to the user, by which is meant that they *guarantee* (as far as possible) that a message launched into the network arrives safely at the destination(s). This guarantee is particularly important, since for many messages there is no immediate reply expected by the sender. This is to be contrasted with the interactive traffic typically supported by packet-switched networks, in which loss of data in transit is immediately apparent to the sender.

(iv) Message-switching networks usually allow a given message to be sent to more than one destination. By contrast, most other data networks (circuit-switched or SAF packet-switched) support only point-to-point, not point-to-multipoint, communications.

Since message-switching is largely application-oriented, and this chapter is concerned with network infrastructure, most of the discussion about message-switching is deferred to later chapters. Additionally, until the appearance of the X.400 Recommendations [6] (see Chapter 6) very few standards for message-switching existed—and those which did exist were largely *de facto* (e.g. IATA/SITA) standards [7]. Many special-purpose message-switching systems exist, notably military ones; and there are message-switching systems available commercially; but all these networks are distinct, using their own particular formats, protocols and techniques. The only features they would have in common are the general message-switching concepts presented above.

To help to clarify the nature of message-switching, two examples are presented briefly.

3.3.1 A Typical Commercial Message-Switch

A familiar example of a message-switching system is one which interfaces to the public Telex network. Such a system will support many interactive terminals which may be used to create messages on the node (Fig. 3.3), using suitable editing programs. In creating the message the user will supply destination addresses (on the public Telex network), indicate the priority of the message (for immediate delivery or to be sent at cheap overnight rates), etc. Messages received from the Telex network will probably be printed by the node (often a legal requirement) and will also be held in the destination user's 'mailbox', whence he may retrieve them next time he logs in to the node. (It will be noted that addressing

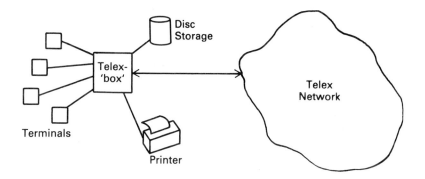

Fig. 3.3 A telex 'box' for handling messages to/from the telex network.

a destination may involve specifying a user's name as well as some network number.)

Such a simple message-switching system, which is really a combination of a mailbox system with Telex, rather than genuine message-switching will usually be capable of upgrading to handle a more extensive infrastructure than Telex interfaces, local interactive terminals and a printer. Figure 3.4 illustrates some possible upgrades

(i) Support of remote access by user terminals over the public telephone network, or a packet-switched network.

(ii) Direct node-to-node connections, via leased channels, to other similar nodes. This is justified if heavy message-traffic can exist between the locations in question.

(iii) Support of special-purpose terminals, and terminals using different formats and codes from the normal asynchronous terminals. For example Teletex [8] (Chapter 6) terminals might be supported, or synchronous terminals such as IBM 3270s.

(iv) Switching of terminals between the local host computers and the message-switching nodes. Users will not want *two* terminals on their desk, but will want to use one to access indifferently a host computer or the message-switching service. The switching could be done in some device front-ending the message-switching node. Alternatively, software in the node could route through traffic, not intended for it, to a host computer.

(v) Interworking with message-handling services on host computers, such as mailboxes; or with centralized accounting functions on the host computers. This supposes the support by the node of the protocols used by the hosts, for example IBM 2780 or 3780 emulation. The hosts in

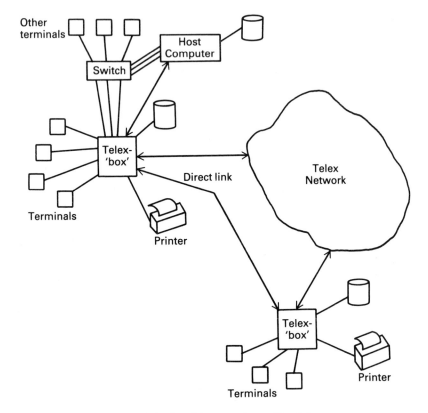

Fig. 3.4   Possible upgrades to Fig. 3.3.

question need not be local; they could be accessed over leased telephone circuits or a packet-switched network.

These, and other features, are readily available on many commercial message-switching systems.

3.3.2 A Large Message-Switching Network

In contrast to the small commercial message-switching system discussed above, the Société Internationale de Télecommunications Aeronautiques (SITA) [7] network is probably the world's largest data network, at least outside the military area. The SITA network is not a purely message-switching network, but also handles interactive traffic. In SITA parlance, type A (interactive) traffic accounts for some 6×10^9

messages, while type B (conventional message) traffic represents 0.5×10^9 per year. (However, type B messages averaging 200 characters, are perhaps 2½ times as large as type A messages.) On average it will be seen that the network handles 15 000 message characters per second, so that peak loads will exceed this considerably—although perhaps not so much as in other networks, since traffic is world-wide, 24 hours per day.

The SITA network serves the airline industry with about 250 airline members, some 200 switching centres, and nearly 20 000 airline offices and over 50 airline reservation systems attached to the network. It is used to provide access to airlines' passenger-reservation systems (SITA itself operates a passenger-reservation system, GABRIEL, for several airlines), to permit the transfer of aircraft movement and flight security information, baggage information, and a wide range of other services.

The network has until recently been based on nine high level switching centres (see Fig. 3.5) originally composed of Univac 1108 computers, now supplemented largely by Phillips DS 714s. Terrestrial and satellite links operating at 9600 bps or 56 Kbps, interconnect these nodes. Type A interactive traffic, which requires relatively fast response times across

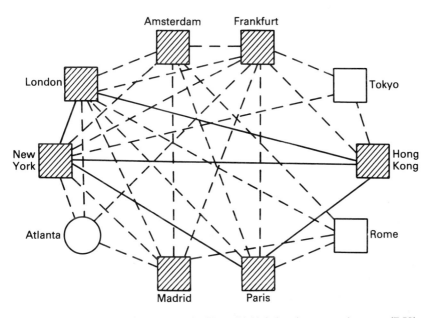

Fig. 3.5 The SITA central network. ▨ = old high level system plus new (DIS) packet-switching system; □ = old high level system; ○ = (DIS) packet-switching system.

the network (< 3 seconds), is being off-loaded on to the data transport network (packet-switching) composed of the newer computers, while the Type B messages continue to be carried by the old high level centres. There are many subsidiary satellite processors, concentrators and time division multiplexors interfacing the high level systems to the users.

Type B traffic, the pure message-traffic, originates from various devices, but historically it is essentially from teleprinters. Using SITA and other protocols (see below) it is carried from node to node to its destination. Each node sending a message (messages may be fragmented if they are long), receives an explicit confirmation from the next node that the complete message has been received there. Until this confirmation is received, the sending node does not destroy its copy of the message. The original sender also receives an explicit confirmation from his local node that the network has received his message; so by delivering a message to the network he is assured that it will arrive at its destination. If it is not possible to deliver the message to the destination, e.g. because it is out of order, the network holds the message until it can be delivered. In any case, all messages are archived by the network with suitable identifications (sequence numbers, date and time of transmission and delivery, etc.) so that an operator can investigate any problems.

This highly reliable message-switching service will itself be upgraded in the future by replacing some of the older high level centres with new hardware and offering new message-handling services.

Finally, Table 3.4 gives an overview of the protocols available for accessing the SITA network.

Table 3.4 Access to SITA Network

User Airline	Data Link	Access Protocol	Service Available
Teleprinter	Telegraph leased circuit	Point-to-point teleprinter Multi-station line	Type B
Telex	Public Type B service	Teleprinter	Type B
CRT Terminal	Synchronous leased circuit	P.1024B P.1024C	Type A
Application computer	Synchronous leased circuit	P.1024, P.1124 synchronous link control SIRCCO	Type A

P.1024 and P.1124 are SITA protocols. P.1024B is designed for terminals compatible with IBM's 1006 Line Control Procedure, while P.1024C is for terminals compatible with the Univac Uniscope 100 Control Procedure. SIRCCO is used for IBM-based reservation computer systems. In future developments the HDLC and SDLC protocols will also be supported.

3.4 PACKET-SWITCHING DATA NETWORKS

Packet-switching networks are SAF networks in which the unit of transfer is a packet, a block of user data less or equal to some maximum size such as 128 octets. The source user is responsible for packetizing his data before delivering it to the network. The network delivers the packets to the specified destinations. The destination user is responsible for reassembling the data from the packets he receives. There are also control packets which do not carry user data.

Since many simple terminals are not capable of handling packets, whether data or control, but work with asynchronous character streams, most packet-switching networks include a Packet Assembler/Disassembler (PAD) [10] function which will perform these tasks for such simple terminals. This PAD function will probably be implemented on all network nodes, and also possibly in remote concentrators (see Fig. 3.6). Simple asynchronous DTEs access these PADS either through

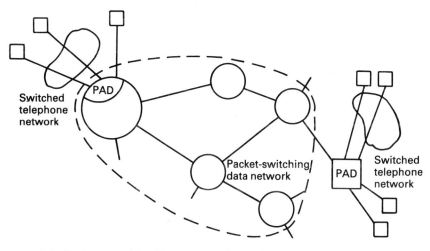

Fig. 3.6 Packet assemblers/disassemblers (PADS). □ = asynchronous terminal.

direct connections or by dialling over the public telephone network with, for example, V.21 modems [9]. Suitable commands from the DTE in the form of strings of readable characters are interpreted by the PAD, which either performs some local operation or generates an appropriate packet for forwarding into the network, in response to the command. A similar procedure applies in the reverse direction: packets received from the network either cause the PAD to perform a local operation, or cause it to forward a stream of characters (e.g. the user data carried in a data packet) to the asynchronous DTE.

As has been discussed in Chapter 1 there are essentially two types of packet-switching: (1) message-switching (datagram) and (2) call-switching (VC).

3.4.1 Datagram Networks

A datagram packet-switch is exactly like a message-switch except that there are restrictions on the size of the message and the network is usually not built to the same standards of security. A datagram is a self-contained envelope with all necessary address, routing, priority and other information on the outside and user data inside. The network routes it to the destination using the normal SAF technique. Usually the network will not add sequence numbers to datagrams or archive them. If several datagrams carry a single fragmented message, it is nothing to the network. It is the duty of the source and destination users to ensure that all datagrams in the message arrive, to put them in the correct sequence if they arrive out of sequence (for example because they took different routes through the network), and to recover from any other errors introduced by the network.

Since the network is unable to identify messages, and still less conversations, the only flow control it can apply to users is over *all* datagrams crossing a particular DTE-DCE interface. If, as is usual, user conversations are multiplexed on that interface then one user's misbehaviour in overloading the network with packets will result in all users of that interface suffering. Similarly, if a destination DTE becomes overloaded by an excess of received datagrams, so that the node local to that DTE begins to accumulate undelivered packets, then that node is unable to protect the destination DTE since it is probably unaware of the *source* of the problem (datagrams will usually carry a source address but not necessarily in a form intelligible to the network, as opposed to the destination). If the node *is* aware of the source of the problem it can only control that source back over the network with considerable difficulty.

In practice datagram networks are uncommon outside the research and academic communities, so we do not discuss them further. There are, however, famous datagram networks such as ARPA [11].

3.4.2 Call-Switching Networks and X.25

Call-switching packet networks insist that the originating user establishes a 'call' to the destination user before he can exchange data packets with him. The call may be thought of as a virtual circuit (VC), or a pipeline between two DTEs. (Multipoint VCs are not permitted on most packet-switching networks.)

The sequence of events during a call is roughly as follows: The caller requests a VC to the called DTE. The network transmits the request. If the called DTE accepts the request, its acceptance is transmitted back across the network to the calling DTE. Data transfer can now take place in both directions over the VC that has been established. Calling or called DTE can request to clear the VC at any time. The opposing DTE is advised, and it should confirm the clearance, this confirmation being relayed back to the first DTE.

Call request and accept, clear request and confirmation commands are special packets recognized both by the DTEs and the network, which between them manage the VC.

The X.25 protocol [3], which is perhaps the best-known of all standard protocols, governs the details of nearly all VC packet-switching networks, in particular public networks. X.25 defines the *interface* to the network. Although this interface specification may, and does, have implications for the internal structure of the network, it is strictly written in terms of the exchange of information between a DTE and a DCE. Various versions of X.25 have been produced since the original 1976 specification appeared, not to mention the various interpretations put on the one specification by different implementors (PTTs included), so what follows makes no claim to be an exhaustive review of X.25; it is only intended to make the general structure clear and to highlight some features which have important implications or consequences. X.25 defines three levels of interfacing

Level 1. This specifies the physical DTE-DCE interface, which should be X.21 (see Chapter 2) [12]. X.21 would normally apply *without* 'selection' (dialling); so that the DCE is directly connected to the local packet-switching node, to which, in effect, the DTE talks at Levels 2 and 3. In practice X.21 bis [12], which is simply a synchronous subset of V.24 [13], is much more frequently used on the DTE/DCE interface than X.21 itself, since the DCE is usually a synchronous *modem* on a leased telephone line to the node.

Level 2. This specifies how the link (nominally DTE-DCE, in reality DTE-Local Node) is established and used. The Link Access Procedure (LAP) of Level 2 is a variant of the familiar HDLC of data communications. LAP has effectively been replaced by LAP-B, a *balanced* version, involving simpler initialization of the link, but still maintaining the asymmetry between DTE and DCE. Thus the software obeying the LAP-B protocol must be explicitly configured to run as a DTE or a DCE. LAP serves to carry (in HDLC I-frames) the packets of Level 3 across the link. Due to its error-recovery mechanisms, LAP can offer an almost error-free infrastructure to the packet-handling superstructure.

Level 3. Level 3 is the packet level of X.25, or more generally 'the network layer', the level at which networking aspects (such as addressing a destination) are handled. The specification defines the types of packets that exist; and how they are used to establish, transfer data on, and clear VCs. Essentially each VC on an X.25 interface is identified by a corresponding logical channel number (LCN). Every packet belonging to that VC bears its LCN in the packet header. In this way many VCs can be multiplexed on a single X.25 interface (see Fig. 3.7).

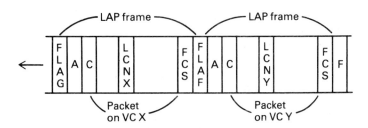

Fig. 3.7   Multiplexing of VCs on a link.

Looking at Level 3 in a little more detail, we consider the basic format of packets. The first three octets are always a header, which may be extended further. Bits 8–5 of octet 1 identify the format in use

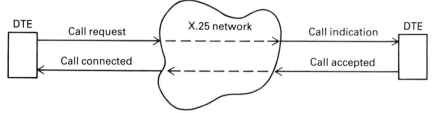

Fig. 3.8a   Call establishment in X.25.

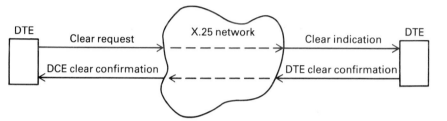

Fig. 3.8b   Call clearing in X.25.

('X.25'), bits 4–1 specify the logical channel *group*, and bits 8–1 of octet
2 the LCN itself. If there is competition for logical channel numbers
between many users, one way of resolving the problem could be to
divide users into groups and let them compete for LCNs (equivalently
for available VCs) within a group. Priority users could belong to a group
with few members. Octet 3 specifies the *type* of packet in question.

Table 3.5 lists the packet types, each one of which has two names
depending on which way it crosses the DTE-DCE interface. As can be
seen from the table, they fall into four categories.

3.4.2.1 Call Set-Up and Clearing

The general concept of call set-up and clearing has been discussed earlier.
It is further illustrated in Figs. 3.8a,b and 3.9. Figures 3.9a,b show *state
diagrams* for calling and clearing in which each transition between states
is labelled with the packet whose transmission caused the transition,
and its source.

The call request (or call indication) packet which is used to initiate
a call carries in it, besides the basic header

Table 3.5 Packet types in X.25 and their coding

Packet type		Octet 8 bits							
From DCE to DTE	From DTE to DCE	8	7	6	5	4	3	2	1
Call set-up and clearing									
Incoming call	Call request	0	0	0	0	1	0	1	1
Call connected	Call accepted	0	0	0	0	1	1	1	1
Clear indication	Clear request	0	0	0	1	0	0	1	1
DCE clear confirmation	DTE clear confirmation	0	0	0	1	0	1	1	1
Data and interrupt									
DCE Data	DTE Data	X	X	X	X	X	X	X	0
DCE Interrupt	DTE Interrupt	0	0	1	0	0	0	1	1
DCE Interrupt confirmation	DTE Interrupt confirmation	0	0	1	0	0	1	1	1
Flow control and reset									
DCE RR	DTE RR	X	X	X	0	0	0	0	1
DCE RNR	DTE RNR	X	X	X	0	0	1	0	1
	DTE REJ	X	X	X	0	1	0	0	1
Reset indication	Reset request	0	0	0	1	1	0	1	1
DCE Reset confirmation	DTE Reset confirmation	0	0	0	1	1	1	1	1
Restart									
Restart indication	Restart request	1	1	1	1	1	0	1	1
DCE Restart confirmation	DTE Restart confirmation	1	1	1	1	1	1	1	1

Note. A bit which is indicated as 'X' may be set to either 0 or 1.

(i) The calling and called network user addresses (NUAs), with information as to the number of digits in these fields.

(ii) A facilities field (with length indication) specifying facilities required on *this* call (e.g. reverse charging).

(iii) A call user data (CUD) in which the caller can place up to 16 octets of data (or 128 if the fast select option (below) exists).

This information permits the network to establish the VC with the facilities required. Several remarks are in order:

(i) The LCN (or VC number) which identifies the VC refers only to the *local* interface. For example, a call request on LCN 5 leaving DTE A may appear as a call indication on LCN 17 on arriving at DTE B. This is necessary, since it is hardly possible to allocate LCNs which are unique over all the network. It means that on call set-up the network must establish a mapping between a source address plus source LCN pair and a destination address plus LCN pair, so that all subsequent packets,

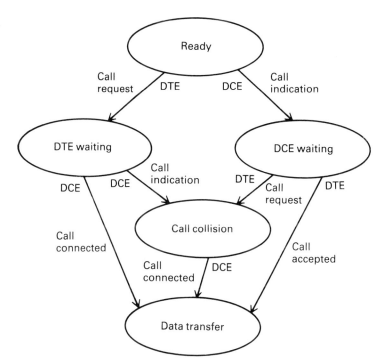

Fig. 3.9a Call establishment in X.25 (state diagram).

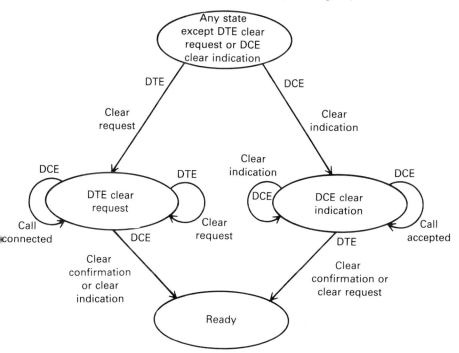

Fig. 3.9b Call clearing in X.25 (state diagram).

identified by LCN only, can be correctly routed and their LCNs mapped. How and where this is done is a problem internal to the network.

One method of effecting this mapping might be to make it take place in the nodes local to each DTE and perform the mapping on all packets entering the network. Thus a packet leaving DTE A on LCN X, crosses the network bearing (somehow) DTE B's address and LCN Y, the address B being stripped before crossing the DCE to DTE interface at B. A packet in the reverse direction crosses the network bearing A's address and LCN X. This method would allow all packets to be routed *independently* through the network. This in turn produces a problem of sequencing at the receiving end: packets could arrive out of sequence depending on the routes chosen. Since in X.25 data packets are supposed to arrive in the sequence sent, it also implies that the node local to B must put out-of-sequence data packets back in sequence. This method of handling mapping allows a VC service to be built on a datagram-like infrastructure.

Another, more usual, method creates the VC out of a series of concatenated VCs between network nodes, along a route fixed for the duration of the call. The mapping is then from LCN to LCN at each node along the route, the mapping tables being established on call set-up. Once the call is set-up, there is no need to carry addresses or LCNs (other than the LCN of the particular internodal link in question). This method in effect supposes that internodal links have protocols which also look like X.25.

(ii) The choice of an LCN on sending a call request follows the 'hunting' procedure discussed in Section 3.2.1. Figure 3.9a shows that a call collision (an outgoing and incoming call on the same channel) is resolved on the DTE-DCE interface in favour of the *outgoing* call. For the network, this implies that there is substantial house-keeping to perform in clearing down the VC partially established right across the network from the remote DTE (unless the local DCE can find another free LCN on which to send the call indication packet to the local DTE).

(iii) If Logical Channel Group Numbers (LCGNs) are used there is a further problem. Presumably a remote caller can be allocated a suitable Logical Channel Group on the local interface; but which one? Are LCGNs defined network-wide, so no mapping is required? If not, how is mapping between LCGNs to be established? In most networks LCGNs are simply not supported.

(iv) Fast select calls. Using the CUD it is possible to convey information to a called DTE without ever establishing the VC. The called DTE simply rejects the call (sends a call clear packet) and takes the data. If, as in the later versions of X.25, he can send information with the clear request packet, the called DTE can actually reply (briefly) to the received message in clearing the call. This fast select option is an additional facility which has to be specifically requested on call set-up.

(v) Calls may be cleared not only by either DTE, but also by the network. This can be effected by a node on the route sending a clear request in *both* directions, i.e. to both DTEs, and absorbing the returning clear confirmation packets.

(vi) Finally, X.25 permits the existence of Permanent Virtual Circuits (PVCs) linking two DTEs. These require no call set-up and clearing, but always exist in the data transfer state.

3.4.2.2 Data Transfer and Interrupts

Data packets, which have a maximum length particular to the network in use, are subject to a flow control mechanism *per VC*. DTEs can also send a short interrupt packet not subject to this mechanism. Only one unacknowledged (i.e. to which no interrupt confirmation packet has been received as a reply) interrupt packet may be outstanding at a time. Interrupt packets can be used to clear congestion, if the flow control mechanism results in no data transfer using ordinary data packets being possible.

Data packets can carry additional 'bits' of information besides data, namely

(i) Qualifier-bit. The Q-bit can be used to distinguish user data from other data. A specific example is given by X.29 [14] (see Section 3.4.3) in which data packets with the Q-bit set contain data for a PAD rather than for the attached DTE.

(ii) The More-bit. The M-bit (see Fig. 3.10). This bit, applicable only to maximum length data packets, states whether this packet can be combined with the next one, if, for example, the call enters a second network with a larger maximum packet-size. Since such a combination depends on the data content, one could legitimately object that the M-bit has no place at the network level since it refers to the user's application.

(iii) The D-bit. The D-bit is concerned with the source of the P(R) of the flow control mechanism. It is discussed immediately below.

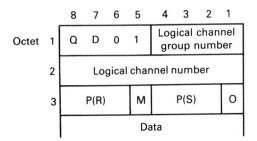

Fig. 3.10   X.25 data packet header.

3.4.2.3 *Flow Control and Reset*

The flow control mechanism is a *window* mechanism. Data packets are numbered 0 to 7 cyclically (or 0 to 127 on some networks) and a sender may send up to W packets (where W is the window size) from his current *window-edge*. For example if W is 3 and his current window-edge is 6, he may send data packets numbered $P(S) = 6$; $P(S) = 7$; $P(S) = 0$ but no more. $P(S)$ is a send number in the data packet header, octet 3, see Fig. 3.10.

The window-edge is updated by the receipt of $P(R)$, in a data packet in the reverse direction, or in a Receiver Ready (RR), Receiver Not Ready (RNR) or Reject (REJ) packet, if there is no reverse data packet to carry the $P(R)$. The value of $P(R)$ is the value of the new window-edge. RR packets are used specifically to carry $P(R)$s to a sender to update his window-edge. RNR packets are used to tell a sender to stop sending data packets, temporarily. REJ packets are used by a DTE only to request a DCE to retransmit data packets from the specified $P(R)$ number, or to 'undo' a previously sent RNR packet.

The reset packet serves to reset the $P(S)$ and $P(R)$ numbers on an interface to zero. It is used in case of errors (particularly those to do with $P(S)$ and $P(R)$ numbers), and a reset confirmation packet in the reverse direction is required to show that the resetting action has taken place. The specification states that when a reset takes place the entire VC is reset (i.e. both DTE-DCE interfaces are reset) and all data packets in transit are thrown away. Thus resetting implies, normally, loss of data with no means of recovery. Again, some comments are in order.

(i) The flow control mechanism is clear, but when a DCE sends a $P(R)$ in a data or other packet, where and when is that $P(R)$ generated? If the P(R) comes from the local node then the DTE is free to send more data packets into the network, whether or not the previous ones have been delivered to the remote DTE, or even sent out across the network. If this technique is used (as is normal) it is possible for a queue to build up right across a network, if the remote DTE does not update its DCE's window-edge. This particularly applies if the VC is a concatenation of X.25-like internodal links. The flow control mechanism then only operates at the source DTE when each link has its maximum number, W, of outstanding data packets—i.e. after, rather than before, congestion has occurred.

Alternatively, the P(R) could come from the remote DTE, with P(S) and P(R) numbers carried right across the network. This technique is employed in some networks. Specifically X.25 allows the user to request this option at call set-up (a facility), and invoke it for a specific data packet by setting the D-bit in it, thereby obtaining a form of end-to-end acknowledgement as well as an end-to-end flow control. (There is of course a possibility that P(S) and P(R) numbers on the two DTE-DCE interfaces are not in phase, making implementation of this facility difficult.) Whatever the source of P(R) numbers, practical programming problems usually result in an RR packet being sent in response to every received data packet, thereby reducing VC capacity.

(ii) How is the window-size, W, determined? On most networks it is fixed when a DTE becomes a subscriber to the network, in accordance with the *throughput class* to which he subscribes. Throughput classes are an ill-defined concept which supposedly represent a guaranteed maximum transnetwork delay, a kind of Grade of Service for SAF networks. Later versions of X.25 allow a calling DTE to negotiate the value of W for each call, and a called DTE to reject or accept a proposed value of W. (This is another 'facility'.) Such values of W must always be less than or equal to some fixed maximum for the network. In fact the facility appears to be of doubtful use, since if the network can support a large W it is easier to provide it always, rather than on a temporary basis with the reallocation of buffers in nodes thereby implied. In practice one may generally say that $W = 1$ severely reduces throughput, $W = 2$ marginally reduces it, $W = 3$ allows maximum throughput apart from exceptional circumstances.

(iii) The RNR mechanism appears unnecessary, if the window mechanism works properly. In practice RNR is often not implemented.

(iv) The REJ mechanism also appears unnecessary, since Level 2 supposedly offers error-free transmission. REJ could be useful if a receiving DTE has too large a window-size and runs out of buffers—but this should not arise.

(v) The Reset mechanism, as has been pointed out, can lose data packets. It is also difficult to implement unless a VC is a chain of concatenated X.25-like channels. If the VC is implemented on top of a datagram network it is extremely difficult to clear all data packets in transit when a reset occurs.

(vi) Another optional facility is the ability to negotiate the maximum data packet size applicable to a given call. Since negotiation is for a *smaller* size than the maximum supported by the network, the facility appears of doubtful use.

3.4.2.4 Restarts

A Restart affects an entire X.25 interface, i.e. all VCs. It clears all SVCs (Switched VCs) and resets all PVCs. It is used to initialize or reinitialize a DTE-DCE interface.

3.4.2.5 Summary on X.25

The above discussion of X.25 highlights some of its features and problem areas. It should be read in conjunction with the specification itself, unless the reader has already got some familiarity with X.25. It would be inappropriate to discuss full details of X.25 here when the official specification is readily available.

3.4.3 PADs and X.3 [10], X.28, X.29 [14]

The concept of a Packet Assembler/Disassembler (PAD) was discussed at the beginning of Section 3.4. It supports asynchronous terminals, builds packets for sending across the network and disassembles packets received from the network for delivery to the terminal. Three CCITT specifications cover this area. They are compatible with X.25, in the sense that the PAD handles X.25-like VCs across the network. The specifications are (see Fig. 3.11):

(i) X.3, which defines the PAD, its operation and the parameters which control that operation.

(ii) X.28, which defines the protocol between the asynchronous terminal (the 'start-stop DTE') and the PAD.

(iii) X.29, which defines the protocol between the PAD and a remote X.25-compatible host (the 'packet-mode DTE') engaged in a VC with a start-stop DTE.

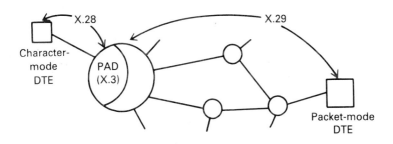

Fig. 3.11 The roles of X.3, X.28 and X.29.

3.4.3.1 The PAD, X.3

A PAD has to obey the X.28 and X.29 protocols. It also has to assemble and disassemble packets. The way it does this is determined by parameters.

To establish a VC, a user accesses the PAD from his start-stop DTE and enters an X.28 dialogue in which he identifies himself, for charging, and the destination address he requires. The PAD builds an X.25 call request packet and sends it to the destination. When it receives the call connected reply it sends a suitable X.28 text string to the user to tell him the VC is established. Thereafter, in the data transfer phase, the parameters take over.

The parameters define: When a packet is to be forwarded to the network; how output to the start-stop DTE is to be formatted; if and how flow control is to be implemented on the interface to the start-stop DTE, etc. Each parameter has an identifier and a value. A selection of parameters is presented below for illustrative purposes:

Parameter	Function
1	Allows the user (i.e. the start-stop DTE user) to escape from data transfer or not, depending on the parameter value; e.g. if the value is zero the user cannot even clear the call, the remote packet-mode DTE must do so.
2	Provides echo to the user or not.
3	Defines the data-forwarding character(s), i.e. those characters which, when typed by the user, result in a packet being sent from the PAD to the network. Example: Carriage return.
4	Defines the data forwarding delay, or the delay in units of 50 ms after which a packet will be forwarded to the network if a user ceases typing.
5 & 12	Define flow control procedures in both directions on the start-stop DTE interface. Essentially: Are X-ON, X-OFF characters recognized by the DTE and/or DCE, or not?
6 & 8	Define whether or not certain output to the user should be suppressed; for example messages from the PAD itself, or unwanted data from the remote host DTE.
7	Defines what the PAD should do if the user types 'break', e.g. send a reset packet, or an interrupt packet across the network.
9 & 10	Define how to handle the terminal, if it requires extra characters after carriage return to allow for mechanical fly-back on a printer, or its width is small.
11	This is a read-only parameter, used by the remote packet-mode DTE, to determine the speed in bits per second of the start-stop DTE, so that output to it may be regulated.

The clearing of calls is a potentially problematic area. Should a start-stop DTE user be allowed to clear a call, or should it occur only when he has 'logged-off' the remote host, and then under the host's control? Should a host be allowed to clear a call, possibly before the start-stop user has received (at the rate of his perhaps slow printer) output previously sent to him? An X.29 command exists for the host DTE to request the PAD to clear the call when ready.

3.4.3.2 *The Start-Stop DTE User Interface, X.28* [14]

This interface and protocol are very simple. Typically a user calls the PAD (e.g. with a V.21 [9] modem via the dial-up telephone network), sends some automatic speed detection characters, logs in (name or 'NUI' and password) and types the address he wants. Once the call is established, everything he types thereafter is built into data packets and sent across the network. To escape from data transfer (if Parameter 1's value allows it) he types (typically) 'Control-P'. He may then clear the call by typing 'LIB' or 'CLR', etc., or enquire what the PAD parameter's values are (PAR?), or set new values (SET), etc. When his command is finished he returns to data transfer automatically, unless the call was cleared.

3.4.3.3 *The Packet-Mode DTE Interface, X.29* [14]

This is even simpler than X.28. X.29 states that the exchange of packets between the PAD and the remote packet-mode DTE is as per X.25. All data packets are treated as going to/from the start-stop DTE user unless the Q-bit is set (see Section 3.4.2.2), in which case they are to/from the PAD itself. The packet-mode DTE may use this feature to read or set PAD parameters, with appropriate formatting, or, for example, to issue commands such as the invitation to the PAD to clear the call, discussed above.

3.4.3.4 *Some Comments on X.3, X.28, X.29*

Many users are unaware how critically the values of PAD parameters affect their bills for use of packet-switching networks. This is because of the charging method which normally applies, in which effectively a charge is made *per packet* (in either direction) irrespective (almost) of its size. If remote echo at a host is used from a start-stop DTE, character by character, the user is effectively sending two 1-character packets per character typed, and paying for it. He could dramatically reduce his charges by using *local* echo at the PAD (parameter 2), a single data-forwarding character (carriage return) and a long data forwarding delay (Parameter 4 equal 2 seconds, say).

Many hosts deliberately set-up the parameters for the user's benefit (?) and then put parameter 1 equal zero. The start-stop user cannot now read, let alone change, the PAD parameters.

Another feature of the parameters is that their values are made known to the DTEs *on request*. If one DTE changes them the other is not automatically informed.

Finally, as with X.25, a full appreciation of these important recommendations can only be obtained by studying them directly. The above comments merely give an outline of how an X.3 PAD operates.

3.5 ARCHITECTURE AND PERFORMANCE OF X.25 PACKET-SWITCHING NODES AND NETWORKS

In Section 3.2 the performance of SAF networks was considered generally. In this section we return to the theme but specifically for X.25 packet-switched networks, following the outline presentation of X.25 in Section 3.4.2.

3.5.1 Architecture of an X.25 Node

Figure 3.12 illustrates the architecture of a typical X.25 node. Lines, or groups of lines, are controlled by dedicated microprocessors. For example, one microprocessor might handle eight asynchronous lines, and provide a PAD (X.3) supporting X.28 and X.29. Another might handle four 9600 bps X.25 lines, with X.21 (or X.21 bis) interfaces, supporting the Level 2 and Level 3 protocols. Another microprocessor could be dedicated to a single internodal link operating at 48 or 64 Kbps using a

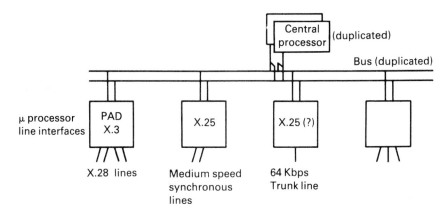

Fig. 3.12   Possible architecture of X.25 node.

V.35 or V.36 modem [15], or a G.703 [16] interface to a PCM slot. The node will be equipped with as many such interfaces as are necessary or possible.

The microprocessor interfaces are probably single cards with on-board program and data memories, the data memories serving principally to hold packets in transit. All cards plug in to a bus, which is probably duplicated for security. On the bus(es) is also a more powerful central processor (probably duplicated) whose function it is to assist on call set-up and clearing, monitor traffic and nodal performance, acquire statistics for billing purposes and support programs allowing a network manager to reconfigure the node by taking lines in and out of service, etc. Typically, a call proceeds as follows

(i) The microprocessor servicing the line on which an incoming call request is received analyses the packet for validity and advises the central processor.

(ii) The central processor determines how the call is to be routed and records the request. It advises the microprocessors controlling the incoming and the chosen outgoing lines that the call request (suitably modified in accordance with the conventions of channel-mapping, etc. that may apply) is to be passed from one to the other.

(iii) The call request packet is passed over the bus to the microprocessor controlling the outgoing line, which outputs it.

(iv) Assuming the call is accepted further on, a call accepted packet returns and is passed from the second to the first microprocessor for return to the call originator, and the central processor is advised that the call now exists, i.e. has been established.

(v) The central processor initializes the necessary memory areas for recording information about the call.

(vi) When data transfer begins, it is directly between incoming and outgoing lines *without* intervention by the central processor.

(vii) When a clear request is detected by the relevant microprocessor the central processor is advised and records the call as cleared, saving the billing and other information.

(viii) When the clear confirmation is detected by the microprocessors the VCs are freed.

Typically, only the node local to the originating DTE will fully record the details of the call for charging. Such charge records will be accumulated and then delivered to some central node on the network where network usage, billing, etc. are performed.

The technique is very similar to that of the time-division Telex switch discussed in Section 2.1.2 (Fig. 2.6), except that (due to the varying length of packets, retransmissions, delays on error-recovery, flow-control, etc.) packets, unlike characters, are not switched through between incoming and outgoing line in strict synchronism. Queues, as emphasized in Section 3.2, can build up.

3.5.2 Performance of an X.25 Network

The performance of the network is obviously dependent on many factors, in particular the speeds and bit-error-rates of the transmission lines in use, and the load on the network. Assuming line speeds are known (obviously), how a given call is routed is known, the nodes are sufficiently powerful to handle the traffic, and the load on the network is light, it is possible to calculate the *theoretical* performance. For example, reverting to the graph of Euronet in Fig. 1.8, where we may take the trunk lines as operating at 48 Kbps and the lines to DTEs as operating at 2400 or 4800 bps, it would be possible to calculate estimated call set-up times and transnetwork delay.

This was in fact done, and the calculated values then compared with real figures obtained from measuring what happened to real traffic. Euronet is defunct, but the general results are of interest and typical for most X.25 networks [17].

Call Set-Up Delays. Theoretical call set-up times were of the order of 120 ms (depending on destination), and actual minimum call set-up times were 2.2 times as long. The difference is ascribed to call set-up processing in nodes, which was 50 ms per node on the route, plus an extra 50 ms at the node local to the originating DTE. Average call set-up times were at least double the minimum times recorded. This was essentially due to line errors resulting in retransmission, and (worse) recovery by timeouts.

Transnetwork Delays. Again these are dependent on destination, but it may be said that for packets of 30 data octets transnetwork delays were theoretically about 300 ms and minimum delays experienced indicated that 10 ms per node on the route could be added to that figure. Average transnetwork delays were three times as great, due to retransmissions and timeouts.

Maximum Throughput. Packet-switching is ideal for sporadic traffic. What happens if a DTE fires data packets at the network as fast as it can? In practice the best results never exceeded 94% of the theoretical rate at which the DTE could send data (limited by line speeds), and was on average only 75%.

It will be appreciated that bit errors on lines affect the performance of an X.25 network critically. On the other hand, despite the apparently important role of reset packets in the X.25 specification, resetting of VCs never occurred unless provoked by deliberate errors. Data packets were only lost as a result of such deliberate resets. One data packet in a million was duplicated; none were corrupted (i.e. there was no residual error after error-correction) nor received out of sequence.

One may summarize the above results by stating that X.25 networks appear to be reliable, in the sense that the service provided is very error-free, but of very variable performance in terms of delays and throughput.

3.6 INTERFACES BETWEEN PACKET-SWITCHED NETWORKS

CCITT has issued the X.75 recommendation [18] defining this interface. It conceptually applies to the situation of Fig. 3.13, in which networks

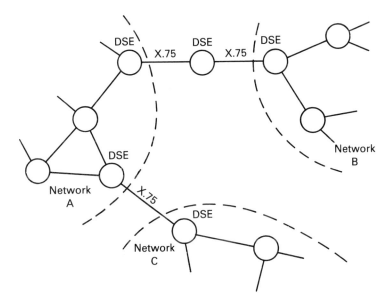

Fig. 3.13 X.75 internetwork interfaces.

have gateway/transit data switching exchanges (DSEs) at each end of the internetwork connection; plus, possibly, another DSE in the middle of this link, if very long (see Recommendation X.92) [13].

X.75 is essentially the same as X.25 and as such will not be elaborated on here. A critical area is the handling of user and network facilities (utilities), since a facility requested by the user on call set-up over two or more networks may be available on one, but not on another network.

One particular feature of X.75 requires mention. Level 2, the link level, allows for the use of more than one physical circuit over which packets are conveyed at Level 3. There may be, and probably will be for security, parallel circuits between the networks; and the Level 2 I-frames, which carry the packets, may be routed via *either* circuit. Accordingly these I-frames are allocated sequence numbers (modulo 4096) before being delivered to the conventional LAP protocol of a circuit; and when they arrive at the other end the packets from the parallel streams are merged into a single stream and put back into sequence, see Fig. 3.14. There is an appropriate addition to the Level 2 protocol to handle this feature and to identify errors that could arise and recover from them if possible. (Note also that the most recent version of X.25 also supports the multilink, i.e. several circuits, function).

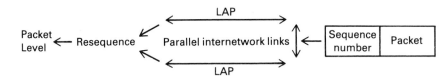

Fig. 3.14   X.75 use of parallel links.

3.7 SUMMARY

In this chapter we have looked at store-and-forward (SAF) switching, including message-switching and packet-switching. Well-known protocols such as X.25 have been presented. The performance of SAF networks and nodes has been considered, both theoretically and in practice. What has not been considered is the network itself: Where nodes should be, which ones should be interconnected, how traffic is routed. This subject is addressed in the next chapter, since the concepts involved are very largely relevant to circuit-switched as well as SAF networks.

REFERENCES

1 Shannon's Theorem is discussed in most books on Information and Communications Theory. See for example: *Basics of Communications and Coding* by William G. Chambers, Oxford Science Publications 1985.
2 See Reference 8, Chapter 1.
3 *Recommendation X.25* CCITT Red Book, **VIII. 3,** Geneva, 1985.
4 *High Level Data Link Control* ISO 3309 HDLC-Frame Structure. ISO DIS 4335 HDLC-Elements of Procedure. (International Standards Organisation.)
5 Some of the problems discussed here are treated in more detail in *The Design of a Small Packet-Switching Node* by A. Patel and M. Purser, Computer Networks and ISDN Systems, Vol 11, No. 4, April 1986.
6 *Recommendations Series X.400* CCITT Red Book, **VIII. 7,** Geneva, 1985.
7 SITA, Societe Internationale de Telecommunications Aeronautiques, 112 Ave. Charles de Gaulle, 92522 Neuilly sur Seine, France. Articles about SITA appear at intervals in the technical press. SITA itself issues booklets and manuals which are of considerable interest.
8 *Recommendation F.200, the Teletex Service* CCITT Red Book, **II. 5,** Geneva, 1985.
9 Recommendation V.21 CCITT Red Book, **VIII. 1,** Geneva, 1985.
10 *Recommendation X.3 (PAD)* CCITT Red Book, **VIII. 2,** Geneva, 1985.
11 There are very many papers on aspects of ARPANET. For example *The ARPA Network Control Centre* by McKenzie A.A., *Proceedings of the Fourth Data Communications Symposium,* October 1975 includes a good overview. Other early datagram networks were the European Informatics Network (EIN) and Cigale (INRIA-France).
12 *Recommendations X.21, X.21 bis* CCITT Red Book, **VIII. 3,** Geneva, 1985.
13 *Recommendation V.24* CCITT Red Book, **VIII. 1,** Geneva, 1985.
14 *Recommendations X.28, X.29* CCITT Red Book, **VIII. 3,** Geneva, 1985.
15 *Recommendations V.35, V.36* CCITT Red Book, **VIII. 1,** Geneva, 1985.
16 *Recommendation G.703* CCITT Red Book, **III. 3,** Geneva, 1985.
17 *The performance of a packet-switched network—a Study of Euronet* B. Alton *et al., Performances of Data Communication Systems and their Application,* by G. Pujolle, North-Holland, 1981.
18 *Recommendations X.75, X.92* CCITT Red Book, **VIII. 4,** Geneva, 1985.
19 *General Information-Binary Synchronous Communications* IBM, Reference G.A27–3004.

Chapter 4
Network Design and Routing of Traffic

In this chapter some of the problems raised at the end of Chapter 3 are addressed. Where should the nodes of a network be located and what capacity should they have? What links, of what capacity should exist between nodes? How should traffic be routed through the network? These questions are fundamental to the design of the network.

Once the network is in existence further questions may be added. How do we know what is happening in the network, both in terms of loading and of failure of links or nodes? How does the network behave in the event of overload, or failure? This is the subject of dynamic adaptation of the network, particularly adaptive routing, discussed towards the end of the chapter.

4.1 DESIGNING TO SUPPORT TRAFFIC

The design of a network is obviously very largely determined by the type and volume of traffic it must carry. Traffic is of two sorts
(1) User traffic, between DTEs connected to the network, to support which the network exists. If the DTEs can be numbered 1 to N, then the user traffic can be defined by a *traffic matrix* $T = (t_{ij})$ in which t_{ij} is the traffic (probably the busy season busy hour traffic rather than the average traffic) from DTE (i) to DTE (j). In the case of circuit-switched networks the traffic from DTE (i) to DTE (j) could be added to that from DTE (j) to DTE (i) to give t_{ij}, so that T is symmetric. This is because, in circuit-switching, a full-duplex channel of fixed capacity is usually assigned to each call and which end is the originator hardly matters. In the case of SAF networks in which the traffic is measured essentially in terms of data units (e.g. packets or octets) per second, and where flows in opposite directions may differ considerably, it could be more realistic to treat T as unsymmetric, i.e. $t_{ij} \neq t_{ji}$.
(2) Internal control and monitoring traffic. This could include signalling traffic for call set-up, routing and clearing; as well as the gathering of statistics for monitoring performance, data for charging, error messages

for consideration by the administration and control commands for changing the status of network components (e.g. deactivating a link), or reconfiguring the network (e.g. distributing new routing tables). This traffic is largely between nodes, rather than to or from DTEs. Certain elements of this internal traffic (e.g. monitoring and control) are likely to be highly inhomogeneous, since the traffic is probably all to or from a central control point where the network administration is located.

In a well-designed network the existence of internal traffic has been foreseen and capacity has been built into the network to carry this traffic. Indeed, in Chapter 2 it was pointed out that in some networks user traffic and internal traffic are carried on separate subnetworks (see Fig. 2.25). On other networks, particularly many packet-switched data networks, internal traffic is added to user traffic largely after the network becomes operational; and, unless controlled, it can easily grow to unacceptable volumes.

In principle, if user and internal traffic are carried on the same network, it would be possible to build the internal traffic into the traffic matrix by treating the nodes and DTEs on the same footing—i.e. they are all 'nodes'—and the traffic matrix element t_{ij} is the traffic from Node (i) to Node (j). We shall adopt this approach. Furthermore, a group of terminals generating little traffic, and served by a concentrator either within a switch or remotely attached to a switch, will usually be regarded as a single node offering the concentrated traffic to the network.

Given, then, a traffic matrix based on nodes (which are sources and sinks of traffic and whose geographical locations are presumably known) the design of a network can be regarded as an operation consisting of three stages

(1) Define a network configuration consisting of these nodes plus perhaps some purely *transit* nodes which serve only to switch traffic, links between nodes and the associated capacities of the nodes and links. Initially, any network configuration which can apparently support the traffic would be chosen, and this configuration would be refined in subsequent iterations.

(2) Apply the traffic to the network configuration. If there is no direct connection between Node (i) and Node (j), to support traffic t_{ij} and t_{ji}, then a route for this traffic through other nodes must be defined. In general, for all elements of the traffic matrix a route must be defined explicitly or implicitly. If the capacities of the nodes and links on the chosen route are not sufficient to carry the sum of all the traffic elements

allocated to them, then alternative routes must be defined. If no route can be found then some of the offered traffic cannot be supported and either the configuration must be changed or the traffic matrix itself modified (e.g. by deciding not to support certain types of traffic). Moreover, traffic is a statistical concept and even if the configuration supports average busy hour traffic flows, there is a certain probability that any node or link may be required to carry more traffic than it can. Thus the definition of the routing strategy includes not only how average traffic is to be routed, but what is to be done (including rerouting) if traffic overflows occur *in real time*.

(3) Evaluate the configuration and the traffic handling determined in steps (1) and (2). Many criteria for evaluation are possible, including

(i) The cost of the configuration.

(ii) The unused capacity of the network. Is it excessive and a waste of money, or is it insufficient to handle peak loads with an adequate Grade of Service?

(iii) The 'performance' of the network. Will call set-up times be too long because of an excessive number of links in routes? Will transnetwork delays be too long?, etc.

(iv) The 'resilience' of the network. How are the traffic-carrying capability and the performance affected by the failure of a node or a link?

(v) The potential for handling traffic growth. If different types of traffic are likely to grow at certain rates over the years, will the basic configuration become unusable, or is it amenable to orderly upgrading?

The result of the evaluation (stage (3)) will be to modify either the configuration of stage (1) (increase capacities, add a new node, remove a link, etc.); or the routing of stage (2) (divert traffic from node 2 to node 17 via a different route, etc.); or possibly both. This modification could be done using some mathematical procedure, such as minimizing the network cost with respect to link and node capacities subject to Grades of Service constraints, which could be analytical or iterative. Alternatively, the modification could be left entirely to the judgement of the designer, who would then perform steps (1) to (3) again, as often as he thought necessary. A mixture of the mathematical and intuitive approaches is also possible.

Although in simple cases there may be a direct analytical solution to the optimal design of the network, given optimization criteria, free variables and defined constraints, this is unlikely to be so in the more general case. Iteration, whether manual or automatic (e.g. in a computer), of the three stages in order to arrive at an optimal solution is normally necessary. There are many reasons why this is so, some of the more important ones being listed below.

Cost. The cost of network components such as links and nodes is seldom a straightforward function of capacity, or length (of a link). Nodes need sites and buildings to house them. These may already exist or may need to be purchased or constructed. Links need cable-ducts, rights-of-way, etc. which again may exist in some cases or must be constructed or purchased in others.

Dynamic Behaviour. It has been emphasized that traffic is a statistical concept, and that there is finite probability of any given traffic flow exceeding any given value. When many elements of the traffic matrix use a common internodal link (or node), and overflow routes are brought into use when its capacity is exhausted, the probabilities of overload of different network components can become very difficult to calculate. A better tool for evaluating the network may be that of simulation in which some function generates traffic according to a defined probability distribution, and the behaviour of the network model is observed over a suitable period of time. The whole design procedure is now: (1) define the configuration, (2) define the routing rules, (3) model the resulting network, load it with simulated traffic, observe the results; and iterate steps (1) to (3).

Resilience and Growth Considerations. In theory, it should be possible to define the probability of failure of nodes and links, or to specify their availability. Similarly, it should be possible to specify the long term growth patterns for traffic in a suitable probabilistic form. From these data the probabilities of all sorts of different traffic patterns on different network configurations could be determined and incorporated into some optimization program. In practice, not only are the complexities of so doing very great, but also the data themselves are likely to be subject to many non-linear and ad hoc constraints. Upgrades of capacity are nearly always discontinuous step functions; and the availability of network components may depend on policy decisions, such as 24-hour 7-day-per-week maintenance rather than 16-hour 5-day-per-week maintenance, which may be taken at any time if it is seen that some critical component is vulnerable.

In short, network design is an art, drawing on scientific tools such as statistics, modelling, simulation, mathematical optimization, etc. These tools are indispensable, but the final result will always depend on human judgement, policy and other constraints difficult to formulate mathematically. We shall, therefore, concentrate on aspects of network design, starting with routing, and continuing with some analysis techniques for connectivity and capacity.

4.2 ROUTING

Given a network configuration of nodes and links and an applied traffic matrix, the capacities required for the nodes and links are clearly a function of how traffic is routed. For instance, if (for whatever reason) no traffic is ever to be routed through a certain link then that link's capacity can be put to zero—the link can be removed.

Conversely, once the configuration and capacities are fixed, real-time traffic should be routed to use nodes and links 'optimally'. It is possible that the optimal decision in a given situation involves a choice of routing not explicitly envisaged when the configuration and capacities were fixed—perhaps because the real traffic flows are different from those embodied in the traffic matrix used at the design stage; perhaps because some network component has failed.

Network design and traffic routing are, as previously emphasized, mutually independent.

The classical solution to this interdependence is to determine fully the rules for routing at the design stage, and to apply them inflexibly in real-time. If the rules are fixed, the network configuration and capacities can be tailored to those rules. This does mean that traffic from A to B always uses the same route; but it does mean that given any putative real-time situation, the routing which will be used can be predicted with certainty. This is the approach used in the telephone network, and generally in circuit-switched networks.

In SAF networks real-time routing decisions are often not deterministic; and even if they are, they can be of such complexity as to be difficult to predict. Routing in SAF networks is often 'adaptive', by which is meant that the decision how to route traffic is taken not only on the basis of whether a route is simply available or not, but also by considering the resultant performance (e.g. transnetwork delay) as seen by the user. The routing decisions 'adapt' to the instantaneous loads on network components.

The dichotomy reflects the natures of circuit-switched and SAF networks. In the former, the situation is black or white—a desired circuit does exist or it does not. In the latter, almost everything is grey—traffic can be queued almost indefinitely.

It is logical to consider routing in circuit-switched networks first, since circuit-switched networks existed first and are the more amenable to analysis.

4.2.1 Routing in Circuit-Switched Networks

The basic technique employed in the routing of traffic in circuit-switched networks supposes that there exists in each node a routing table, or its equivalent. This table defines which output link to select for any chosen destination of a new call. Since it would be scarcely feasible to hold all possible destination addresses in each node, the numbering scheme for addresses groups those addresses in areas, regions, national zones, etc.— in the manner familiar to telephone subscribers.

For example, the X.121 Recommendation [1] for the numbering of addresses on data networks (see Fig. 4.1) employs 14 digits, as follows
(i) 3-digit data country code (DCC).
(ii) 1-digit network identifier within the country.
(iii) 10-digit network number (NN) of the DTE.
(Note that the first four digits together are referred to as the Data Network Identification Code, or DNIC).

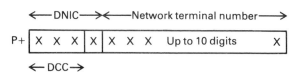

Fig. 4.1   X.121 Addressing.
Note: P = prefix (for International Data Call); DCC = Data Country Code; DNIC = Data Network Identification Code.

Thus a node receiving a call requesting routing to an X.121-compatible address can look firstly at the first 3 (or 4) digits to decide if it is for another country or not. If it is an international call, the node need not look at the remaining 11 (or 10) digits, but simply forward them along the route designated for international calls.

X.121 does not define numbering plans within a country; but in the hierarchical schemes, commonly used at least in telephony, the first few digits of the NN would be a regional or area code and indicate to the node whether the call is local, or to be routed to another area. In the latter case, the trailing digits would be forwarded to the chosen region or area without inspection by the node.

In old-fashioned networks where destination addresses were sent as pulses suitable for actuating Strowger step-by-step switches, the receiving, examining and forwarding of addresses was slow. Electro-mechanical 'registers' were used to hold this 'selection information' (addresses) in the nodes. If setting up a call involved passing through many nodes the delays could be appreciable, and were both annoying to the user and expensive (because of the relatively long holding times) in their use of resources such as registers. Much ingenuity went into speeding up this call set-up process. One obvious approach is to start the analysis of a destination address before it is fully received. If the first few digits show that the call is not for a local destination, then an outgoing route can be selected at once, and they and the following digits can be forwarded on it directly, without the need to accumulate them before forwarding. (They will probably be accumulated nevertheless, as they may be required for metering and charging.)

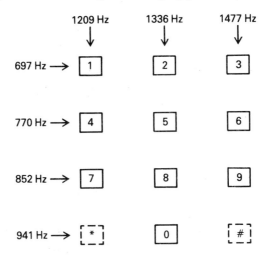

Fig. 4.2 Frequencies for push-button telephone selection.

Two other methods of speeding up selection have since been developed for the telephone network. One is Dual-Tone Multiple Frequency (DTMF) selection (Fig. 4.2), as used in some push-button telephones, usually on PBXs. The selection information is transmitted in a shorter time by the telephone than is possible with step-by-step selection. The other, of course, is Common Channel Signalling (CCS), discussed in Chapter 2; in which signalling information, including selection information, is sent on high speed digital channels distinct from the voice channels.

Yet another strategic consideration when considering routing is: Where should routing decisions be made? One approach, called 'right-through routing', relies on the originating nodes selecting the route to the destination and forwarding an appropriate command to all other nodes along the route which are supposedly unintelligent. A more normal procedure is to allow each node to examine all or part of the selected destination address and make its own decisions ('destination routing').

4.2.1.1 Alternative Routing

A strictly hierarchical network (Figs 4.3a, 4.3b) is a 'tree', with only one route from a source to a destination. In Fig. 4.3 a call from subscriber X to Y can be handled by the local exchange, but a call from X to Z goes from local to primary switching centre to secondary switching centre, and back down again. The primary switching centre might correspond to an area, the secondary to a region.

Such a strictly hierarchical scheme is clearly inflexible. It is also vulnerable to component failures. In practice, where the traffic justifies it, links will exist between nodes on the same level (see Figs 4.4a, 4.4b), and even between nodes on different levels. Various *alternative* routes will now be possible between a given source-destination pair. When should such extra links be introduced and how should they be used to provide alternative routes?

To answer this question we give an illustration, based on Figs 4.3 and 4.4. We assume for simplicity that the cost of a channel is proportional to its length, and that the distances AB, AC, AS, BS, CS between the indicated switching centres are all equal (α), and that SD = 2α, AD = $3\alpha/2$. This assumption in effect states that a direct channel from A to C, for example, has half the cost of one via S. (The calculations which follow could obviously be adjusted to handle different cost ratios.) We also assume target Grades of Service on all links of 1%. Suppose the offered traffic between the nodes in question is

$$A \leftrightarrow B, A \leftrightarrow C, A \leftrightarrow D \quad : \quad 4 \text{ Erlang}$$
$$A \leftrightarrow S, B \leftrightarrow S, C \leftrightarrow S, D \leftrightarrow S \quad : \quad 7 \text{ Erlang}$$

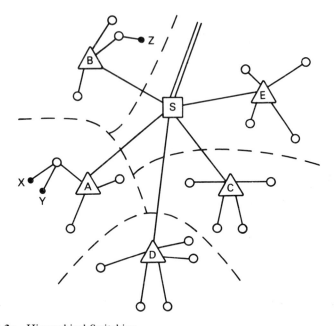

Fig. 4.3a Hierarchical Switching.
Note: ○ = local code switching centre; △ = primary switching centre; □ = secondary switching centre.

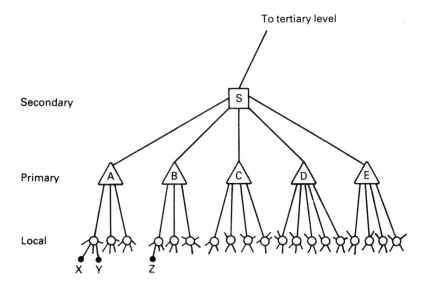

Fig. 4.3b Hierarchical Switching.

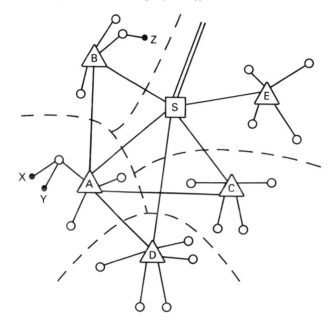

Fig. 4.4a Hierarchical Switching with additional links.
Note: ○ = local code switching centre; △ = primary switching centre; □ = secondary switching centre.

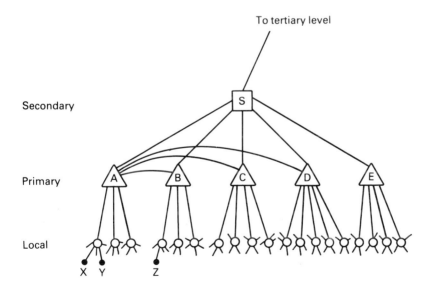

Fig. 4.4b Hierarchical Switching with additional links.

Three possibilities are considered

(1) No direct links. All traffic from A to B, C and D goes via S. This implies that AS is offered $7+3\times4 = 19$ Erlang; and BS, CS and DS are each offered $7+4 = 11$ Erlang. Using the Erlang-B formula it is easily found that the capacity of AS should be 28 circuits; and BS, CS and DS should each have capacity 18. The total cost is then (proportional to)

$$100\alpha = (28\alpha+18\alpha+18\alpha+2\times18\alpha),$$

taking distances into account.

(2) Direct links for all direct traffic. In this case AS, BS, CS and DS are each offered 7 Erlang, while new direct links AB, AC and AD are offered 4 Erlang each. The required circuits* are 14 on each link to the secondary centre S, and 10 on each direct link, to achieve a 1% Grade of Service. The cost is

$$105\alpha = (3\times14\alpha+14\times2\alpha+2\times10\alpha+10\times1.5\alpha).$$

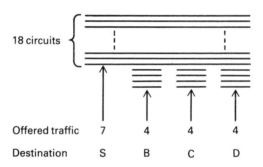

18 circuits

Offered traffic   7   4   4   4

Destination   S   B   C   D

Fig. 4.5   Routing from A to specified destinations.

(3) Direct links plus alternative routing. In this case we choose, somewhat arbitrarily, that four circuits will be provided on each of the direct links AB, AC, AD. These circuits will be the first choice, 'high-usage' route for traffic between those primary centres. Overflow traffic will be routed via S. The probability of overflow when 4 Erlang are offered to four circuits can be calculated to be 31%. Thus AS is offered $7+3$ $(0.31\times4) = 10.72$ Erlang; while BS, CS and DS are each offered $7+(0.31\times4) = 8.24$ Erlang. For 1% Grade of Service AS requires 18 circuits; BS, CS and DS require 15 circuits. Taking into account the direct circuits, the cost is

$$92\alpha = (18\alpha+2\times15\alpha+15\times2\alpha+2\times4\alpha+4\times1.5\alpha).$$

*Numbers of circuits have been rounded to the nearest integer.

This cost is less than those of (1) or (2).

The significance of alternative routing should now become clear. By judicious choice of the capacities (in terms of numbers of circuits) on first-offered routes, such as the direct routes AB, AC and AD, it may be possible to design a network which is *less expensive,* as well as being more flexible and resilient to component failures.

Of course the example is only an example, and one could query: Would three or five direct links be cheaper than the four chosen between A and B, C, D? Should we not use a 2% GOS on the direct links, since that is the overall GOS on 2-link routes via S?, etc.

Such considerations alter the numerical results, but do not alter the general conclusion: Designing a network to support an explicit alternative routing strategy can result in economies, essentially due to the non-linear nature of the Erlang-B formula.

Figure 4.5 illustrates alternative routing in another manner. The horizontal lines represent circuits picked 'from the bottom up' when free. The figure corresponds to the example discussed.

Figure 4.6 illustrates the same example again. The arrows indicate to which routes we turn as an alternative when the high-usage trunks are fully occupied.

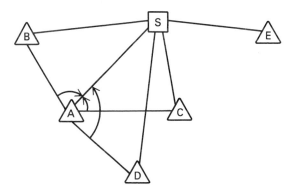

Fig. 4.6   Alternative routing from A to B,C,D.

4.2.1.2 *Alternative Routing—additional considerations*

Alternative routing is not as straightforward as might at first appear. The general objective is to define a strategy which will enable one or more alternative routes to the specified destination to be selected by a node, if the preferred route is unavailable. The strategy is to be implemented in real-time. The strategy must also produce predictable results off-line, so that links can be dimensioned to handle the overflow traffic they will receive; and so that they can be costed accordingly. Once the links are costed, their capacities can be further adjusted to minimize costs, as discussed above.

The first point to make is that costing can be complex. The cost of a channel depends on more than its length. Associated costs to be taken into account can include: Interfacing to the switches; additional switch capacity to handle the new channel; the possible need for new carrier equipment, cabling or ducting to carry the channel, etc.

Secondly, the definition of the alternative routing strategy itself must take into account the practicability of its implementation in real-time; and must avoid certain dangers, such as routes with an excessive number of links and switches in them and routes involving loops or which 'ping-pong' to and fro between two adjacent nodes.

With regard to the practicability of real-time implementation, it is normal that, where a node contains routing tables (i.e. is not unintelligent and relying on 'right-through routing' commands from other nodes), those tables should contain entries only *for destinations*. The route to a destination from a given node should not depend on the *source* of the call. Thus a routing table contains destinations (either individual, or grouped such as 'Region 6' or 'International'); and against each destination a list, in order of preference, of output links to distinct neighbouring nodes on the permitted routes to that destination.

For example, in Fig. 4.7, it is supposed that a call is made from X (entering the trunk network at P1) to Z (P6). Routing table entries could be

Node	Table Entry
P1	P6:2,3
S2	P6:1,7,6
S3	P6:2
T2	P6:3
T1	P6:3,4
S1	P6:4
Q1	P6:2

The first entry signifies that at node P1 there are two output links towards P6, namely numbers 2 and 3 in order of preference.

From the tables we see that the first choice route from P1 is to S2. What if no route out of S2 can be found, because all channels are occupied? The answer is (usually) that the call is cleared. The link 3 from P1 to S3 is not attempted. It is only attempted if P1 finds its output link 2 to S2 fully occupied; *not* if S2 cannot further route the call. This restriction is not essential, but is usual because

(i) It simplifies routing implementation.

(ii) It reduces the time taken to establish calls, by reducing the number of routing options available.

(iii) It enables simple dimensioning of links. In our example the link P1–S1 carries overflow traffic from P1–S2. We do not have to consider overflow traffic from links onwards out of S2, which might be referred back to P1.

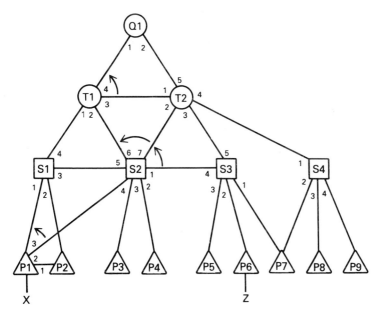

Fig. 4.7 Possible alternative routing from X to Z.
Note: the numbers beside a node identify the outgoing links.

The example of Fig. 4.7 is that of a hierarchical network with primary, secondary, tertiary and quaternary levels. The routing alternatives from P1 to P6 have been chosen according to a set of rules for such hierarchical networks. These rules could, in principle, automatically generate the routing tables when applied to the network configuration.

When considering any node and a required destination to be reached from that node, the rules are

(1) If there is a direct connection to the destination it is the first preference.

(2) If there is a direct connection to another node at the same hierarchical level, provided that node is a direct 'ancestor' (in the tree) of the destination, it is the next preference. This rule ensures that the route does not wander at length round a level. Since the network is a hierarchy, there is a maximum-minimum number of links between any pair of nodes; and this is found by going up the hierarchy and down again. For our network, no nodes are more than six links apart. It is this rule which disallows S1 routing the call to S2, when the destination is P6, although in the particular example it might be a good strategy.

(3) If choices (1) and (2) are unavailable, the next preference is to go to the next higher level, to the node nearest to the destination. Thus, for destination P6, S2 picks T2 in preference to T1 (if the route to S3 is unavailable). If no channel is available to the node nearest to the destination, the next nearest is chosen, etc.

(4) Descending a level is only permitted when the descent is directly towards the destination. Thus, for destination P6, T2 can only choose S3, S2 is not allowed. This avoids the possibility of the call 'ping-ponging' between S2 and T2 if links S2–S3 and T2–S3 are unavailable.

In this example the route P1–S1–T1–Q1–T2–S3–P6 is the 'final' or 'backbone' route from P1 to P6. Whatever capacities the other links may have, this backbone route should have a Grade of Service acceptable for the traffic offered, including (of course) the overflow traffic for which the backbone route is the final alternative route.

The above rules are typical for alternative routing in a hierarchical network. Other rules can be used, but all would have the objectives

(i) To ensure that all routes are shorter than some acceptable maximum length.

(ii) To avoid 'ping-ponging' and looping.

(iii) To ensure ease of implementation and modelling of traffic flows.

4.2.1.3 A Refinement to Overflow Calculations—Wilkinson's Method [2]

If A Erlang are offered to M circuits the overflow traffic is the offered traffic multiplied by the probability of overflow

$$\text{Overflow traffic} = A.E(M, A). \tag{4.1}$$

where $E(M, A)$ is given by the Erlang-B formula (Equation (1.11) of Chapter 1).

However, it is a well-known phenomenon that the probabilistic characteristics of overflow traffic differ from those of 'first-offered' traffic. Assuming there are infinitely many channels available, first offered traffic has a Poisson distribution ($M \rightarrow \infty$), in which the variance is equal to the mean (A). But overflow traffic from M circuits has a distribution in which the variance is greater than the mean. The traffic is more 'peaked'—obviously because overflows are likely to occur in bursts.

Supposing that there are M high-usage channels and an infinite number of overflow channels, it would be useful to know

$$P_{i,j}(t) \; 0 \leqslant i \leqslant \mathrm{M}, 0 \leqslant j$$

where $P_{i,j}(t)$ is the probability at time t of i high-usage and j overflow channels being occupied. Simultaneous equations for $P_{i,j}(t)$ can be developed. For example, for $0 < i < M$, we can write

$$P_{i,j}(t+\mathrm{d}t) = (1-\lambda \, \mathrm{d}t - i\mu \, \mathrm{d}t - j\mu \, \mathrm{d}t)P_{i,j}(t) + \lambda \, \mathrm{d}t \, P_{i-1,j}(t)$$

$$+ (i+1)\mu \, \mathrm{d}t \, P_{i+1,j}(t) + (j+1)\mu \, \mathrm{d}t \, P_{i,j+1}(t)$$

where the arrival rate of calls is λ and the hold-time is $1/\mu$ (see the derivation of Equations (1.3) to (1.6) of Chapter 1).

Making the usual steady-state assumption, $\mathrm{d}P(t)/\mathrm{d}t = 0$, we get

$$(\lambda + (i+j)\mu)P_{i,j} = \lambda P_{i-1,j} + \mu(i+1)P_{i+1,j} + \mu(j+1)P_{i,j+1} \tag{4.2}$$

Equation (4.2) is valid for $0 < i < M$, and other equations can be derived when $i = 0$ or $i = M$. These equations are difficult to solve directly.

It can be shown, however, that, if

$$P_j^* = \sum_{i=0}^{M} P_{i,j},$$

the mean and variance of P_j^* are

$$\text{Mean}\,(P_j^*) = \alpha = A \,.\, E(M, A) \tag{4.3}$$

$$\text{Variance}\,(P_j^*) = \alpha(1 - \alpha + A/(1+M+\alpha-A)) \tag{4.4}$$

Equations (4.3) and (4.4) characterize the overflow traffic offered to an alternative route, precisely enough for all practical purposes. Note that Equation (4.3) agrees with Equation (4.1).

Wilkinson's technique applies when a link receives overflow traffic from *several* sources, plus (perhaps) first offered traffic. The technique provides a method for determining the characteristics of the *total* traffic offered to the link. Essentially, the theory rests on two facts

(1) The mean and variance of the total offered traffic are simply the sums of the means and variances of the individual overflows. This is a consequence of the general form of the equations.

(2) Since the mean and variance characterize the offered traffic, we can model the system by *any* process which gives the same mean and variance of offered traffic to the link receiving the overflows.

Wilkinson's technique is a technique for calculating the required number of channels on the link receiving the overflows. It is based on the foregoing observations and proceeds as follows

(i) For each source of overflow calculate the mean, α_i, and variance, v_i, of the overflow traffic using Equations (4.3) and (4.4). (For first-offered traffic Variance = Mean = A, as can be seen if $M = 0$.) The subscript 'i' refers to the 'ith' source of overflow, out of N such sources. Calculate

$$\alpha = \sum_{i=1}^{N} \alpha_i, \ v = \sum_{i=1}^{N} v_i.$$

(ii) Find a *single* source of overflow which gives the same mean and variance. In other words, find an A', M' such that $\alpha = A'.E(M', A')$ and $v = \alpha(1-\alpha+A'/(1+M'+\alpha-A'))$. Wilkinson has developed graphs to facilitate these 'reverse' calculations.

(iii) The traffic offered to the link receiving the overflows can now be regarded as the overflow when A' is offered to M'. To achieve a Grade of Service on this link with (say) C channels, we solve for C when A Erlangs are offered to $(C+M')$ channels in the usual way

$$GOS = E(C+M', A')$$

Applying the technique to the example of (Section 4.2.1.1), Figs 4.4, 4.5 and 4.6, for the overflows from AB, AC, AD to AS we have

	Mean	Variance
First-offered AS traffic	7.00	7.00
Overflow from AB	1.24	1.91
Overflow from AC	1.24	1.91
Overflow from AD	1.24	1.91
	$\alpha = 10.72$	$v = 12.73$

The individual overflow characteristics are evaluated from

$$\alpha_i = A_i.E(M_i, A_i) = 4.E(4,4) = 4 \times 0.31 = 1.24$$
$$v_i = \alpha_i(1 - \alpha_i + A/(1 + M + \alpha_i - A_i))$$
$$= 1.24(1 - 1.24 + 4/(1 + 4 + 1.24 - 4))$$
$$= 1.91.$$

This is equivalent to a single overflow from 13.48 Erlang offered to 3.0 channels. Check

$$\alpha = 10.72 = 13.48E(3.0, 13.48)$$
$$v = 12.73 = \alpha(1 - \alpha + A/(1 + M + \alpha - A))$$
$$= 10.72(1 - 10.72 + 13.48/(1 + 3.0 + 10.72 - 13.48)).$$

For 1% GOS on the link AS, with 13.48 Erlang offered, 21.27 channels are required in total. Removing the 3.0 already accounted for, 18.27 remain, which (rounded up) gives 19 channels. Comparing this with the original result (Case (3) of Section 4.2.1.1) it is seen that AS requires an extra channel to compensate for the 'peaked' nature of the overflows. (Nevertheless the alternative routing solution (3) is still more economic than solutions (1), no direct links, or (2) using direct links only.)

We may summarize these paragraphs on alternative routing in circuit-switched networks by stating that: Given an alternative routing strategy, which is 'sensible', i.e. avoids loops and implementation complexities, it is possible to calculate the required capacities of all links with a relatively high degree of precision. Wilkinson's method permits even the 'peaked' nature of overflows to alternative routes to be taken properly into account. The routing strategy itself could be applied to a given network configuration to generate automatically the routing tables, used in real-time.

4.2.2 Routing in SAF Networks

We shall consider firstly the case of pure message-switching or datagrams, in which each message or packet is routed through the network independently. The routing techniques used may later be applied to Virtual Circuit (VC) packet-switched networks; or techniques peculiar to VC networks may be developed.

The fundamental objective of routing is, of course, to ensure that a message sent from source A to destination B, actually reaches B. However, there may be many secondary objectives, such as

(i) The route from A to B should be chosen to minimize the transit time of the message in question.

(ii) The route from A to B (and all other routes from sources to destinations) should be chosen to minimize the average transit time of messages over all routes.

(iii) The route from A to B should be chosen to optimize the use of network capacity, i.e. maximize throughput.

(iv) The route from A to B should be chosen to maintain an even distribution of loads on links and nodes, in so far as is possible.

(v) The routing strategy should be such that failure of a link or node on the chosen route will cause minimum disturbance to the service as seen by the user.

Even within these secondary objectives there are distinct approaches. For example, for (i) above, the route might be chosen to minimize the transit time of the message, given typical network loading from other traffic; or it might be chosen to minimize the transit time given *actual* network loading at that instant. (Query: is instantaneous knowledge of network loading possible?).

It may safely be said that no single SAF routing technique meets all the objectives of the sort outlined above. Each technique has its merits and its disadvantages, and each network designer will have to balance performance achievable in accordance with his particular objectives, against the complexities and costs of implementing the routing strategy.

In the following sections we consider some of the more widely used or publicized routing techniques under three headings: Routing based on fixed tables; Routing based on tables which are dynamically updated; Other routing techniques. Finally, routing of traffic in VC SAF networks is considered.

4.2.2.1 Routing based on Fixed Tables

In this approach, each node contains one or more tables defining the outgoing link to be taken from that node to reach a specific destination. It may be supposed that the tables have been developed, for and with the network configuration, to meet some optimization criterion, in accordance with the discussion at the start of this Chapter (Section 4.1). In all but the simplest cases, alternative routes to each destination, from each node, will be built into the tables.

This is precisely the approach used in circuit-switched networks (see

Section 4.2.1.1), which addresses the problem of the potential unavailability of a high-usage route, when all circuits are occupied or when a network component (e.g. a link) fails.

However, in SAF networks, an alternative route may be chosen on grounds of performance as well as of non-availability of the high-usage route. For example, the rule might be: If more than three messages are queued for output on the first choice high-usage route, consider the first alternative route; if more than three messages are queued for the first alternative route, consider the second alternative route, etc. It is supposed that the final-choice route has adequate capacity to support the overflow traffic from the preferred alternatives, albeit at a reduced performance—'performance' in this case being the speed at which the message crosses the network. It should be possible to calculate (given a traffic matrix whose components give the number of messages per unit time from A to B), the probability of this reduced performance. For example: transnetwork delay could be designed to be less than 500 ms for 85% of messages, the remaining 15% representing those messages which are sent via the final route and encounter queues longer than some minimum length on it.

Consider firstly a simple system in which λ messages per second are offered to a link with a service rate of μ messages per second ($\mu > \lambda$). If M messages are present in this system, queued or in process of transmission, newly arriving messages are routed to an overflow alternative link with service rate μ'. Let $P_{k,j}$ be the probability of k items in the first system, j in the overflow system. Then, making the usual assumption about a steady state solution ($dP_{k,j}/dt = 0$), the following equation holds

$$(\lambda+\mu^{(1)}+\mu'^{(2)})P_{k,j} = \lambda P_{k-1,j}+\mu P_{k+1,j}+\mu' P_{k,j+1}+\lambda P_{k,j-1}^{(3)} \qquad (4.5)$$

Notes. (1) This term is present unless $k = 0$, (2) This term is present unless $j = 0$, (3) This term is only present if $k = M$, (4) All $P_{k,j}$ with $k < 0$ or $j < 0$ are zero and (5) All $P_{k,j}$ with $k > M$ are zero.

An explicit solution for $P_{k,j}$ is not readily obtained. However the probability of j messages in the overflow system, independent of the state of the high-usage system can be represented by

$$P_j^* = \sum_{k=0}^{M} P_{k,j} = \left(1-\frac{\lambda'}{\mu'}\right)\left(\frac{\lambda'}{\mu'}\right)^j \qquad (4.6)$$

where $\lambda' = \lambda\dfrac{A^M(1-A)}{(1-A^{M+1})}$ and $A = \lambda/\mu$

Equation (4.6) states that the overflow link performs as a normal queue, with arrival rate equal to the 'raw' arrival rate (λ) multiplied by the probability of the high-usage link already having M messages. Simulation studies show that Equation (4.6) holds well. In particular the theoretical mean length of the overflow queuing system, $A'/(1-A')$ with $A' = \lambda'/\mu'$, agrees very well with simulations. However the variance, as found in simulations, is larger than the predicted $A'/(1-A')^2$.

This situation is analogous to that analysed by Wilkinson for circuit-switched systems (see Section 4.2.1.3) and reflects the 'peaked', i.e. non-random, arrival of messages to the overflow system. However, ignoring this problem of 'peaking', we may reasonably say, as a first approximation, that overflow traffic is characterized by the raw arrival rate multiplied by the probability of overflow occurring.

Generalizing, if one link is fed by overflow traffic from N other links, of which link (i) has arrival rate λ_i, and overflow probability P_{M_i} (M_i being the number of messages at which overflow occurs), we may state that the link has arrival rate λ',

$$\lambda' = \sum_{i=1}^{N} \lambda_i P_{M_i} \tag{4.7}$$

with $P_{M_i} = A_i^{M_i}(1-A_i)/(1-A_i^{M_i+1})$ and $A_i = \lambda_i/\mu_i$ (4.8)

First-offered traffic can be included by putting $M_i = 0$, so that $P_{M_i} = 1$.

We may use Equation (4.7) to dimension links in SAF systems in a manner similar to the method employed for circuit-switched networks. Given the arrival rate, λ_i, for a link; the service rate, μ_i; and some maximum delay criterion we can determine M_i—the number of messages being processed or queued at which overflow to an alternative link must occur if the criterion is to be met. The probability of overflow P_{M_i} can be calculated from Equation (4.8). The resultant overflow is one of the summation terms in Equation (4.7). Summing all the overflows to find λ', we can calculate the probability of exceeding the delay criterion for the alternative route if μ' is known. μ' can be adjusted to make this acceptable. Clearly, with appropriate costing factors for line speeds and line lengths, some optimum set of line speeds (μ' and the μ_i) can be found to meet the delay criteria.

As an example consider Fig. 4.8. There are (full-duplex) traffic flows of 400-bit messages as follows

$$A \longleftrightarrow S, B \longleftrightarrow S \qquad 12 \text{ messages/second.}$$
$$A \longleftrightarrow B \qquad\qquad\qquad 3 \text{ messages/second.}$$

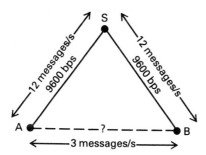

Fig. 4.8 Is a circuit AB required?

We suppose, for simplicity, allowable line speeds are 9600 bps or 2400 bps only; and that the time taken inside a node is 100 ms per message. The objective is to ensure that 85% of all messages traverse the network in less than 500 ms.

The question is: Should a link AB exist and what speed should it have? There are three possibilities

(1) No direct link AB. All traffic is routed through S. The offered traffic to AS (and BS) is 15 messages per second, and since capacity (μ) is 24 messages per second, loading is 5/8. For traffic from A to B through S the delay in ms is

$$\text{Delay} = 3 \times 100 \text{ (in the nodes)} + (N_{AS} + N_{SB})\frac{1000}{24} + \frac{2 \times 1000}{24},$$

the second term being queuing behind N_{AS} messages on the link AS, N_{SB} on the link SB; and the third term being actual message transmission times.

The total delay for A to B traffic is thus

$$383.3 + 41.7(N_{AS} + N_{SB}) \text{ ms.}$$

For this to be less than 500 ms $N_{AS} + N_{SB} \leq 2$. With a loading of $A = 5/8$ on AS and BS the probability that $N_{AS} + N_{SB} \leq 2$ is

$$\text{Prob}(N_{AS} = N_{SB} = 0) + 2.\text{Prob}(N_{AS} = 1, N_{SB} = 0)$$
$$+ 2.\text{Prob}(N_{AS} = 2, N_{SB} = 0)$$
$$+ 1.\text{Prob}(N_{AS} = 1, N_{SB} = 1)$$

since the configuration is symmetrical. Using the formula

$$\text{Prob}(N) = (1-A)A^N$$

it is found that there is a 52% probability that the delay A to B exceeds

500 ms. (There is only a 4% probability that the delay A to S or B to S exceeds 500 ms.)

(2) Direct Link AB, with no Overflow. The load on the links AS and BS is now $12/24$ (= 1/2), and the delay (A to S or B to S) is

$$2\times100+N_{AS}\times(1000/24)+(1000/24)$$

$$= 241.7+41.7\times N_{AS}.$$

$$\therefore N_{AS} \leqslant 6 \text{ to meet the 500 ms criterion.}$$

Prob ($N_{AS} \leqslant 6$) = 99.3% with $A = 1/2$, so there is no problem on the links AS or BS.

However, on the link AB, if the speed is 2400 bps the load is also 1/2, since capacity is 6 messages per second. The delay is

$$2\times100+(N_{AB})(1000/6)+(1000/6)$$

$$= 367+N_{AB}\times167.$$

For the delay to be less than 500 ms $N_{AB} = 0$. The probability of this is only 50%. Therefore the link must be 9600 bps, not 2400 bps, if the delay criterion is to be met.

(3) Direct Link AB with Overflow via S. On AB the load is 1/2 and we have seen that we should only route messages directly if $N_{AB} = 0$. Therefore $M_{AB} = 1$; i.e. overflow occurs if 1 message is present. Using Equation (4.8) with $M_{AB} = 1$ and A (the offered load) = 1/2 we have

$$P_1 = 1/3 = \text{Probability of overflow.}$$

Therefore, using Equation (4.7) with $N = 1$, $\lambda_1 = 3$, $P_{M_1} = 1/3$, the overflow traffic is 1 message.

On the route A to S to B the traffic (including first-offered traffic) is now $12+1 = 13$ messages per second, and the load is 13/24. The delay is

$$3\times100+(N_{AS}+N_{SB})\,(1000/24)+2\times(1000/24)$$

$$= 383.3+41.7(N_{AS}+N_{SB}),$$

so

$$N_{AS}+N_{SB} \leqslant 2, \text{ as before.}$$

The probability ($N_{AS}+N_{SB} \leqslant 2$) = 62.4%, calculating as in (1) above with $A = 13/24$. So there is a 37.6% probability that 1/3 of the A to B traffic will exceed 500 ms in transit, i.e. a 12.5% probability for all the

A to B traffic. This meets the objective that 85% of all traffic has a transnetwork delay less than 500 ms. (There is no problem with A to S or B to S traffic.)

The example illustrates once again how a routing strategy influences network design. Without alternative routing a 9600 bps link AB would be required (see Case (2)), since routing all traffic through S is also unacceptable (Case (1)).

A further form of SAF alternative routing, known as 'hot-potato' should be mentioned. In this technique messages are passed through a node as quickly as possible—hence the name. From the ordered list of alternative routes out of a given node to a given destination, the highest priority route for which there is no output queue is chosen. If all alternatives have non-empty output queues, then the route with the shortest queue is chosen.

4.2.2.2 Routing Tables which are Dynamically Adapted

Fixed routing tables are designed to handle average traffic flows offered to a given network configuration; and, conversely, the configuration is designed to support the traffic flows at the link-by-link level which arise as a result of the fixed routing tables used. If, however, conditions change from those foreseen, either because the offered traffic or the configuration changes, then it is sensible to consider how the routing tables may be adapted to the new conditions.

The term 'adaptive' routing is used here to mean: Procedures for adapting the list of preferred routes from each node to each destination, in response to network conditions. Many such adaptive routing procedures exist, and some are reviewed briefly hereunder [3].

Centralized routing. The first approach to adaptive routing which naturally presents itself is to have some central controlling site which analyses the current network configuration, traffic flows and delays (i.e. lengths of queues of messages for internodal links) and then generates new 'optimal' routing tables for each node. These new tables are then sent to the nodes for use. This updating of the routing tables in the nodes takes place at instants which may be regularly spaced in time; or which may be determined by some significant event, such as a marked change in traffic patterns or failure of a network component. Two problem areas clearly exist

(1) The additional traffic on the network resulting from sending current

configuration and loading data to the centre, and returning new routing tables to the individual nodes, itself distorts network loading. To a certain extent this can be foreseen and catered for, but at the least it represents a significant amount of inhomogeneous traffic. Even if carried on separate CCS channels this traffic can hardly be ignored.

(2) There are inherent delays in the 'timeliness' of the procedure. By the time the information has reached the centre, been processed, and new routing tables have been returned to the nodes, they may be out of date. The situation in the network may have changed again. Moreover, until the next updating interval occurs, further changes may arise. Indeed, the new routing tables will *provoke* further changes which may, to a large extent, be foreseen by the centre which performs the optimization algorithm, although changes originating with users can hardly be foreseen. Simulations have shown that so-called 'magic' centralized routing, in which the delays in receiving information and delivering new routing tables are taken to be zero, does not produce the improvements in performance which might be expected, essentially because of the necessarily finite intervals between updates of the tables [4].

Thus centralized adaptive routing is useful for handling longer term changes in the network and its traffic. It is not really suitable for handling short-term fluctuations, which would require very rapid updating of routine tables with the consequent generation of heavy traffic by the function itself.

How do such centralized 'optimization' algorithms work? Assuming that the criterion is to minimize transnetwork delays, the algorithm might proceed as follows

(i) Determine the delays on each network link, from existing queue lengths.

(ii) For each source-destination pair find the shortest route (in time) through the network, taking into account other constraints such as loading on nodes. Algorithms for finding shortest paths exist, see Section 4.3.

(iii) Apply the current offered traffic flows (the current traffic matrix) to the network, using the routing found in step (ii). (It may be that two or three, rather than one, shortest routes are desirable so that heavy traffic may be split between them; i.e. the algorithm also simulates the alternative routing strategy.)

(iv) The combination of the existing delays and the additional traffic as determined in (iii) produces new values for the delays. The process can be iterated from step (i) until a stable traffic pattern is, hopefully, achieved.

Of course, there is nothing to guarantee that stability will be achieved. Solutions may oscillate to and fro, and it may be necessary to 'dampen' them, for example by weighting the importance of existing queues with respect to those arising from future traffic. Furthermore, the finding and use of all the individual shortest routes may not necessarily be the best strategy. It could be better to minimize average transnetwork delay; or simply to attempt to ensure that all transnetwork delays are less than some maximum figure.

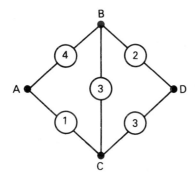

Fig. 4.9 A simple network.
Note: the numbers give the capacity of each link in messages per second.

As an example, consider the network of Fig. 4.9. The numbers attached to each link give that link's capacity in messages per second in each direction. Thus four messages can be sent from A to B, and from B to A, in a second. Figure 4.10a gives the delays involved in sending a message between any pair of directly connected nodes (in the absence of other traffic); and Fig. 4.10b gives the shortest route and associated delay between any pair of nodes. (Note: 'X' means that the shortest route is the direction connection; 'B' signifies that the shortest route is via B. Thus the shortest route from A to C is via B, and the associated delay is 7/12 second.) Using Fig. 4.10b as a basis for routing, *all* traffic to/from A would go via B.

Figure 4.11 illustrates a possible instantaneous state of the network. The numbers represent the number of messages queued or being processed in each direction on each link. Thus three messages are queued or being processed on the link to B from C. The situation could have arisen if routing based on Fig. 4.10b were used.

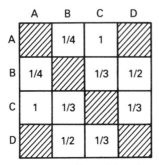

	A	B	C	D
A	░	1/4	1	░
B	1/4	░	1/3	1/2
C	1	1/3	░	1/3
D	░	1/2	1/3	░

Fig. 4.10a Direct delays in seconds.

	A	B	C	D
A	░	X 1/4	B 7/12	B 3/4
B	X 1/4	░	X 1/3	X 1/2
C	B 7/12	X 1/3	░	X 1/3
D	B 3/4	X 1/2	X 1/3	░

Fig. 4.10b Delays on fastest routes.

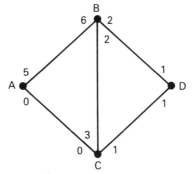

Fig. 4.11 A possible state of the network.
Note: the numbers signify the messages queued for being processed on each link in each direction.

Figure 4.12a gives the delays involved in sending a message between any pair of directly connected nodes. The delay for C to B, for example, is $(3+1)\times1/3 = 4/3$ seconds. Figure 4.12b gives the shortest route and associated delay between any pair of nodes, assuming the basic conditions

	A	B	C	D
A	░	3/2	1	░
B	7/4	░	1	3/2
C	1	4/3	░	2/3
D	░	1	2/3	░

Fig. 4.12a Direct delays given queues of Fig. 4.11.

	A	B	C	D
A	░	X 3/2	X 1	C 5/3
B	X 7/4	░	X 1	X 3/2
C	X 1	X 4/3	░	X 2/3
D	C 5/3	X 1	X 2/3	░

Fig. 4.12b Delays on fastest routes.

of Fig. 4.11. In this case we see that, if Fig. 4.12b is used as a basis for routing, traffic from A to C or D is routed via C; whereas if Fig. 4.10b were used that traffic would be routed via B.

So far we have two bases for routing tables: Figure 4.10b which takes into account only link capacities; and Fig. 4.12b which also takes into account the current instantaneous state of the network of Fig. 4.11. A third situation exists if we consider offered traffic in the form of a traffic matrix, from which we can *predict* queues and hence delays.

	A	B	C	D
A		1	2/3	1/3
B	1		1/2	1/2
C	2/3	1/2		1
D	1/3	1/2	1	

Fig. 4.13   Offered traffic (messages per second).

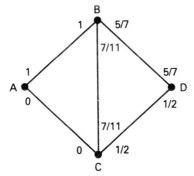

Fig. 4.14   Queues resulting from traffic of Fig. 4.13.

Figure 4.13 is a traffic matrix, giving messages per second between any pair of nodes. If this traffic matrix is applied to the network using the routing implied by Fig. 4.10b (no traffic on the link AC) the queues of Fig. 4.14 will result. (Note: the number of messages queued and being processed is given by $A(1-A)$, where A is the link loading. Thus link A to B carries $1+2/3+1/3 = 2$ messages per second; capacity is 4; loading $A = 1/2$; therefore $A/(1-A) = 1$.) Figure 4.15a gives the corresponding delays on the direct links, and Fig. 4.15b gives the shortest routes and

	A	B	C	D
A		1/2	1	
B	1/2		6/11	6/7
C	1	6/11		1/2
D		6/7	1/2	

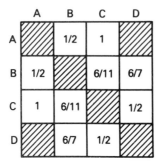

Fig. 4.15a Direct delays given queues of Fig. 4.14.

	A	B	C	D
A		X 1/2	X 1	B 19/14
B	X 1/2		X 6/11	X 6/7
C	X 1	X 6/11		X 1/2
D	B 19/14	X 6/7	X 1/2	

Fig. 4.15b Delays on fastest routes.

associated delays between any pair of nodes. Figure 4.15b is yet again different to Figs 4.10b and 4.12b. It recommends routing traffic from A to C directly, but traffic from A to D via B, not C.

Figure 4.15b was derived assuming best routes given by Fig. 4.10b, i.e. no traffic on the link AC. But Fig. 4.15b *recommends* that the direct traffic between A and C should travel on this direct link. Therefore we should iterate the procedure, applying the traffic matrix of Fig. 4.13 to the network according to the optimum routing given by Fig. 4.15b. However if we do this, and route A to C traffic via AC, then it is found that the shortest delay is via B. In short, the iterative procedure does not converge, but oscillates. An optimum stable solution will only be reached by load-splitting; that is, sending some of the A to C traffic via B, some directly on AC.

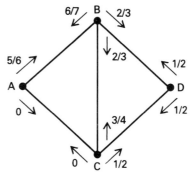

Fig. 4.16 Flows (messages per second) corresponding to Fig. 4.13.

The three cases of Figs 4.10, 4.12 and 4.15 give three different routing patterns, depending on the assumptions taken, viz
(1) There is no traffic in the network, except the 'test' message.
(2) There are existing queues as given by Fig. 4.11.
(3) There exists other traffic, defined by traffic matrix of Fig. 4.13, and the routing of Fig. 4.10b or Fig. 4.15b, each routing used resulting in recommending the other.

The analysis can be pursued further. Suppose for example we combine the existing traffic (Fig. 4.11) with the predicted traffic of the matrix (Fig. 4.13). This can be done by converting the queues of Fig. 4.11 into message flows which would give rise to these queues, as in Fig. 4.16. Suppose the 'combination' is given by

Flow on link $= \delta$(Existing Flow)$+(1-\delta)$
(Flow derived from traffic matrix). $\qquad$ (4.9)

In deriving the flow from the traffic matrix we assume routing as per Fig. 4.12b (A to D traffic via C). The resulting flows and queues, with $\delta = 0.5$, are shown in Figs 4.17a and 4.17b respectively. The delays on direct links are given by Fig. 4.18a and the shortest delays and routes by Fig. 4.18b. Once again we see that the recommended routing of Fig. 4.18b (A to D traffic via B) differs from that used. Again, if the recommendation is followed, the solution oscillates.

The above trivial example serves to show that optimum routing is certainly non-trivial. The calculations were based on a very simple network, ignoring nodal delays and alternative routing. Nevertheless, three solutions were found (one unstable) based on three different hypotheses, and an infinity of other solutions is indicated if Equation (4.9) is used

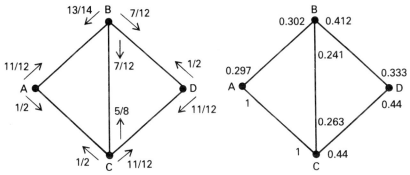

Fig. 4.17a Flows from combining Figs 4.16 and 4.13.

Fig. 4.17b Resulting queues.

Chapter 4

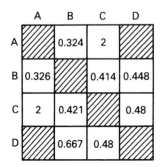

	A	B	C	D
A	░	0.324	2	░
B	0.326	░	0.414	0.448
C	2	0.421	░	0.48
D	░	0.667	0.48	░

	A	B	C	D
A	░	X 0.324	B 0.738	B 0.768
B	X 0.326	░	X 0.414	X 0.448
C	B 0.747	X 0.421	░	X 0.48
D	B 0.993	X 0.667	X 0.48	░

Fig. 4.18a Direct delays resulting from Fig. 4.17.

Fig. 4.18b Delays on fastest routes.

with varying values of δ. When $\delta = 0.5$ the solution is unstable unless load-splitting is used.

Delta-routing. The concept of delta-routing is due to Rudin [3]. In the previous example a combination of existing traffic and forecast traffic (from the matrix) was used to predict network loading. The combination was controlled by a parameter, δ, and the resulting queues, for $\delta = 0.5$, are shown in Fig. 4.17b. It was supposed that all this was done at the centre at which new routing tables are elaborated.

In delta-routing the concept is to combine central decision-making with *local* decision-making, with the objective of handling long-term variations at the centre and short-term ones locally; thereby reducing both the frequency of central calculations and the resultant traffic between the centre and the nodes. The method employed in delta-routing is the following

(i) At the centre, using 'current' queue lengths for all network links, find the shortest and next shortest route (via a distinct outgoing link) to each destination from each node.

(ii) If the shortest route differs from the next shortest by more than a factor δ, this shortest route (as found at the centre) is built into the routing tables and imposed on the relevant node. If the difference is less than δ, then the centre recommends both routes to the node, and leaves the ultimate choice to the node itself.

(iii) At each node, for each destination, the central choice of route is used (if it exists). If the centre recommended *two* outgoing links, then the node picks that with the shorter queue.

Simulations have shown this approach to be successful in optimizing transnetwork delays in the face of traffic (or configuration) changes. The reader is referred to the original paper for further details.

Non-centralized routing. Various techniques exist for developing adaptive routing tables in a node based on local or regional, rather than centralized, information. A particularly well-known approach (used in Arpanet) is for each node to receive from its neighbours estimates of the shortest delays to all destinations from those neighbours. A given node can then, by adding the delay to a particular neighbour (derived from the queue length for the link to that neighbour), estimate the shortest delay to all destinations via that neighbour. The node can choose the link to the neighbour, via which the overall delay to a given destination is shortest, as the route to that destination. These 'shortest delays' in turn form estimates of delays from that node to all destinations, and can be passed to its neighbours.

This is precisely the technique used in deriving the shortest routes of Fig. 4.12b from the queues of Fig. 4.11; except that we supposed the routing was done centrally rather than in the distributed fashion described above. However, in the distributed case problems can arise when information is updated. For example suppose, suddenly, the queue at C for the direct link to A increases to a large size, 5 (say), resulting in an estimated C to A delay of 6. C will compare the delays to A via B ($4/3+7/4 = 37/12$) and to A via D ($2/3+5/3 = 7/3$) and decide that the best route to A is via D. But the route from D to A is back via C! The error arose because D did not receive the updated information about the state of the C to A link when C received it. It is necessary to incorporate delays or other 'damping' factors into the use of recently updated routing tables to ensure that the new information has permeated the network [5].

Backward-learning. Yet another adaptive routing technique is that of 'backward-learning'. In this technique the delay from A to D (say) is estimated by measuring at A the delay from D to A. If traffic is not symmetric these two delays may be quite unrelated, so the technique is more useful for estimating the *lengths* of paths (i.e. the number of links in them) rather than delays. For example, if each message carries its source address and a 'handover' count, incremented by one for each link traversed, a node receiving messages incoming from a given link can determine the minimum handover count associated with that link and any given source. Comparing this with the minimum handover counts from the same source, but different incoming links, the node can decide which incoming link gives access to the shortest route from (and hence to) the source.

Of course, if traffic from the source is always routed along the same path to the node there will be no range of handover counts to compare. The technique thus supposes that a certain amount of 'random' routing is used to explore the network's configuration. This approach could be usefully employed following a failure of network components, or a complete restart of the network.

4.2.2.3 Some Other Routing Techniques

It is possible to imagine many other routing techniques. Two are mentioned here.

The first is random routing [6]. In random routing messages are sent out from a node on a randomly selected available link. Provided that the network never divides itself into separate 'islands' due to component failures, the message should eventually reach its destination, even in the event of severe failures. Of course the transit times will be long (they can be estimated) and the network will be more heavily loaded in consequence.

The second technique is 'flooding' [7]. In this case each message is uniquely identified and also given a time-stamp on entering the network. When the message reaches a node copies of it are dispatched on *all* outgoing links (except the one on which it arrived). Within some maximum time period at least one copy will reach the required destination. The destination will throw away duplicate copies it may receive. Nodes will destroy all copies where time-stamp shows them to be older than the maximum time period allowed for reaching destinations. This technique obviously loads the network; thus negating, by increasing queuing delays, the potential advantage of finding the fastest route automatically. It is, however, clearly attractive for wide-spread broad-casting of messages to multiple destinations.

4.2.2.4 Routing and Virtual Calls (VCs)

In the previous discussion of routing in SAF networks the object to be routed was an independent message or datagram. How should the related collection of packets associated with a VC be routed?

One approach to the problem is simply to superimpose a VC service on a datagram network. With each VC there will be associated an entry and an exit node (possibly one and the same). At the entry node packets are built into datagrams, with an appropriate sequence number. They are then routed across the network by whatever datagram technique is used. Different packets belonging to the same VC may take different routes and arrive at the exit node out of sequence. The exit node puts them back in sequence for delivery to the destination DTE, using the sequence numbers mentioned above. Although there are obvious problems in dealing with resets (as in X.25) and other error conditions, the approach is perfectly valid and is used in some commercial packet-switching VC networks.

A less obvious problem associated with resequencing is that of the availability of buffers at an exit node. A 'deadly embrace' can occur if all buffers are exhausted when VCs are awaiting missing packets to insert in sequence for delivery to the user. The missing packets cannot be received until the exit node has free buffers; and the exit node cannot have free buffers until the missing packets arrive and the sequences can be delivered to the user. Algorithms exist to handle this problem, but they imply the existence of some sort of entry-to-exit-node protocol, to prevent more packets entering the network when the danger of a 'deadly embrace' exists.

The more usual approach to routing VCs is to allocate a fixed route to all packets belonging to the VC for the duration of the VC's existence. This route could be chosen exactly as in circuit-switching, with no reference to packet flows. A routing table (with alternative routes) defines which link to take from a node to a given destination. That link will be chosen, provided a virtual channel is available for it, irrespective of the queues or delays involved. If no virtual channel is available the alternative routes will be chosen. Flow control procedures for the VC (on the network interfaces, within the network, or possibly end-to-end between users' DTEs) will limit the number of packets in transit. For example, if an X.25-like protocol exists *between* nodes then there is a window mechanism limiting the number of packets belonging to a VC which can arrive at any node along its route. Use of the X.25 D-bit (see Section 3.4.2.3) can provide another very useful protection against overload.

A more flexible approach to handling the routing of VCs is the following. Routing tables, fixed or periodically adjusted using modified forms of the adaptive techniques discussed in Section 4.2.2.2, determine how VCs are routed in each node. However, an alternative route to the preferred route will be chosen not only if no virtual channel is available, but also if the preferred outgoing link is heavily loaded.

Suppose the arrival rate of VCs for a given outgoing link from a node is $\bar{\lambda}$ and the VC-duration is $1/\bar{\mu}$. Suppose also that the arrival rate of packets per VC is λ and the service rate of packets on the link is μ. We put $A = \lambda/\mu$.

The probability of k VCs being present is P_k, as is given by Equation (1.6) of Chapter 1,

$$P_k = P_0 \prod_{i=0}^{k-1} \bar{\lambda}_i / \prod_{i=1}^{k} \bar{\mu}_i \qquad k < 1/A \tag{4.10}$$

$$P_k = 0 \qquad\qquad\qquad k \geq 1/A$$

with $\bar{\lambda}_i \, dt$ being the probability of arrival of a new VC, and $\bar{\mu}_i \, dt$ the probability of termination of a VC, in time dt, when i VCs are present. We have also imposed the restriction that the number of VCs present is never allowed to equal or surpass $1/A$. In other words, if $\bar{k}$ is the largest integer such that $\bar{k} < 1/A$, then $\lambda_i = 0$ for $i \geq \bar{k}$. If $\bar{k}$ VCs are present, all newly arriving VCs are allocated alternative routes.

As in Chapter 1, we take $\bar{\mu}_i = i\bar{\mu}$. We also impose an additional constraint on $\bar{\lambda}_i$; namely that allocation of a new VC to an alternative route will take place if there are M or more buffers in the output queue for the link. This gives

$$\bar{\lambda}_i = \bar{\lambda}\,(1 - \text{Probability of } M \text{ or more buffers in use}) = \bar{\lambda}\,(1 - (iA)^M).$$
$$i < \bar{k}$$

Substituting $\bar{\lambda}_i$, $\bar{\mu}_i$ in Equation (4.10) we have

$$P_k = \left(\frac{\bar{\lambda}}{\bar{\mu}}\right)^k \frac{P_k}{k!} \prod_{i=0}^{k-1} (1 - (iA)^M) \qquad k \leq \bar{k} \tag{4.11}$$

$$P_k = 0 \qquad\qquad\qquad k > \bar{k}.$$

The probability of the system being in the state in which new VCs are sent to alternative routes (the 'Probability of overflow') is

$$\text{Probability of overflow} = P_{\bar{k}} + \sum_{k=1}^{\bar{k}-1} P_k (kA)^M \tag{4.12}$$

As an example, consider an output link from a node for which the arrival rate of VCs is once every 5 minutes and the holding time is 10 minutes. Then $\bar{\lambda}/\bar{\mu} = 2$. If the number of packets per second per VC is 3, and the link can handle 12 packets per second, then $A = 1/4$, so $\bar{k} = 3$. We also put $M = 2$.

Since

$$\sum_{k=0}^{\bar{k}} P_k = 1$$

we have from Equation (4.11)

$$P_0\left(1+2+\frac{(2)^2}{2!}\left(1-\left(\frac{1}{4}\right)^2\right)+\frac{(2)^3}{3!}\left(1-\left(\frac{1}{4}\right)^2\right)\left(1-\left(\frac{1}{2}\right)^2\right)\right) = 1$$

or

$$P_0\left(1+2+\frac{15}{8}+\frac{15}{16}\right) = 1,$$

so

$$P_0 = \frac{16}{93}.$$

Then from equation (4.12), the probability of overflow is

$$P_0\left(\frac{15}{16}+2\cdot\left(\frac{1}{4}\right)^2+\frac{15}{8}\left(\frac{1}{2}\right)^2\right) = \frac{16}{93}\cdot\frac{49}{32} = 0.26.$$

So the rate of arrival of VCs for the alternative routes is $0.26\bar{\lambda}$, or once every 19 minutes.

Thus, using an alternative routing strategy for VCs, in which all traffic on a VC follows a fixed route (chosen when the VC is established in such a way as to minimize queuing delays), it is possible to calculate the probable traffic loads on the alternative routes. The network may then be dimensioned to support the traffic flows produced by the users and the routing strategy.

4.2.3 Routing on Failure of Network Components

Before leaving the topic of routing, a word should be said about what happens when a link or node fails. If the network is circuit-switched, or supports VC packet-switching with a fixed route for the duration of a VC, then the calls affected by the failure are simply cleared.

If, however, the network uses datagram routing, it should adjust automatically to the failure; except for those messages already queued for failed links or in failed nodes. Special software will be required to reroute messages on a queue for a failed link. This software reverses, as it were, previously taken routing decisions. A failed link must obviously be marked as such to the routing procedures so that they explicitly avoid it, rather than simply relying on examining queue lengths. Messages lost in a failed node can not normally be recovered, except by end-to-end control procedures between DTEs, using retransmission of unacknowledged messages.

4.3 NETWORK ANALYSIS

The subject of network analysis is extensive and, in its purest form, a branch of graph theory [8]. Here we are only interested in some specific aspects of the topic. For example, in choosing routes and alternative routes between a given node and destination, one might have a use for a systematic procedure for finding all possible routes from which to make the choice.

In graph theory, links between nodes are usually called edges, and routes which have no edges in common are called 'edge-disjoint'. It could be useful to be able to enumerate readily all the edge-disjoint routes between any pair of nodes, since that number is indicative of the resilience of the network in the event of failure of a link. A stronger requirement is to consider only 'vertex-disjoint' routes ('vertex' = 'node'). In choosing routes for inclusion in routing tables the preference could be for 'edge-disjoint' or 'vertex-disjoint' routes, on grounds of reliability in the face of failure. However, we have previously assumed that a route from an (intermediate) node to a destination is independent of the source of the call or message. This assumption causes problems if we look for disjoint routes. For example, in Fig. 4.19, there are two vertex-disjoint routes from A to E (A–B–D–E and A–C–E). If these are chosen, then we cannot use B–C–E as an alternative to B–D–E for traffic from B to E, unless we distinguish traffic at B for E according to its source.

Other problems of network analysis which we have already met are: Finding the distance (in terms of minimum number of links) between

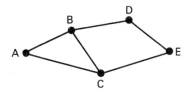

Fig. 4.19   A simple network.

any pair of nodes (see Section 1.3); Finding the shortest route (in terms of delays) between any pair of nodes.

Solutions to the type of problems illustrated above are useful not only when designing a network, but also when it is in use in real-time. For example, given the current use of channels in a circuit-switched network one might perform a 'contingency analysis': If a particular link fails, are there sufficient suitable channels on other links available for the calls using the first link to be rerouted via those on other links? Finding the shortest-delay routes is another typical real-time problem in adaptive routing.

In the following paragraphs some relevant methods of network analysis are discussed.

4.3.1 Finding the 'Capacity' Between Any Pair of Nodes

Figure 4.20 illustrates a network of six nodes, with links labelled with their 'capacity'. This could be the 'flow' the links could carry (in bps for digital data, or even litres per second of liquid). Another, perhaps more convenient, way of defining 'capacity' in the example is to say it is the number of channels on the link.

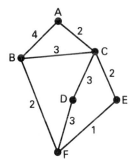

Fig. 4.20   A network and its link capacities.
Note: the figures represent the capacities for the links (i.e. the number of channels).

How many channels exist between A and F, for example? More precisely, how many distinct parallel routes, each route using one channel per link on the route, can be established simultaneously between A and F? An algorithm to answer this question might run as follows

(i) Start at the source and select an outgoing link, arbitrarily the first time. On subsequent passes through the algorithm, use the same link unless it is no longer available, in which case pick the next link anti-clockwise until all links have been used.

(ii) Pick as many channels as are still available on the link.

(iii) Proceed to the end of the link to reach a new node.

(iv) At the new node, record the path taken to arrive there from the source and the number of channels on that path. If the new node is the required destination, record that these channels are taken, i.e. no longer available, and return to (i). Otherwise proceed to (v).

(v) Pick an outgoing link from the node. The first time, this can be done arbitrarily, provided it does not lead directly to a node further back on the current path. In later passes through the algorithm the outgoing link must also be marked as 'available' to be selected. A link is available unless all its channels have already been taken, or it leads to another node out of which there is no available link. Subject to these constraints, links from the node can be picked anticlockwise, as in (i).

(vi) If no outgoing link which does not rejoin the path is available, then mark the link via which this node was reached as unavailable, and step back to the previous node on the path. Repeat step (v) for this node. If an outgoing link is available proceed to step (vii).

(vii) Take N channels on the chosen link, where N is the lesser of the number available on the link and the number used on the path from the source to the node. (In the former case, adjust the path record to include the lower number of channels possible.) Go to step (iii).

This is a modified version of the Ford–Fulkerson algorithm [8]. It will cease at step (i), when all links from the source have been explored. Figure 4.21 illustrates the application of the algorithm to Fig. 4.20. The numbers in circles on paths indicate the channels taken by that path.

It is interesting to note that the total number of parallel channels between A and F is six. If the network is cut in half in any way, so that A and F are in distinct halves, then the sum of the capacities of the cut links is never less than six. This illustrates the maximum-flow minimum-cut theorem of Ford and Fulkerson. The maximum flow between a pair of nodes is the minimum of the sum of the capacities of the cut links,

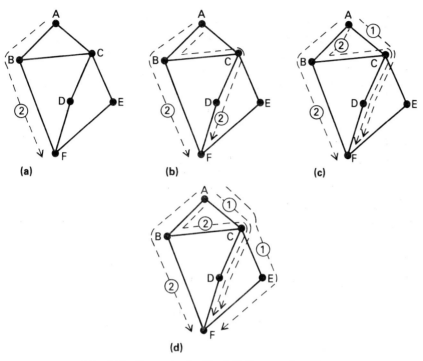

Fig. 4.21 Stages in the Ford–Fulkerson algorithm.

over all possible cuttings of the network in half in which the nodes are in distinct halves.

A different approach to finding the number of channels linking nodes is given below. It is based on matrices in a manner similar to the method of Section 1.3. The method yields progressively the number of channels of length 1 link between a pair of nodes; then the number of channels of length 2 links between the pair, the channels being distinct from the previously found channels; then the number of channels of length 3 links, etc.

We start from a connectivity matrix, C, which includes the number of channels on each link. We define a matrix $C_{(n)}$ whose elements (ij) give the number of channels of length n links, interconnecting the nodes i and j, provided that there exist no connections of less than n links. Associated with $C_{(n)}$ is a matrix $D_{(n)}$ which contains unity in position (i,j) if there exists a path of length n or less between nodes i and j, zero otherwise.

If, for a given pair of nodes i and j, we can find a $C_{(n)}$ in which the (ij) element is non-zero (for the lowest possible n), then we have found all channels of length n between i and j. If these channels are *removed* from the original connectivity matrix the calculations can be repeated to find all channels of length $(n+1)$, etc.

The method of calculating $C_{(n)}$ is repetitive. $C_{(1)}$ is put equal to C, the connectivity matrix, and then formulae for calculating $C_{(n+1)}$ from $C_{(n)}$ can be applied. These are

$$C_{(n+1)} = (C \cdot C_{(n)}) \ (AND) \ \bar{D}(n)$$

$$D_{(n+1)} = \text{Boolean} \ (C_{(n+1)}(OR) \ D_{(n)}). \tag{4.13}$$

The operators used are: In the matrix multiplication $C \cdot C_{(n)}$ the product of two elements $a \cdot b$ is defined as $a \cdot b = \text{Min}(a,b)$, and the sum $(a+b)$ is the ordinary sum. The *AND* operation with $\bar{D}_{(n)}$, the complement of $D_{(n)}$, means zeroize all elements in $C \cdot C_{(n)}$ corresponding to zeros in $\bar{D}_{(n)}$. This effectively means eliminate from $C_{(n+1)}$ any connections of length n or less. In calculating $C_{(n+1)}$, it must be made symmetric by choosing the lesser of the two values $C_{(n+1)i,j}$, $C_{(n+1)j,i}$ if they differ. (This deals with channels converging on to a single link from two or more links.) The calculation of $D_{(n+1)}$ consists in placing unity where $D_{(n)}$ or $C_{(n+1)}$ have non-zero values, zero elsewhere. The calculation begins with $D_{(0)} = I$, the identity matrix, and $C_{(1)} = C$, the connectivity matrix showing channels per link.

Since $C_{(n)i,j}$ gives the channels of length n between i and j, provided there are no shorter ones, we can subtract those channels from the original matrix C to find a new C', which has no channels of length less than $(n+1)$ links between i and j. Now the process can be repeated to find those channels of length $(n+1)$, which in turn can be subtracted to give C'', etc. In this way we can find all independent channels between i and j and hence, by summation, the capacity of the network to carry traffic from i to j.

In subtracting channels we must be able to identify them. This is easily done by analysing the matrix multiplications in reverse. Thus

$$C_{(n)i,j} = \sum_k \text{Min}(C_{i,k}, C_{(n-1)k,j}).$$

The values of k which gives non-zero terms are points on the route(s) i to j. We can, for each k, proceed to find the next point from

$$C_{(n-1)k,j} = \sum_m \text{Min}(C_{k,m}, C_{(n-2)m,j}).$$

A tree corresponding to the routes is constructed, and the actual values to be subtracted from C can be written on the branches. Consider Fig. 4.20 again, as a simple example.

$$C_{(1)} = C = \begin{array}{cccccc} \mathbf{A} & \mathbf{B} & \mathbf{C} & \mathbf{D} & \mathbf{E} & \mathbf{F} \\ 0 & 4 & 2 & 0 & 0 & 0 \\ 4 & 0 & 3 & 0 & 0 & 2 \\ 2 & 3 & 0 & 3 & 2 & 0 \\ 0 & 0 & 3 & 0 & 0 & 3 \\ 0 & 0 & 2 & 0 & 0 & 1 \\ 0 & 2 & 0 & 3 & 1 & 0 \end{array} \begin{array}{c} \mathbf{A} \\ \mathbf{B} \\ \mathbf{C} \\ \mathbf{D} \\ \mathbf{E} \\ \mathbf{F} \end{array} \qquad D_{(1)} = \begin{array}{cccccc} 1 & 1 & 1 & 0 & 0 & 0 \\ 1 & 1 & 1 & 0 & 0 & 1 \\ 1 & 1 & 1 & 1 & 1 & 0 \\ 0 & 0 & 1 & 1 & 0 & 1 \\ 0 & 0 & 1 & 0 & 1 & 1 \\ 0 & 1 & 0 & 1 & 1 & 1 \end{array}$$

$$C_{(2)} = \begin{array}{cccccc} 0 & 0 & 0 & 2 & 2 & 2 \\ 0 & 0 & 0 & 5 & 3 & 0 \\ 0 & 0 & 0 & 0 & 0 & 6 \\ 2 & 5 & 0 & 0 & 3 & 0 \\ 2 & 3 & 0 & 3 & 0 & 0 \\ 2 & 0 & 6 & 0 & 0 & 0 \end{array} \qquad D_{(2)} = \text{All elements are unity.}$$

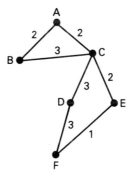

Fig. 4.22 The network with A–F channels of length 2 removed.

This states that the diameter of the network is 2; and that there are, for example, two parallel channels of length 2 between nodes A and F, and none of shorter length. How many channels are there altogether between these nodes? We identify the channels of length 2 as $A-(2)-B-(2)-F$ from the product $C \cdot C_{(1)}$, and remove them to give a new network as in Fig. 4.22. Repeating the calculations

$$C_{(1)} = C = \begin{array}{cccccc} 0 & 2 & 2 & 0 & 0 & 0 \\ 2 & 0 & 3 & 0 & 0 & 0 \\ 2 & 3 & 0 & 3 & 2 & 0 \\ 0 & 0 & 3 & 0 & 0 & 3 \\ 0 & 0 & 2 & 0 & 0 & 1 \\ 0 & 0 & 0 & 3 & 1 & 0 \end{array} \qquad D_{(1)} = \begin{array}{cccccc} 1 & 1 & 1 & 0 & 0 & 0 \\ 1 & 1 & 1 & 0 & 0 & 0 \\ 1 & 1 & 1 & 1 & 1 & 0 \\ 0 & 0 & 1 & 1 & 0 & 1 \\ 0 & 0 & 1 & 0 & 1 & 1 \\ 0 & 0 & 0 & 1 & 1 & 1 \end{array}$$

$$C_{(2)} = \begin{array}{cccccc} 0 & 0 & 0 & 2 & 2 & 0 \\ 0 & 0 & 0 & 3 & 2 & 0 \\ 0 & 0 & 0 & 0 & 0 & 4 \\ 2 & 3 & 0 & 0 & 3 & 0 \\ 2 & 2 & 0 & 3 & 0 & 0 \\ 0 & 0 & 4 & 0 & 0 & 0 \end{array} \qquad D_{(2)} = \begin{array}{cccccc} 1 & 1 & 1 & 1 & 1 & 0 \\ 1 & 1 & 1 & 1 & 1 & 0 \\ 1 & 1 & 1 & 1 & 1 & 1 \\ 1 & 1 & 1 & 1 & 1 & 1 \\ 1 & 1 & 1 & 1 & 1 & 1 \\ 0 & 0 & 1 & 1 & 1 & 1 \end{array}$$

$$C_{(3)} = \begin{array}{cccccc} 0 & 0 & 0 & 0 & 0 & 2 \\ 0 & 0 & 0 & 0 & 0 & 3 \\ 0 & 0 & 0 & 0 & 0 & 0 \\ 0 & 0 & 0 & 0 & 0 & 0 \\ 0 & 0 & 0 & 0 & 0 & 0 \\ 2 & 3 & 0 & 0 & 0 & 0 \end{array} \qquad D_{(3)} = \text{All elements are unity.}$$

Note that $C_{(3)F.A}$ and $C_{(3)F.B}$ were forced to 2 from 3, and to 3 from 4 respectively to preserve symmetry. This is because paths from node F to nodes A or B reconverge at node C.

This result shows that there are two parallel channels of length 3 between nodes A and F. The tree diagram is

$$A\text{--}(2)\text{--}C \genfrac{<}{>}{0pt}{}{(1)\text{--}E\text{--}(1)}{(1)\text{--}D\text{--}(1)} F$$

The two channels between nodes C and F can be allocated arbitrarily within the capacity restrictions. We have allocated one via node D, one via node E. Subtracting these from Fig. 4.22 we get Fig. 4.23 and now

$$C = \begin{array}{cccccc} 0 & 2 & 0 & 0 & 0 & 0 \\ 2 & 0 & 3 & 0 & 0 & 0 \\ 0 & 3 & 0 & 1 & 2 & 0 \\ 0 & 0 & 1 & 0 & 0 & 1 \\ 0 & 0 & 2 & 0 & 0 & 1 \\ 0 & 0 & 0 & 1 & 1 & 0 \end{array} \qquad \text{giving } C_{(4)} \begin{array}{cccccc} 0 & 0 & 0 & 0 & 0 & 2 \\ 0 & 0 & 0 & 0 & 0 & 0 \\ 0 & 0 & 0 & 0 & 0 & 0 \\ 0 & 0 & 0 & 0 & 0 & 0 \\ 0 & 0 & 0 & 0 & 0 & 0 \\ 2 & 0 & 0 & 0 & 0 & 0 \end{array}$$

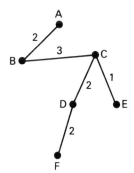

Fig. 4.23 The network with A–F channels of length 3 removed.

There are two channels of length 4 between nodes A and F. Summarizing the channels between nodes A and F we have: two of length 2, two of length 3 and two of length 4.

The total channel capacity between nodes A and F is thus 6. This is the same result as that obtained with the modified Ford–Fulkerson algorithm, but yielding some more detail as to path lengths. Another possible advantage of the matrix method over the algorithmic approach is that it is easier to implement. It is more 'automatic' and involves making fewer decisions.

4.3.2 Finding Fastest Routes Between Nodes

The matrix method of Section 4.3.1 gives shortest routes, in terms of the number of links on the route, between any pair of nodes. If, however, the objective is to find the route with the least time delay (supposing that the delay on each link is known) other methods are required.

Firstly, in practice, it is very unlikely that a network will be so bizarrely designed that a route with many links will have a shorter delay than one with few links, between the same pair of nodes. Thus a simple approach to finding the fastest (least-delay) route is to consider a set of the shortest (least-links) routes (found by the matrix method), calculate their associated delays, and pick that with least delay. However, there are problems with this method. Consider the network of Fig. 4.24, in which each link has only *one* circuit, as in message-switching for example. The matrix method will deliver the 2-link route ABF and the 3-link route ADEF, from A to F but not the 3-link route ABCF—which could be the fastest.

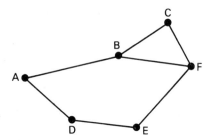

Fig. 4.24   A simple network.

Another approach to finding the fastest route is to modify the calculations of the matrix algorithm. For example, in matrix multiplication the product of row $r = (r_1 r_2 \ldots r_n)$ and column $c = (c_1 c_2 \ldots c_n)$ is $r_1 \cdot c_1 \oplus r_2 \cdot c_2 \oplus \ldots \oplus r_n \cdot c_n$. In ordinary algebra '$\cdot$' = multiply, $\oplus$ = add. In the method of Section 4.3.1, $a \cdot b = \mathrm{Min}(a,b)$, $\oplus$ = add. For fastest routes, where we wish to find least delays, and we suppose elements in the matrix are delays, then we can take $a \cdot b = a+b$, and $x \oplus y = \mathrm{Min}(x,y)$. The matrix method, thus amended, will give the fastest route of length n which is *independent* of the fastest routes of lengths 1,2, ... to $(n$-$1)$. In short the method ignores some routes which are not mutually independent.

Thus to find all the fastest routes between nodes a more direct approach is necessary. One method is a simple systematic search as follows

(i) Start from the source and pick an available output link. An available link is one whose ramifications have not yet been fully explored. (If none exists, the search has ended. From the file of recorded paths pick the fastest.) Proceed to the next node on the chosen link.

(ii) If the next node on the chosen link is the required destination, record the path to it and the association delay in a file. Mark the link as unavailable and return to the previous node. Go to (iii). (If the next node is not the destination go from (i) to (iii) directly.)

(iii) If there is no available output link from the node, or only ones which directly join a node further back on the current path from the source, mark the link just used from the previous node as unavailable and return to that previous node. Mark all 'unavailable' links other than those which emanate from a node on the current path (including from the source) as 'available'. If there is an available output link, select one and proceed to the next node on it. Repeat (iii).

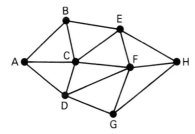

Fig. 4.25 Find all routes from A to H.

The procedure explores successively all routes emanating from one link from the source, then from another link, etc. Figure 4.25 is used as an example. The procedure runs as follows
—File ADGH, mark GH na (not available).
—File ADGFH, mark FH na.
—File ADGFEH, mark EH na.
—ADGFE will now fail, since all available paths from E double back. So mark FE na. Make EH available.
—File ADGFCEH, mark EH na.
—ADGFCE will now fail. So mark CE na. Make EH available.
—File ADGFCBEH, mark EH na.
—ADGFCBE will now fail. So mark BE na. Make EH available.
—ADGFCB will now fail. So mark CB na. Make BE available.
—ADGFC will now fail. So mark FC na. Make CB, CE available.
—ADGF will now fail. So mark GF na. Make FC, FE, FH available.
—ADG will now fail. So mark DG na. Make GF, GH available. (At this stage all routes beginning ADG have been tested and filed.)
—File ADFH, mark FH na.

It is clear that this procedure would be very lengthy, and in practice (certainly on-line) some sub-optimum technique similar to those discussed previously would probably be sufficient. The procedure could be speeded up by marking as unavailable any links at the end of paths in excess of some plausible maximum number of links [9].

4.4 CONCLUSION

In this chapter the topics of routing and network design (by which is meant the configuration and its capacity) have been discussed. The interdependence of the topics has been emphasized. Conventional alternative routing techniques, as used on circuit-switched networks, can be carried over to SAF networks. SAF networks are also susceptible to more adaptive techniques, to take into account the delays caused by buffering and queuing of messages. It is possible to offer VC packet-switched services on a datagram network employing these adaptive routing techniques. A more usual course is to use alternative routing (based on fixed tables) per VC, with all packets on that VC following the chosen route.

In building the routing tables, whether on- or off-line, it is necessary to know the characteristics of the routes being considered—their lengths and their associated delays. Analytical tools, of some complexity, exist to facilitate this.

REFERENCES

1 *Recommendation X.121* CCITT Red Book, **VIII. 4,** Geneva, 1985.
2 Wilkinson RI (1956) Theories for Toll Traffic Engineering in the USA *Bell Systems Technical Journal,* **35,** 421–514.
3 Rudin H (1976) On Routing and Delta Routing *IEEE Transactions on Communications* **COM-24,** No. 1.
4 Adams RA *et al.,* (1973) Simulation Study of a data communications network *Plessey Telecommunications Research Ltd.* Report No. 97/73/03/TR.
5 McQuillan J M *Adaptive Routing Algorithms for Distributed Computer Networks* (MIT Ph.D. Thesis).
6 Prosser RT (1962) Routing procedures in Communications Networks *IRE Transactions on Communications Systems* **CS-10** 322–335.
7 Boem BW and Mobley RL (1969) Adaptive Routing Techniques for Distributed Communications Systems *IEEE Transactions on Communications* **COM-17,** 340–349.
8 Wilson RJ (1972) *Introduction to Graph Theory* Oliver & Boyd. It includes a discussion of the Ford–Fulkerson algorithm.
9 Other algorithms for finding the shortest routes are discussed in:
Hoffman AJ and Winograd S (1972) Finding all the shortest distances in a directed network. *IBM Journal of Research and Development,* **16,** 412–414.
Domschke W (1972) *Kurtzeste Wege in Graphen Algorithmen, Verfahrensvergleiche.* Verlag Anton Hain.

Chapter 5
Services, Interfacing and ISDNs

In Chapters 2 and 3 circuit-switched and SAF networks were considered; and in Chapter 4 there was a discussion of how such networks should be designed, configured and dimensioned to support the offered traffic (taking into account the routing used). Most of the discussion was concerned with low level details of the internal construction of networks, or, in certain places, with details of interfacing to the networks.

In this chapter the emphasis is on the functions, facilities and services provided by networks, as seen from the outside. There are two classes of outside 'observers' of a network.
(1) The persons responsible for managing the network.
(2) The users of the network and its services.

5.1 NETWORK MANAGEMENT

The reader may be somewhat surprised that network managers should be considered as 'outside' the network. However, in modern networks, the manager it usually almost as detached from the network as a user. Although maintenance staff will be required to attend to faults in switches, lines, etc., it is frequently not necessary that they should be on site unless actually carrying out maintenance. Monitoring, control, tests and diagnoses can all be made from one or more consoles comfortably situated in an operator's or manager's office remote from the racks of telecommunication equipment.

Monitoring and control of a network require that a person (network operator or manager) can receive information on the performance of network components (switches, lines, etc.); and that the person can send commands to those components to test, reinitialize, take them out of service, etc. If the network is capable of carrying *data*, then the network itself can be used to convey the information to, and the commands from the operator or manager.

A network which is essentially carrying voice traffic might have a few specialized operator consoles strategically situated at fixed network addresses, using dedicated channels to the nodes. The dedicated channels could be voice channels, adapted for data, or possibly CCS channels. At the other extreme, on an all-data network, there might exist no specific operator consoles. Any terminal, connected anywhere on the network, would be allowed to serve as an access point for a network operator or manager. The operator functions, however, would be under secure password control; so that only someone who had passed that control would be able to monitor or modify the network. These functions may be put under four main headings

(1) Event reporting, in which errors, significant changes of status, etc. are reported as soon as they occur.

(2) Control. This is the function which allows an operator to modify the network, e.g. take a node out of service.

(3) Performance statistics, or tabulated data on loading and usage of lines, switches and so forth, which is made available at regular intervals (e.g. weekly) to the management.

(4) Data on individual users from which the charges payable by those users can be calculated.

The first two functions are typically available to an 'operator', a person responsible for the minute-by-minute correct operation of the network. The second two functions are more pertinent to the network management, which is responsible for longer-term planning and commercial matters.

The general mechanism for providing these functions is that, within any network node, there will be what may be called a Monitor Process. Individual entities in the node, such as a communications protocol module or an on-line diagnostic package, will receive commands from, and deliver error and statistical reports to, the monitor process. The monitor process, in turn, communicates with one or more Network Management Centres (NMCs). An NMC is a common sink, where monitoring data from many nodes may be collated, and is a source of operator commands to those nodes. Finally, a network operator or manager has access to the NMC from a console, local or remote, with suitable security control (Fig. 5.1). The advantage of this approach is that in each node to be monitored or controlled there is only *one* process to which all communications should be addressed; and that by giving operators access to those processes only via an NMC, all the processing and collating of data (which may undergo frequent modifications) and the support of the dialogues with the operator, can be held and main-

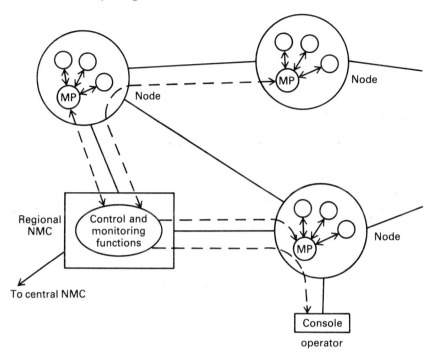

Fig. 5.1 Management of a network.
NMC = network management centre; MP = monitoring process; O = other process.

tained at a single point—the NMC. Of course other approaches are possible, for example, giving operators direct access to nodes and providing no NMCs (except possibly for acquiring customers' charging data), but usually these approaches give rise to more complex development and maintenance of the control and monitoring function itself.

If more than one NMC exists, the various NMCs would usually have a regional responsibility in the network, with only one central NMC given the extra functions enabling it to provide information on the network as a whole. Having regional NMCs provides more security in case of an NMC failure; monitoring and control traffic on the network will be homogeneous, and therefore less likely to cause overloads and similar problems.

Readers familiar with telemetric systems, as are commonly used with electricity transmission and distribution services and other public utilities (water, gas), will realize that the monitoring and control of a telecommunication network differs very little from that of any other sort of network. The central and regional NMCs correspond to central and regional Load Dispatch Offices (LDOs). The monitoring processes correspond to Outstations or Remote Terminal Units (RTUs), responsible for the low level functions of Supervisory Control and Data Acquisition (SCADA). The network manager and operator may access the NMCs via simple terminals; but the coloured graphics displays, usual in the man-machine interfaces of LDOs, are not unknown in telecommunications networks. The state-estimation, load-flow, contingency analysis, and other high-level programs run at an LDO do not all have their parallels in existing NMCs, but most of the concepts involved might usefully be transferred to telecommunication networks. Indeed, the only essential difference between the supervision of telecommunication networks and traditional telemetric systems is that in the former the supervisory infrastructure is very largely based on the network which is to be monitored. In the latter case, the supervisory and the monitored networks are distinct, both in nature, and physically.

5.1.1 Monitored Data

There is little point in elaborating on the details of the information monitored or the items controlled. In any specific network it is easy to state what is required. In the short term, the network operator wishes to know if and when links or nodes have serious errors, what are the causes of them. He also requires control tools to enable him to deal with the situation (run a diagnostic, abort or restart a process, etc.). In the longer term, the management wants to observe traffic on the network to see where more capacity may be required. Data such as: busy-hour Erlangs of traffic at a node, packets-per-second switched through, average length of SAF buffer queues, a traffic-matrix derived from actual observation, are clearly of interest.

However, a special word should perhaps be said about data for charging purposes. The tariffication of telecommunication networks usually has three bases
(1) Charges to new users on first becoming a subscriber, e.g. for the issuing of Network User Identifiers (NUIs) or passwords.
(2) Standing charges, for the continuing support of facilities for the subscriber whether he uses them or not, e.g. a DCE and its permanent link to a network node.

(3) Usage charges based on the duration of calls (as in most circuit-switched networks) or on the volume of information transmitted (as in most packet-switched networks), or on both.

Additionally, a user may have to pay access charges, incurred on another network (e.g. the telephone network), which he must use to gain access to the network he really wants (e.g. a data network).

The only item which requires *on-line* monitoring is item (3). For every user the network, in practice the originating node, must record information necessary for charging for every call made or message sent. The information typically required is

(i) The sender's identity.

(ii) The destination(s).

(iii) The start and finishing times of calls, or the time of sending a message.

(iv) The volume of user data sent or received per VC (packet-switching) or per message.

(v) Any special facilities used on this transmission, such as reverse charging, high priority, etc.

Difficulties can arise when a service to the user, such as Teletex [1], Videotex [1], message-handling [2] or information retrieval (q.v.), is built on top of the normal network infrastructure. In principle, use of the additional service will also be charged to the user, and the user will receive two bills, one for use of the new service, one for use of the basic network. But this is not always fair, let alone convenient. For example, suppose a message-handling service (e.g. X.400 q.v.) involves relaying messages between message-handling exchanges interconnected over an X.25 network (Fig. 5.2). Each inter-exchange link incurs separate X.25 charges, as do the user-to-exchange links; but really a single X.25 call might serve the purpose if the message-handling service were designed differently. Again, many services (e.g. the postal service) carry large quantities of unsolicited traffic, or 'junk mail'. An electronic mail service can hardly charge the recipient for this, but such charging is bound to happen if sending and receiving are lumped together for charging purposes—as is the case for X.25.

A solution to this problem is to subsume the infrastructure charges into the service charges, either explicitly or implicitly. 'Explicitly' means that the infrastructure bills the service on behalf of the user, giving the service the necessary data about call duration and volumes. 'Implicitly' means that the infrastructure bills the service without necessarily

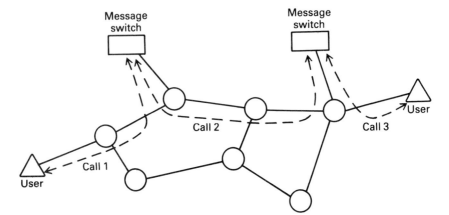

Fig. 5.2 A service (message-switching) which might involve several calls.

identifying individual users and the service estimates the infrastructure costs imputable to each user.

Such considerations show that flexibility is required in charging systems. A caller may be billed; or alternatively reverse-charging, in which the called number is asked whether he agrees to pay, may be used. There may be toll-free numbers, to which reverse-charging always applies; or perhaps it is only applicable to certain specified potential originators of calls for that toll-free number. There may be credit-control of users, who may not incur debts larger than a certain amount before being 'cut-off' the network automatically. There may exist special customers in the form of other value-added services supplied by the network administration, who receive bills in a different form and at different tariff rates. There may be users of those special services, who are only billed by those services and not by the network itself.

To permit the necessary flexibility in the methods of charging users, the usage data which is acquired must be very comprehensive, if frequent rewriting of software is to be avoided.

5.2 INTERFACING TO THE NETWORK

In Chapters 2 and 3 interfacing to circuit-switched and SAF networks were, respectively, considered. Most of the discussion was concerned with the requirements of the networks—the formats for the data, the details of the call set-up and clearing, etc. Of course, very many DTEs are built to conform strictly to interfacing standards such as X.25 or X.21. Nevertheless, there is often a need for an organization to provide access to an external network for its internal computer users, without forcing each individual's equipment to be compatible with that network.

Moreover, individual access by individual users is expensive. As discussed in Section 5.1.1, there are standing charges per registered user, of which perhaps the most significant are those associated with the physical connection between the user and the external network: the DCE, the line, the port on the node. Considerable savings may result if these costs can be shared between users within an organization. A configuration such as that of Fig. 5.3 is indicated. Here a unit, labelled Concentration and Switching Point (CSP) serves not only to concentrate traffic from individual users within the organization on to the access paths to an external network, but also to switch traffic locally between users, be they at terminals or computers.

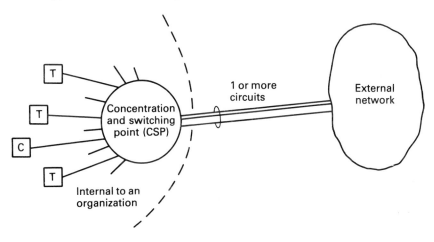

Fig. 5.3 A concentration and switching point.
T = terminal; C = computer.

Two approaches to providing a CSP immediately present themselves (1) Local Area Networks (LANs). A LAN (see Fig. 5.4) serves as an 'in-house' switch for (data) traffic and is readily supplemented with a 'gateway' to an external network. Within the gateway conversion between the formats and standards required by the two networks takes place, when traffic passes from one to the other. It should be noted that most LANs, such as Ethernet [3] or the Cambridge Ring [4], operate

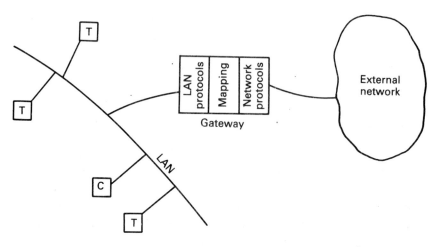

Fig. 5.4 A LAN gateway to an external network.

with some sort of *SAF-switching,* in which a common medium (e.g. a coaxial cable) is shared on demand between would-be users. Traffic from a sender is queued at the sender's device until the demand for transmission capacity is granted.

(2) Private (Automatic) Branch Exchanges (PBXs or PABXs). A PBX is the second obvious contender for the role of CSP. A PBX is an in-house telephone exchange, providing precisely those functions of concentration and switching (and also many more, such as traffic recording) required for the CSP—but for *telephones.* However, a PBX can be adapted to handle data traffic, including selection of the destination, etc., and hopefully less equipment overall is required since there will be no separate data CSP. Moreover, with ingenuity, it is often possible to use existing telephone cabling for data, sharing the one internal extension line between a telephone and a data terminal, and even sharing exchange lines (i.e. to the external network) between voice and data. PBXs are, however, usually circuit-switched, so there may be questions about the efficiency with which they handle sporadic interactive traffic.

Before discussing LAN and PBX-access to networks in more detail, a general problem should be mentioned: Direct Inward Dialling (DID). Whereas a terminal may readily 'dial-out' (i.e. originate a communication to an external network) via a CSP by generating the appropriate numbers for the external network, DID requires that the external network delivers destination numbers to select local terminals 'behind' the CSP. This supposes that the external network is in some way compatible with the numbering plan for the terminals within the organization.

For example, suppose the numbering plan of a public network is based on 8-digit decimal numbers, and a private CSP has ten exchange channels to the public network and 100 internal extensions. Each of the ten exchange channels, as seen from the public network has, in principle, a distinct 8-digit number.

For DID to be possible one of four broad approaches must be followed (1) Either some or all of the ten exchange channels are paired with specific extension lines (permanently or for a period) so that incoming calls on those exchange channels are switched directly through to the specified extensions. In effect the extension lines in question are direct exchange lines, which happen to be routed through the CSP.
(2) Or the remote caller is allowed select more than eight digits (for example ten digits), the trailing two digits serving to identify which of the 100 extension lines he requires. These trailing digits must be accepted, transmitted and delivered to the CSP by the public network, transparently. The implication is that every node in the public network must be able to handle addresses of arbitrary length (less than a certain maximum), since it is hardly feasible for each node to know what the length of every number should be, on the basis of its first few digits. Handling of such arbitrary length addresses is supported in the call request packet of X.25, see Section 3.4.2.1.
(3) Or the public network only handles 8-digit addresses, but the numbering scheme is such that *six* digits are sufficient to identify the required CSP, the remaining two being used by the CSP to pick the extension line required. In effect, the CSP customer has one hundred 8-digit public numbers but only ten exchange channels. Seen from the public network, all the exchange channels could bear the same address, of which only the first six digits are significant to the network, an arbitrary free channel being picked whenever a new call arises. (Alternatively each exchange channel could have a distinct 6-digit address, but this is clearly more wasteful of public addressing space.) This is the approach commonly used in telephone networks, where DID exists.
(4) Or DID is a two-stage process. In the first stage the remote caller establishes a connection to the CSP itself. In the eyes of the public network the call now 'exists'. In the second stage, the caller explicitly requests the CSP to switch the connection through to a particular extension. This approach is used in various 'Internet' protocols for data

networks, in which local private networks use datagrams, transferred between them over public X.25 channels. It is also the traditional approach to handling a private telephone exchange, but with a *manual* switchboard and operator.

The DID problem exists essentially when call-switching is employed, since a 'call' has to be established to the terminal on an internal extension line. The problem does not really exist with message-switching, since each message carries both data and a destination address, and it is easy to supplement the destination address with the identity of the internal extension line, if necessary putting it in the data field if the public message-switching format does not allow it in the address field.

5.2.1 Access to a Network from a LAN

Figure 5.4 illustrates the general form of the interconnection of a LAN to an external network, such as a public data network.

If SAF-switching is used within the LAN we may assume that any block of data (message or packet), travelling to or from the external network, may be safely transferred across the LAN itself between the gateway and another device, encapsulated in a suitable 'LAN-packet'. This LAN-packet will carry a pair of addresses: the LAN-source and the LAN-destination. If the block is heading for the external network the LAN-destination address will be that of the gateway; if it is an incoming block the LAN-source will be the gateway.

When the external network uses message-switching, outgoing blocks can be put directly in the necessary format (including the destination address on the external network) by the LAN-source. More probably the basic information necessary for this can be placed in the block by the LAN-source, leaving the gateway the task of actual conversion to the external format. Incoming messages from the external network will probably only carry the address of the gateway as a destination address. The encapsulation for forwarding on the LAN requires identification of a LAN-destination, usually from within the text of the message using such conventions as 'for the attention of . . .'.

If the external network uses call-switching the situation is more complex. Supposing simultaneous external calls are possible, the problem is to identify one particular call (which might be one VC on a multiplexing X.25 interface, or one single physical circuit) with one device across the LAN. In the general case there could be a 'port' or sub-address *within* that device, associated with the call. This mapping between external call and internal device-port naturally takes place in the gateway. How is it first established? One method is as follows

(1) Outgoing calls
(i) The LAN-source sends some sort of call-request command to the gateway. The command carries the required external destination address and the LAN-source's internal port number.
(ii) The gateway picks a free channel to the external network and establishes the call. It may now make an entry in a mapping table: (LAN-source+port) = (Gateway+External channel).
(iii) The gateway can then send some sort of call-connected reply to the LAN-source. This reply must carry the identity of the LAN-source's port. The reply could also convey the external channel identifier, to be used by the LAN-source for all future data transfers to/from that port while the call lasts (Fig. 5.5a) or the channel identifier could be concealed from the LAN-source, and only the LAN-source's port used as the identifier of the call within the LAN (Fig. 5.5b).
(iv) Depending on which of the options in (iii) was used, all further traffic on the LAN associated with the call is identified by the LAN-source and the gateway addresses; and the external channel number, or the LAN-source's port number.

(2) Incoming calls
(i) An external call comes in on some channel. We suppose the LAN-destination is identifiable, as discussed previously. Then the gateway sends some sort of call-indication command to the LAN-destination bearing the channel number.
(ii) The LAN-destination picks a free port (or one indicated by supplementary information in the call-indication).
(iii) The LAN-destination returns some sort of call accepted command to the gateway, carrying both the external channel number and the LAN-destination's port number.
(iv) The gateway can now establish the mapping table (Gateway+External channel) = (LAN-destination+port); and future LAN traffic can be identified either by the channel or by the port number, as discussed previously.

The LAN-device can access the gateway and the external network using 'remote subroutine' calls, such as establish-a-call or await-an-incoming-call, across the LAN. In this case the natural method of

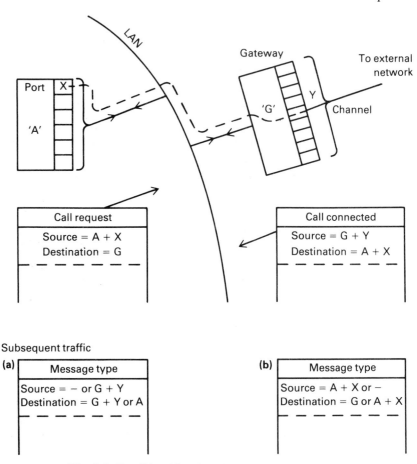

Fig. 5.5 Possible addressing when using a LAN gateway.

identifying the call across the LAN is using the external channel number, and since this is of course used on the interface to the external network, the mapping table in the gateway is really unnecessary. Alternatively, the gateway software can be an independent process, rather than a set of subroutines, to the corresponding process in the LAN-device; and the call-identifier within the LAN could be external channel number or LAN port number.

Such a system of addressing is unsymmetrical, since the identifier belonging to one end of the call across the LAN is used to identify the call right across the LAN. If calls can be made between two LAN devices, or if there is more than one gateway on the LAN and calls can be made between gateways, there is no clear reason for deciding *which* end will supply the call identifier. Policies such as choosing for call identifier the local port (or channel) of the call originator, or of the sender of each individual block across the LAN, can be made to work, but are messy.

The essence of this sort of addressing problem, which frequently occurs in networks, is that, in International Standards Organization (ISO) jargon, a 'connection-oriented' service (i.e. call-switching), is being built on top of a 'connectionless' (i.e. message-switching) infrastructure, in which there is no transnetwork channel which may serve to identify the calls. If the LAN is connection-oriented, as are some based on the frequency division multiplexing of channels on a common CATV cable, the ports or channels in the devices at each side of the LAN can effectively be plugged into the transnetwork channel for the duration of the call—and the problem of call identification disappears. We can simulate this on a connectionless infrastructure by inventing a trans-LAN channel number for each call, but it is difficult to ensure the necessary uniqueness of this number.

The standard solution to identifying a call or 'connection' across a connectionless infrastructure is to use the *two* pairs
(1) Source device address+port or channel within the source
(2) Destination device address+port or channel within the destination.

These are exchanged on call establishment, the originator sending (1) and receiving (1) and (2) in the reply. Thereafter every message transferred incorporates (1) and (2) in its header. For example, the ISO DP8473 [5] for a connectionless protocol specifies that the International Protocol Data Unit (IPDU) carries both source and destination addresses, and a large amount of other information, in its header (see Fig. 5.6). These addresses are not of fixed length; instead, the header also carries length indicators for them. In a particular application the convention could be that the first so many digits of these addresses were the device addresses, used for routing in the network, and the trailing digits were the port or channel numbers within the device. (A glance at Fig. 5.6 will show that message headers are not exactly small, and that the efficiency of procedures based on such protocols is bound to be low.)

Finally, it should be noted that these addressing problems concern the implementor rather than the user. Most LANs (and indeed many value-added services on larger networks) provide a name-server, which

Octet

Network layer protocol identifier				1
Length indicator				2
Version/protocol ID Ext.				3
Lifetime				4
SP	MS	E/R	Type	5
Segment length				6,7
Checksum				8,9
Destination address length indicator				10
Destination address				11 to $m-1$
Source address length indicator				m
Source address				$m+1$ to $n-1$
Data unit identifier				$n, n+1$
Segment offset				$n+2, n+3$
Total length				$n+4, n+5$
Options				$n+6$ to $p-1$
Data				p to z

Fig. 5.6   Format of Internet protocol (ISO 8473) packet.

is a look-up table mapping users' or services' names into network addresses (see Fig. 5.7). The user, or application programmer, uses a name or names for the destination of his call or message. The system software looks up the associated address(es) in the name-server, and inserts them into the required field, replacing the name. The name-server may be centralized, requiring the use of the LAN to access it, or it may be distributed over each node, or a mixture of centralized and distributed name-servers may be used—and commonly is used.

Name	Network address
L. O'BRIEN	332131500004
EUROKOM	272431540003
	27243159000630
DIANEE	270448112
|	|
|	|

Fig. 5.7   Example of a simple name-server.

5.2.2 Data Access to a Network from a PBX

A PBX switches voice traffic, so it is clear that if data are carried in the bandwidth and on the same channels as those by voice, as is the case when modems are used, then the PBX can switch such data traffic. Selection of the destination of a call can be made manually using a telephone before switching over to the modem. Alternatively the DTE could have an automatic dialling unit, generating the necessary selection signals without manual intervention. For internal calls the modems could be limited-distance modems, or simply digital signal boosters on the telephone pair. It is also possible to support simultaneous voice and data (sometimes referred to as 'voice-over-data'), for example using the method described in Section 5.2.2.1.

If the PBX switches voice traffic in analogue form this is indeed the way in which data traffic is normally supported. If, however, the PBX switches voice in digital form, and can support digital extensions and exchange lines, other possibilities arise for handling data. Data will be carried in digital form directly between DTEs, without the need for digital to analogue conversion, and selection can also be performed digitally with, for example, the required destination address being generated from the keyboard of a DTE. This digital information will of course not have the same structure or bit rate as the digital channels used to carry it (64 Kbps is normally needed for voice) but it can easily be embedded in such channels using appropriate framing.

If the exchange lines are also digital this method of handling data traffic can in principle be extended to the public network. However, until ISDNs become available (see Section 5.4) the public telephone network only uses digital transmission and switching as and where it may be convenient and economic. There is no guarantee of a caller obtaining an all-digital path to his remote destination. Even if such an all-digital path can be found, and the PBX can extract from the user's data stream the necessary selection and other signals with which to communicate with the public network, there still exists the likelihood that the data format of the sender's PBX (i.e. the method of embedding data in the 64 Kbps channel) is incompatible with that at the receiving PBX or DTE. In short, until the advent of ISDNs, data transmission in *digital* form over the telephone network is not practicable.

The conclusion is that a digital PBX should provide appropriate interfaces to external networks, for incoming and outgoing data calls.

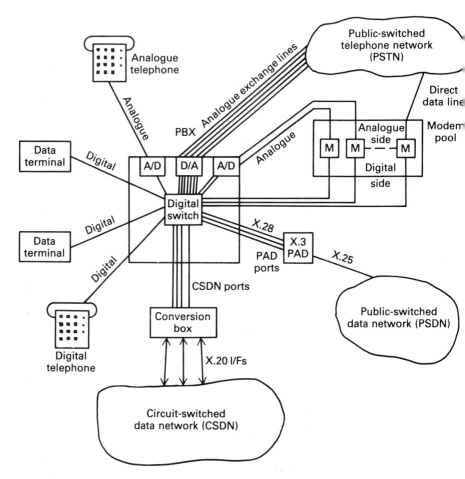

Fig. 5.8 Interfaces of networks from a PBX.

These interfaces will have a certain number of 'ports' giving access to the data channels on the external network and the PBX provides access to these ports which are in effect simply extension numbers. Examples of such interfaces (see Fig. 5.8) could be

(i) An X.3 PAD for access to an X.25 PSDN.

(ii) A box providing various X.20 or X.21 interfaces to a CSDN.

(iii) A pool of modems for use with the PSTN. In this case a modem's analogue interface will not, in general, be connected directly to the PSTN, unless this exchange line is exclusively used for data. Instead, the analogue interface will be connected back into the PBX where it may be switched to any suitable exchange line, on demand.

However, one currently available form of external digital data interface for a PBX is when the external link is directly to another PBX from the same manufacturer—a 'tie line' between PBXs. In this case, formatting of data and signalling will be compatible, and, for example, a G.732 2 Mbps link carrying thirty 64 Kbps channels, could be interfaced to both PBXs. These inter-PBX channels could be used as special external lines, chosen by the originating PBX (instead of the public network) when numbers associated with the destination PBX are selected. This implies that the DID facility is available on both PBXs to allow the appending of extra digits to the numbers in order to identify the destination extensions. Alternatively, a unified numbering plan for extensions over both PBXs can be developed, with the inter-PBX channels being competed for (hunting) when the destination extension is found not to be local. Such schemes can be extended to a network of PBXs, see Fig. 5.9.

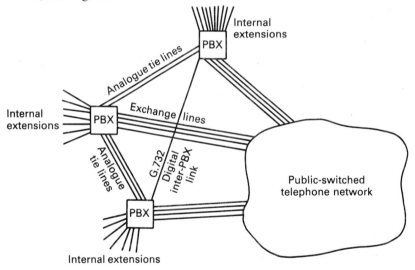

Fig. 5.9   A network of PBXs.

5.2.2.1 Handling of Data by the PBX

The handling of data by the PBX has been mentioned briefly already. In general, extra equipment is required at each end of the extension line to which a DTE is attached. We call this equipment a Data Interface

Module (DIM), which attaches to the DTE, and a Data Line Control
Unit (DLCU) which plugs into the PBX. The DIM may be considered
to be a special DCE, providing a conventional V.24, or possibly V.36
interface (see Fig. 5.10).

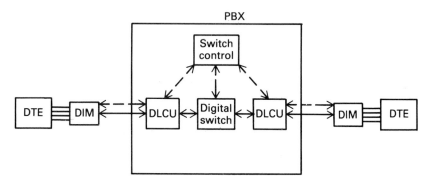

Fig. 5.10   PBX support of data traffic.
← – → = signalling and control; ⟷ = data.

This additional equipment serves four purposes
(1) The embedding of the user data stream (asynchronous or synchronous) in the 64 Kbps digital channel before entry to the switch, and its
extraction from that channel after leaving the switch.
(2) The support of the necessary signalling, when making and when
answering a call.
(3) The boosting of the digital signals to/from the DTE for carrying on
what may be relatively long extension lines.
(4) The handling of bit-rate and clocking problems, to ensure that the
connected DTEs both operate at the same speed, and in synchronism
when synchronous transmission is used.

The nature of the DIM and DLCU depends, among other things,
on the number of 'extension pairs' used, and whether or not the DTE
and DIM have an associated telephone. In one well-known PBX [6], in
which extension lines consist of two pairs of wires there are essentially
two options
(1) Use one of the two pairs as a balanced 'send' circuit, the other as a
balanced 'receive' circuit in conformance with the CCITT V.11 interface.
No additional analogue telephone is involved. This may be called 'stand-
alone' mode.

(2) Use one of the two pairs as a normal analogue circuit for a telephone, and the other as two independent send and receive (unbalanced) circuits, running at 64 Kbps.

In stand-alone mode, when data traffic is asynchronous, call set-up is usually directly from the keyboard of a terminal, so the source DLCU will need to perform automatic speed detection to be able to recognize the selection digits. These digits it will pass to the switch control to operate the switch. The destination DLCU will respond to the connection by sending out some signal on the destination extension line to test for the availability of the destination DTE. At the other ends of the extension lines will be another DIM. The destination DIM will respond suitably to the destination DLCU, probably displaying some 'incoming call' message at the terminal at the same time. The source DLCU will report success back to the source DIM, which will also probably display a message to the user. In short, the DLCUs with the DIMs perform a variant of the usual call set-up procedures common to nearly all networks.

In the data transfer phase, the embedding of the data in the 64 Kbps channel and its later extraction will be done by the DIMs. Usually the data will not require the full 64 Kbps, and spare capacity can be allocated to the signalling procedures for call set-up and clearing. Without this spare capacity, signalling on the DIM-DLCU link is in-band, giving rise to transparency and allied problems.

Seen from the DTEs, the DIMs appear to be modems (DCEs) so that the normal procedures (such as auto-answering) can be used without modification if DTE is a computer. A computer as DTE might also incorporate automatic speed detection, enabling it to adjust to the speed of the calling DTE—otherwise speeds must be prearranged to be compatible.

Figure 5.11 illustrates asynchronous access to the public telephone network via a modem pool. The modems of the pool are connected on the digital side to the switch via a combined DLCU-DIM, with the DIM in this case acting as a DTE (not a DCE, as before), and on the analogue side via an ordinary telephone line unit (LU).

Outgoing calls from an internal DTE hunt to find a free modem and its associated DLCU and LU. The source DLCU can inform the destination DLCU what modem speed is required. The destination DLCU in turn informs the LU at the modem's analogue interface what external number is required, on the basis of information received from the source DLCU via the switch control. The LU makes a 'telephone' call to the

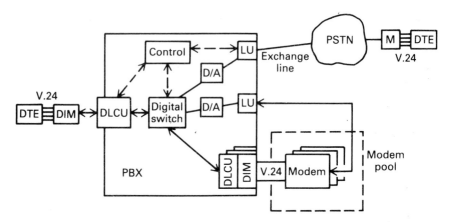

Fig. 5.11   Handling of external calls by a PBX.

external line via the switch in the normal manner. When the call is established the LU must signal that this has occurred back through the DLCUs to the calling DTE, and then send all (data) traffic via the modem. Ideally, the calling DTE sees its DIM as the remote modem, with all the appropriate signals present on the V.24 interface. These signals must be carried to and from the real modem via the switch.

Incoming calls (on specified exchange data lines) are routed to a free modem in the pool. In the absence of DID the call is first established between the external DTE and the modem's DLCU, which will then await a string of digits from that DTE to select the internal destination DTE via the switch—the process of call set-up is in two stages. If DID is available, then the switch control must recognize the received destination number as a data number, pick a modem and establish that part of the connection, and then extend the connection onwards through the switch to the required internal DTE.

If synchronous data flows are to be supported by the PBX the question immediately arises: What synchronous line procedures are to be used, or does the PBX handle the synchronous data transparently?

Although some PBXs do have available optional devices for emulating specific equipment and obeying the associated protocols (such as IBM 3270 terminals and SNA), the normal approach to support of synchronous traffic is to handle it transparently. This means that signalling (e.g. digits for the selection of the destination, etc.) should be out-of-band, because the switch does not and cannot recognize the meaning of in-band traffic.

When the call is established the isochronous clocking necessary for synchronous transmission must be transmitted through the extension line(s), implying special methods for encoding or framing the data, so that the clock can be extracted at the remote end. The source of clocking will normally be the digital switch, which is an isochronous device itself; so that the clock must be delivered to the DIMs for delivery to the DTEs on the V.24 interface, for both received and transmitted data. However, if modems in the pool are used the source of timing signals for incoming data is the modem, and this clocking has to be carried across the switch to the receiving extension. Unless the synchronous data rate is considerably slower than the 64 Kbps rate of the switch there are going to be problems. At slow bit rates the data traffic can simply be sampled 64 000 times per second and the resulting distortion will not be significant. But at higher bit rates (e.g. 48 Kbps) it is hardly possible to fit the data stream into the switch's time frames, if both are driven by different unsynchronized clocks, unless some more elaborate technique such as that discussed in Section 5.2.2.3 is used.

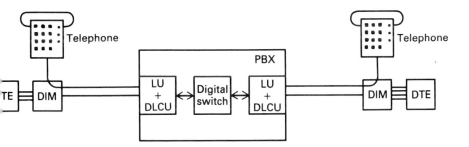

Fig. 5.12 Use of associated telephone for data connections.

Figure 5.12 shows the situation where the DIM has an associated analogue telephone. This can be used for call set-up of the data connection, as well as for voice traffic. The advantage of this approach is that, if synchronous data traffic is to be switched, there is no need for the DLCU to be made compatible with the formats of the particular line procedures used by the DTE, since the selection and call progress information will be from and to the telephone rather than the DTE. Several manufacturers of PBXs can supply an integrated 'Work Station' corresponding to the three pieces of equipment—terminal, DIM and telephone.

5.2.2.2 Use of Digital Telephones

The arrangement of Fig. 5.12 supposed that the telephone was analogue (e.g. push-button), so that one extension line pair carries analogue voice traffic and the other relatively low speed full-duplex digital traffic. If a digital telephone is used, which supports digital 64 Kbps flows plus additional signalling directly, then the extension line can be regarded as purely digital. Such extension lines can be designed to support *simultaneous* use of the line by voice and data traffic on a single pair.

An example of such a digital telephone with data facilities may be taken from another well-known manufacturer of PBXs [7]. Figure 5.13 illustrates the configuration and Fig. 5.14 the message formats. The single pair is used in half-duplex fashion. Every 125 μs (8000 times per second) a 12-bit burst is sent to the digital telephone and a 12-bit burst sent back in reply. The bit rate within the bursts is 256 Kbps, so each bit is slightly less than 4 μs in length, and two-phase shifted encoding is used on the line. Synchronism is controlled by the PBX.

Each burst carries a synchronizing flag, 8 bits for the voice channel, 1 bit for signalling and 2 bits for the simultaneous data channel. The data channel thus has a raw bit rate of $2 \times 8000 = 16000$ bps. Within the data channel the data are framed as illustrated in Fig. 5.15. A 4-bit flag is followed by an 8-bit length indicator and then by 9-bit blocks of

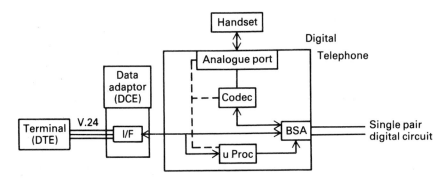

Fig. 5.13 A digital telephone with data adaptor.
BSA = burst signalling acceptor; Codec = coder/decoder for A/D voice.

data (8 data bits and 1 modifier bit). The modifier bit is used to carry, for example, V.24 interface signals to/from the DTE, from/to a modem in the modem pool.

The length indicator can be used to send different amounts of data in each burst. Consider a synchronous data stream of, say, 9600 bps carried over such a channel with clocking from the source DTE. Bits can be buffered in the DIM and placed in the data channel when multiples of 8 have been accumulated. Since the channel rate is just below 16 Kbps (allowing for the non-data bits in Fig. 5.15 and the source rate is 9600 bps there is no problem. The data channel established across the PBX to the destination DTE will only require two of the 8 bits available every 125 μs in the switch. At the destination the data bits can be extracted from the data channel by the DIM and buffered for delivery to the DTE. The receiver signal element timing circuit on the DTE interface will be driven by the destination DIM. It will have nominally the same bit rate as the remote DTE's transmitting clock, and can adjust itself to be precisely the same by observing the long-term state of the DIM's output buffer. If the transmitting DTE's bit rate is slightly faster than the receiving DIM's, the output buffer will tend to fill, so the receiving DIM will increase its bit rate; and vice versa.

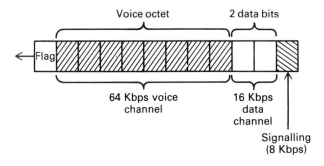

Fig. 5.14 Format of a 12-bit burst on a digital telephone I/F.

In this system, which would normally carry simultaneous voice (64 Kbps) and data (16 Kbps), it is possible to dispense with the voice channel and use the combined 80 Kbps for data. Owing to framing and timing requirements, as discussed above, the actual maximum sychronous data rate supported is 48 Kbps.

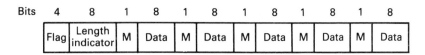

Fig. 5.15   Format of data on a data channel.
M = modifier bit.

5.2.3 LANs versus PBXs

The question naturally arises whether a LAN or a PBX is the best solution to interfacing a large number of devices on a site to an external network, while at the same time providing switching between them locally.

As discussed previously, (see Section 5.2) LANs generally use SAF techniques. A typical LAN, operating at 10 Mbps, offers most of that bandwidth to a requesting device—although the device may have to tolerate a significant and variable delay between making the request and receiving the service. The LAN is ideal for bursty traffic, e.g. from interactive terminals. A PBX, on the other hand will, typically, only offer a voice channel (e.g. 64 Kbps) to a device requesting service. However, since the PBX is circuit-switched, the 64 Kbps remains exclusively available to the device for as long as it maintains the call. A PBX capable of supporting 1200 switched through calls will have a total bandwidth of $2 \times 64 \times 1200$ Kbps $= 153.6$ Mbps, compared with the LAN's 10 Mbps. Additionally the circuit-switched technique ensures maintenance of a steady data rate, ideal for digitized voice, synchronous data in large blocks and bulk data in general, such as that generated by facsimile machines or file transfer applications. Thus the LAN and the PBX serve different traffic types.

However, a single terminal could generate *both* traffic types, alternately or simultaneously. For example the digital telephone-plus-terminal of Section 5.2.2.3 could be supporting simultaneously a voice conversation (ideally circuit-switched) and an interactive dialogue with a computer (ideally SAF-switched). But if the terminal multiplexes these two types of traffic on a single circuit, how are they to be separated for switching?

One ingenious solution to this problem is provided by more recent PBXs which support SAF-switching and circuit-switching [8]. The terminal can then use the bandwidth available to it in the way it wants, dynamically. The scheme is based on a high speed time-division-multiplexed (TDM) bus, carrying (for example) 640 slots per frame, 8000 frames per second. Circuit-switched traffic is allocated the same slot(s) in each frame, providing 64 Kbps channels—or multiples thereof. SAF traffic is allocated, on demand, bursts of adjacent slots. For example, one could reserve slots 1 to 240 in each frame exclusively to SAF traffic giving a minimum bandwidth of $240 \times 8000 \times 8 = 15.36$ Mbps. The remaining slots allow up to 400 simultaneous 64 Kbps channels, for circuit-switched traffic. If these 400 channels are not all taken up at any given moment, the unused slots can be allocated in principle to increase the SAF bandwidth.

The general scheme is illustrated in Fig. 5.16. Data, voice, combined voice and data terminals access the TDM-bus via star connections to controllers attached to the TDM bus. These extension lines operate at 1.5 Mbps on two telephone pairs. The controllers can act as concentrators for circuit-switched traffic. They provide buffering for SAF traffic. The TDM-bus provides a PCM-link for circuit-switched traffic to a conventional digital PBX, which may be located some distance away. The TDM-bus also provides access to a public X.25 network for SAF traffic via an appropriate gateway.

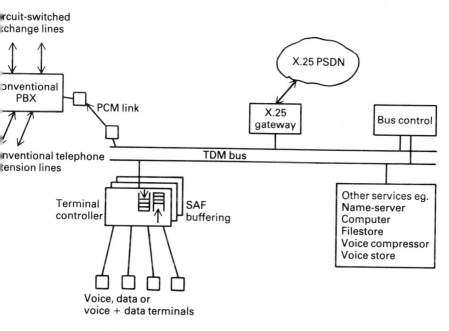

Fig. 5.16 PBX support of SAF and circuit-switching.

Further services may be available on the TDM-bus, such as an applications computer, a name-server, or a file store, to be accessed by interactive terminals using SAF techniques.

One special service could be voice-messaging, in which digitized voice messages are stored for later playback or distribution to other destinations. This voice-messaging service consists of two components (1) A voice compressor/decompressor, to which circuit-switched 64 Kbps channels are connected. The compression function is to receive digitized voice messages, compress them (eliminating silences, etc.) and then transfer them (using SAF-switching) to the voice store. The decompression function is the reverse procedure.

(2) A voice store, accessed via SAF-switching on the TDM-bus, which holds the compressed messages and also provides the search, retrieval and similar functions. Digitized voice messages, even after compression by a factor of 10 to 1, are obviously large, since 1 minute of voice = $8000 \times 60/10 = 48$ Kilo-octets.

To understand further the operation of the TDM-bus it is necessary to discuss time-division switching, mentioned in Chapter 2, in a little more detail, considering only circuit-switching first.

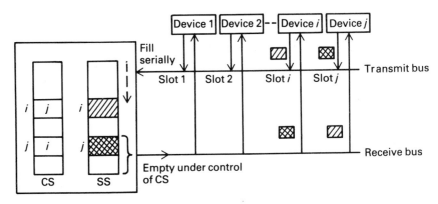

Fig. 5.17 Time-division switching with dedicated slot allocations.

Two approaches are possible. The first is illustrated in Fig. 5.17. Each device is allocated a fixed slot (or group of slots) in the frame in which it transmits or receives information. This means that, to communicate with another device, the information must be transferred to another slot. This could be done by a time-switch, which buffers each slot from a 'transmit-frame' on one 'transmit-bus', and re-outputs them (in a new order depending on the connections) in a 'receive-frame' on another 'receive-bus', less than one frame interval later. For example, at slot time i, information is read into Speech Store (SS) position i of the time-switch. Under control of the Control Store (CS), when slot time j arrives, that information is output to the receive-bus. Since each circuit-switched connection will be full-duplex, a similar arrangement applies for traffic from device j to device i, and each connection will use two time-slots on the transmit-bus, two on the receiver-bus, or four slots in all.

The connection could be set up by in-band signalling, in which the originator (device i say) puts the requisite call request information in slot i when no call is in progress; and the time-switch analyses the request, checks that device j is free, sets up the CS accordingly, signals device j (in-band), etc.

Alternatively, out-of-band signalling can be used. Typically this would be done by reserving one or more time slots for control purposes and using them for polling by the time-switch. The polling consists of cyclicly enquiring of each device if it wants to do something, such as set up or clear a call, and receiving the reply in another control slot. In this case, each device would have access to these control slots as well as to its own time-slots.

The second approach is illustrated in Fig. 5.18. Here transmission is directly between the two devices with no buffering in the controlling time-switch. Indeed, all the time-switch does is allocate a common slot (x, say) to the direction i to j, and another slot (y, say) to the direction j to i. Only two slots are used on a single bus. Call set-up and clearing will be by out-of-band signalling in control slots, using polling by the controlling time-switch.

This second approach is the one normally used for a TDM-bus supporting circuit- and SAF-switching, as it allows the allocation of continuous slots (accessible by any device) to be given to SAF traffic. For example if there are 640 slots we could allocate them as follows

Slot 1	Control (polling)
Slots 2 to 156	Exclusively SAF, giving a minimum bandwidth of $157 \times 64\,000 = 10$ Mbps
Slots 157 to 640	Circuit-switching, giving up to 242 full-duplex 64 Kbps connections.

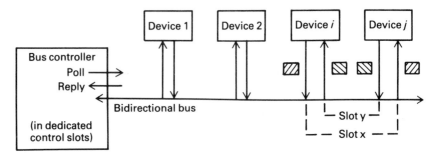

Fig. 5.18 Time-division switching with slot allocations made dynamically.

Call set-up could take six frame-times (poll the call originator, get reply, poll destination, get reply, advise originator, get confirmation) or $6 \times 125 = 750$ μs. In this call set-up process we could either establish a circuit-switched connection; or authorize the would-be originator to send an SAF burst in slots 2 to 400 of the frame following this confirmation, assuming no more than 120 full-duplex circuit-switched connections exist at that time.

In practice, an SAF transfer may be prolonged over several frames, using a series of bursts in the allocated slots. Also, more than one slot will usually be required for polling and control, since a significant amount of information needs to be exchanged between the devices and the controlling time-switch.

A point to note is that the control can be anticipatory. A new SAF transfer can be planned while an existing one is in progress. Nor is there any contention for the bus as exists, for example, in CSMA-CD schemes such as Ethernet, in which devices seize the bus when it is apparently free and then check (Collision-Detection) whether it has been seized by another device. The result is that, under load, the bus is used very efficiently.

It would be foolish to suppose that the definitive solution to the handling of circuit-switched and SAF traffic on the interface to long-haul networks will be provided by the approach, however ingenious, discussed above. In particular, the approach only really integrates the two techniques informally on the user's site. Distinct long-haul networks, with distinct interfaces, are assumed to exist for each type of traffic. The users' real requirement—to be able to divide up the bandwidth available to him, dynamically and optimally, on both local and long-haul connections—will only be met when full ISDN services (see Section 5.4) become available.

5.3 SERVICES AND FACILITIES IN DATA NETWORKS

A network offers services to its users. For example, in the previous section we discussed how a local CSP, in the form of a PBX with a LAN-like TDM-bus, might offer circuit-switching and SAF-switching to the user. More precisely, looking at Fig. 5.16, a circuit-switched service based on 64 Kbps channels and a packet-switched service based on X.25 were offered for long-haul communications; while for local communications the same circuit-switching service was offered, and SAF-switching in bursts up to 10 Mbps (centrally controlled) was possible using a procedure whose details we did not define.

The above services are examples of 'bearer' services, which provide certain types of connections between users, which operate at certain speeds, and which, ideally, comply with some minimal quality of Grade of Service.

A wider view of services may be taken. For example, one might try to clarify 'teleservices', i.e. telecommunication services, according to their characteristics as far as user applications are concerned; rather than limiting oneself to considering only the nature of the bearer services. From this viewpoint telephony is a teleservice. Other teleservices are telex, videotex, message-switching, etc. Some such teleservices are directly provided by public authorities on top of the basic bearer service. Other teleservices may be supplied by users themselves and the only public service such users need is a suitable bearer service. In general, each teleservice will require one or more suitable bearer services to support it; although some teleservices (e.g. teletex) supposedly run on top of nearly all 'official' bearer services.

A service may be considered as a self-contained and complete concept. A 'facility', on the other hand, is a part of a service—and usually an optional or non-essential part. For example, reverse-charging is an optional user facility available with many services. A more serious 'facility' is the X.3 PAD facility for allowing start-stop DTEs to use an X.25 PSDN.

The CCITT has attempted to bring order to the concept of services (essentially transmission and switching services) for data networks in Recommendation X.1, and that of facilities in Recommendation X.2

[9]. In the ISDN Recommendations (Series 1.200) [10] these attempts are extended further to include teleservices as well as bearer services. The need for order is clear. If a service or a facility is to be available internationally, then each country must support it in a manner compatible with every other country.

Nevertheless, the least one can say is that services are not universally available. For example the teletex service, which transfers formatted printed pages (in electronic form) between two teletex-compatible terminals, is only available in a few countries (notably Germany), and may never become available in many others. A similar observation applies to circuit-switched data networks. More seriously, minor incompatibilities exist between *existing* public packet-switched data networks, even within Western Europe; while at the bearer level complete incompatibility exists between the CCITT G.732 PCM multiplex and the T-1 technique used in the USA.

As for facilities within or additional to the basic services, the incompleteness of coverage and the incompatibilities between implementations are too numerous to catalogue. For example, a simple facility such as reverse charging does not always operate internationally; while the important X.3 PAD facility only handles national subscribers. (By this is meant that a subscriber to, say, the Irish PSDN, Eirpac, can use an X.3 PAD in Ireland to access an X.25 host in Ireland or England; but cannot use an X.3 PAD in England to do the same thing, without becoming an explicit subscriber to the UK PSS. In short, when travelling abroad one cannot use a PSDN, as one can use the telephone.)

In the following sections we review briefly some classes of services and facilities, which if not always available and mutually compatible, are at any rate deemed to be desirable by CCITT and others.

5.3.1 Data Services

Here we shall only consider the data services officially recognized by CCITT. In Section 5.4 ISDN services will be considered, and in Chapters 6 and 7 we consider a whole range of 'services' within the framework of the OSI Reference Model, including Application and the so-called Telematic Services.

Recommendation X.1 recognizes the following classes of data service
(i) Start-stop asynchronous circuit-switched or leased circuit data transmission, using the X.20 or X.20 bis interface. 300 bps and an 11-unit

code (IA5 alphabet plus one start, two stop bits) is one official speed and format. Administrations may also support speeds in the range 50 to 200 bps, with other codes.

(ii) Synchronous circuit-switched or leased circuit data transmission, using the X.21 or X.21 bis interface. IA5 is used for signalling and selection, and permissible speeds are 600, 2400, 4800, 9600 and 48000 bps.

(iii) Packet-switched data transmission using the X.25 interface. Approved speeds are 2400, 4800, 9600 and 48000 bps. Recently 1200 bps has also been approved for 'dial-up X.25' over telephone circuits.

(iv) Start-stop use of packet-switched networks using X.28. Three classes of service are defined: 50 to 300 bps using ten or eleven units per character; 75/1200 bps with ten units and 1200 bps with ten units. The first class is based on the V.21 modem; the second on the V.23 modem with 75 bps from the DTE and 1200 bps from the DCE (a typical Videotex use); and the third class is based on the V.22 modem.

(v) Finally a 64 Kbps data transmission service, on an ISDN, is recommended. This service will support circuit and packet-switching.

It will be appreciated that the circuit-switches form a range of independent services, apparently running on separate 'subnetworks' of the circuit-switched data networks, since interworking between different speeds is not possible. The packet-switched services on the other hand can all interwork, one speed with another, including asynchronous X.28 with synchronous X.25.

The above data transmission and switching services use bearer services such as G.732 digital links or analogue voice channels with appropriate modems. However the data services may themselves be regarded as bearers or carriers of higher level services.

This concept of layering of services, in which each layer provides enhancements to a lower layer service so that it may offer a more comprehensive service to a higher layer user (itself usually a further service provider), will be explored more fully in Chapter 6.

5.3.2 Facilities in Data Networks

The number and scope of facilities available in networks are very large. If we consider as an example the telephone network, and in particular a PBX, a range of facilities, most of which could usefully be applied to data networks, also immediately springs to mind. Some such facilities are

Hunting. An incoming call picks a free exchange line (not necessarily with the same number as the number selected) out of a group of such lines all leading to the same user (e.g. his PBX).

Call forwarding. Traffic to a given destination is rerouted to another, perhaps when the destination is busy or otherwise unavailable, perhaps because the user has moved to a new location.

Waiting or 'camp-on'. Incoming traffic to a busy destination is held until the destination is free.

Abbreviated selection. Callers can designate and use abbreviated numbers for frequently called destinations.

Automatic redialling. A call to a busy destination can be made to repeat at regular intervals (without user intervention) until communications are established.

Pick-up. This is similar to forwarding, but instead of a user redirecting his own calls elsewhere, 'pick-up' means that another user can decide to take the first user's incoming traffic. (This is useful if the second user sees that the first user's terminal or telephone is unattended and ringing.)

Conferencing. Multi-party conversations may be set-up, e.g. with 5 or 6 participants.

Charge estimation. The cost of a call is calculated at once and is available to the user on request.

This list could be extended almost indefinitely. For example, the facilities available to the attendant switch-operator of a PBX have not been mentioned at all. The point to make is that, given software control of a switch or network, a very wide range of facilities can be made available, covering dialling, routing of incoming calls, monitoring, accounting, etc.

In the case of data networks, facilities may be classified in various ways. We can list them by service class within the two broad classes of circuit-switching and packet-switching provided by public administrations. For example certain facilities, such as extended packet sequence numbering in which the range is 0 to 127 rather than 0 to 7, is only meaningful with X.25 packet-switching.

Facilities can also be grouped according to whether they are available on demand (e.g. per call) or only on a contractual basis when one becomes a subscriber. For example one might require charging information to be given about all calls, or one might want it only on demand.

Again, a facility may be 'essential', in that all networks are supposed to support it, so that it may be considered to be available internationally.

This does not mean that all (or any) calls use it; it is a so-called 'mandatory option'! Other facilities may be classified as 'additional', which means that they may or may not be provided.

In Recommendation X.2, the CCITT tabulates long lists of facilities for data networks using the above categories. Some of the more important ones are mentioned below

Direct call. This is the equivalent of a leased line; no selection of the destination is necessary. In X.25 Packet-Switched Data Networks (PSDN) it is provided by a Permanent Visual Circuit. Since many facilities are negotiated at call set-up time, and a direct call has no set-up, use of the direct call facility excludes use of many others.

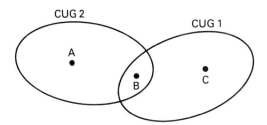

Fig. 5.19 A user (B) as member of two closed groups.
B can send to/receive from A and C; A and C cannot send to/receive from C or A.

Closed user groups. Users may come together in Closed User Groups (CUGs) known to the network. A CUG may be completely exclusive— members may only send traffic to and receive traffic from each other. However a user could belong to more than one CUG, see Fig. 5.19. More usually a CUG will also have outgoing access, allowing members to call the outside world, but not to be called from it. Alternatively a CUG may only have incoming access, so that, for example, employees of a company (the CUG) can only call each other, or receive incoming calls—thus keeping costs down. In PSDNs a member of more than one CUG may specify to which CUG he is to be regarded as belonging, when he makes a call.

Reverse charging. This facility may be requested by a caller when he makes a call; in which case the request must be acceptable to both the network and the called destination, to be granted. DTEs can also declare themselves prepared to accept reverse charge calls (like toll-free telephone numbers) at subscription time. An important aspect of reverse charging is that it provides one method of handling unidentifiable DTEs.

For example, a packet-mode DTE using 'dial-up X.25' over the telephone network to access a PSDN (according to the X.32 Recommendation), should in principle identify itself to the PSDN for charging purposes. This implies (i) that the DTE is a subscriber to the PSDN already and (ii) that the technical problems involved in securely identifying the DTE to the PSDN have been overcome. However, if the called number accepts reverse charging, there is no reason why the network (whatever about the called destination) should need to identify the caller.

Routing control. By 'routing control' we mean those facilities such as hunting, call forwarding ('redirection'), etc. which have already been discussed in connection with PBXs.

Modification of parameters. Various facilities are available, particularly in PSDNs, to modify network parameters either at subscription time, or per call. Examples of parameters susceptible to modification are the window size, the maximum packet size, the 'D-bit', etc.

Reservation of channels. Channels can be reserved for outgoing or incoming access only. This applies both to X.25 VCs or to circuit-switched calls.

On-line information. Users of a network often require additional information to be supplied on-line, such as the cost of the call, explicit identification of the calling or called DTE by the network, or the current state of certain network parameters (e.g. PAD parameters). Facilities exist to permit this sort of information to be requested and provided.

Multipoint working. The only multipoint communication facilities recognized by CCITT are those for leased data circuits—the familiar multidrop line. Since these multipoint systems are operated by the user (with polling or similar software), and the network only provides the physical connections, it may fairly be stated that CCITT does not support multipoint communications—whether under centralized selective control, decentralized control, or in the form of unrestricted broadcasting. It would appear that facilities, similar to those provided by leased circuits, could easily be provided by PVCs on PSDNs. More generally, multipoint addressing is an obviously desirable feature for electronic mail. It may be argued that most E-mail services do provide multipoint addressing facilities. This is so, but they do it at the cost of setting up many parallel calls (or equivalent). It would appear to be more sensible to provide a network facility for setting up *one* call with many destinations. This topic is discussed further in Chapter 7.

There are other types of 'essential' or 'additional' facilities available on data networks, and it is hoped that the above list at least serves to give an idea of the scope of the subject. The reader is referred to Recommendation X.2 for fuller details.

Finally, the reader is also referred to the X.10 Recommendation which discusses access to data networks. Data networks can be accessed directly ('direct connection') or by dial-up connections over the public switched telephone network (PSTN). However, many more possibilities are allowed. For example, PSDNS may be accessed via Circuit-Switched Data Networks (CSDNs) or ISDNs, in various ways.

5.4 INTEGRATED SERVICES DIGITAL NETWORKS (ISDNs) AND THEIR INTERFACES

In Section 5.3 services and facilities for data networks were briefly reviewed and the point was made that the term 'service' could be interpreted in a much wider fashion. Not only are circuit-switching and packet-switching (data) services, but telephony can also be called a service, as could telex, or indeed videoconferencing.

In many ways these services are very different from each other, but in some ways they are similar. All the services use an infrastructure, an underlying 'bearer' network, which nowadays is digital; but at a slightly higher level, telephony and, for example, packet-switching are disjoint. Moreover, as discussed in Section 5.2, whatever happens inside an institution's premises with regard to switching and transmission, the interfaces to the external world will be distinct for voice, telex, circuit-switched and packet-switched data, etc. (See Fig. 5.20.) This is plainly unsatisfactory. If a single pair of wires can support an internal user's digital telephone and terminal on a PBX extension, it is hardly sensible or economic to separate all traffic at the interfaces to the public networks.

There are many concepts involved in that of the Integrated Services Digital Network (ISDN), but it may be said that one of the basic ones is to replace Fig. 5.20 by Fig. 5.21, so that the user, as well as the distinct services, may also see and exploit the common bearer network.

An ISDN is 'integrated' because many different services are available through the same infrastructure, and in particular through a single network interface to the user. It is 'digital' because it is based on digital transmission, in fact on the basic concept of the 64 Kbps channel familiar from PCM (e.g. G.732). It is a network because it provides transmission and switching (if required).

In CCITT's own words (Recommendation I.120) 'A key element of service integration for an ISDN is the provision of a range of services using a limited set of connection types and multipurpose user-network interface arrangements'. It is this limited set of connection types and interface arrangements which will be discussed in the remainder of this Chapter. However, higher level aspects of ISDNs will be returned to in Chapter 6. It should also be pointed out that 'an ISDN will contain intelligence for the purpose of providing service features, maintenance and network management functions'; so that the ISDN concept also addresses the topic of Section 5.1.

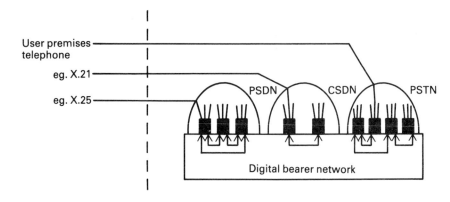

Fig. 5.20   Different interfaces to different networks, using common bearer services.
■= switch on network in question.

Most countries in Western Europe have plans for putting into service an ISDN in the late 1980s or early 1990s. The extent of coverage of the population by the ISDN will gradually increase. It is clearly a formidable undertaking to provide new interfaces to each subscriber's premises, so it may be some years before a particular user is confronted by an ISDN interface. Nevertheless the scope and speed of remote connections will be so greatly changed, in comparison with what is possible to-day, that the future user would do well to prepare himself in advance. In particular, designers and programmers of computer systems might consider how they will handle channels whose speeds range from 64 Kbps upwards into the Mbps range and higher.

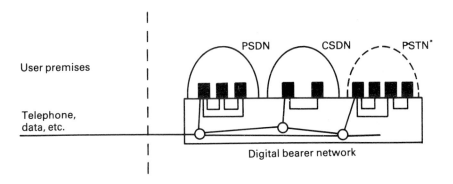

Fig. 5.21 A single interface to different networks, using common bearer services.
○ = ISDN switch; ■ = switch on network in question.
*Eventually the PSTN will be subsumed in ISDN i.e. all switching of telephony will be performed on ISDN switches.

5.4.1 ISDN Interface Structure

In the I-Series Recommendations which cover ISDNs, the 1.400 series is concerned with interfacing to subscribers' terminal equipment (TE). There are many functions required of such interfaces for example
(i) The interface should support a wide range of user equipment from simple terminals, to telephones (possibly with extension lines), to sophisticated PBXs or LANs.
(ii) Multiple simultaneous conversations of different types (e.g. voice and data) should be possible across the interface.
(iii) Through the interface, users should be able to access a variety of network services. In particular access should be possible to other networks, for example a packet-switching network.
(iv) Existing user equipment, with (for example) X.21 or V.24 interfaces, should be able to connect into the ISDN through some sort of Terminal Adaptor (TA) in the interface.
   CCITT Recommendations I.411 and I.412 discuss the general structure of ISDN interfaces, which is illustrated in Fig. 5.22.
   Network Termination 1 (NT1) is the 'end of the line' to the network, providing basic functions such as line monitoring, clocking, power transfer, and low level multiplexing of physical channels at point 'T'.
   Network Termination 2 (NT2) is an intelligent device, such as a PBX, providing concentration of terminal connections, local switching,

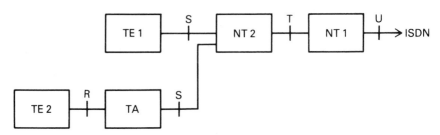

Fig. 5.22 Reference diagram for ISDN interfacing.

higher level multiplexing of conversations on to physical channels, protocol handling and offering interface(s) at point 'S' to Terminal Equipment 1 (TE1) or TAs.

It is possible that NT2 and NT1 functions are amalgamated into a
single piece of equipment, in which case the interface at point T ceases
to exist, and the subscriber only sees interface at point S, Fig. 5.23a. It
is also possible that the NT2 function does not exist, for example if an
'exchange line' is directly connected to subscriber's TE (telephone,
perhaps), possibly with a multidropped extension or two; see Fig. 5.23b.
In this case points S and T are coincident.

Terminal Equipment 2 (TE2) which employs non-ISDN interfaces
such as X.21, can be connected to an ISDN via the TA, to which it
connects at point 'R'.

Many more variants on the basic configuration of Fig. 5.22 are possible, besides the two illustrated in Fig. 5.23.

The interfaces that may exist at points S and T are of course digital,
and they can operate at various speeds, offering various types of channels
to the user. The channel types are

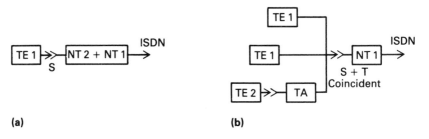

Fig. 5.23 Possible interface configurations for an ISDN.

The B channel. This is a transparent 64 Kbps full-duplex channel which can be used for voice, data or other digital information. It does *not* carry signalling information (which would typically be carried by a D channel). It may be used to gain access to circuit-switching or packet-switching networks. Although the B channel is transparent itself, that does not mean that it automatically provides a transparent end-to-end path between users. That depends on the bearer channels used in the network. For example, a bearer channel might be designed for encoded voice (e.g. according to G.711), and not support unrestricted 64 Kbps data. In establishing a connection using a B channel, the caller can specify the type of through bearer channel he requires. Equipment operating at a rate lower than 64 Kbps can use the B channel by employing rate adaption techniques (I.460). For example, an 8 Kbps user would use bit 1 of each B-channel octet.

The D channel. This operates at 16 or 64 Kbps and is used for signalling. The D channel employs relatively complex protocols for the establishment, support and clearing of connections on other channels, such as B channels. The D channel may also carry data in certain circumstances.

The E channel. This is a 64 Kbps channel used to carry signalling information, like the D channel, except that the protocols (at the lower level) are different from those of the D channel, being those of Signalling System No. 7 (Q.710).

Higher speed channels, or H channels. These channels carry user information, and do *not* carry the associated signalling. The HO channel at 384 Kbps is equivalent to six 64 Kbps channels. The H12 channel at 1920 Kbps is equivalent to the user portion (30 slots) of the European 32-slot PCM frame at 2048 Kbps (G.732). The H11 channel at 1536 Kbps is a complete North American 24-slot PCM frame.

Table 5.1 Channels on ISDN interfaces

	Bit rate of the Network Interface		
	192 Kbps	1544 Kbps	2048 Kbps
Valid Channel Mixes	2B+D(16)	23B+D(64) 23B+E 4HO 3HO+D(64) H11	30B+D(64) 30B+E 5HO+D(64) H12+D(64)

These channels can be used in various combinations on ISDN interfaces, depending on the raw bit rate of that interface. The possibilities envisaged are illustrated in Table 5.1.

The use of the D rather than the E channel is preferred. Provision is also made for the case when NT2 (e.g. a PBX) has multiple physical interfaces to the ISDN, to allow a *single* D (or E) channel to carry the signalling for the channels on more than one physical interface.

5.4.2 Physical Interfaces to ISDNs

From Table 5.1 it will be seen that three types of physical ISDN interfaces are recommended

(1) The 'basic' 192 Kbps interface supporting two B and one 16 Kbps D channels. It is based on balanced (i.e. a pair of) metallic circuits, for each direction of transmission, with multidropping of user terminals (TEs) from the circuit to the NT. The configuration can be used in point-to-point mode with only one TE active at a time; or in point-to-multipoint mode with more than one TE active at a time. It is discussed more fully below.

(2) The 1544 Kbps 'primary rate' interface, of the North American PCM standard. This uses the G.703 electrical interface and G.704 framing. The twenty-four 8-bit slots plus a single framing bit (F) form the frame. Slot 24 is used for the D or E channel, if present.

(3) The 2048 Kbps 'primary rate' interface, of CCITT, discussed in Chapter 2 (G.703 and G.732). Of the 32 slots, time-slot 0 is for framing, as is usual, and time-slot 16 is for the D or E channel.

We do not discuss the 'primary rate' physical interfaces further, but take a closer look at the 'basic' interface, which is described in Recommendation I.430.

Figure 5.24 shows a typical wiring arrangement for the basic interface, with power being delivered from the NT to the TEs. Since the basic rate is 192 Kbps, a bit lasts 5.2 μs. If the attached devices are to work in synchronism so that the NT, for example, does not see a significant phase shift between data arriving from different TEs, there are limitations on the length of the wiring. Specifically two sorts of configuration are envisaged: the short passive bus with an overall length of some 200 m and the TEs distributed arbitrarily along its length; and the extended passive bus in which TEs are clustered at one end at a maximum distance of 50 m apart, and the NT is up to 500 m away at the other end. For

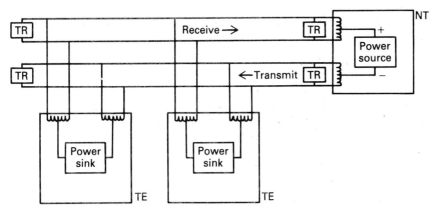

Fig. 5.24 Basic ISDN interface wiring example.
TR = terminating resistor.

point-to-point configurations (only one TE) a bus length of 1 km is possible.

Clocking on the line is controlled by the NT, with the TEs deriving their transmission clock from the received clock from the NT. The coding is as per Fig. 5.25, in which a binary '1' is seen to be no signal, while binary '0' alternates positively and negatively. This is alternate mark inversion, or AMI. The nominal pulse height is 750 mV. A 48-bit frame structure is used, see Fig. 5.26. The start of frame (the F bit) is marked by a violation of the AMI sequence and the auxiliary framing bit (FA) is used as a further framing check. Additional DC balancing bits (L) exist in the frame.

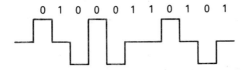

Fig. 5.25 Coding on basic ISDN interface.

The TE's transmit frame is phase-shifted by two bits with respect to the frame it receives from the NT and is slightly different in format. Both frames are 250 μs long and carry two octets from each of the two B channels, plus four (D) bits from the D channel. The frame sent by the NT also contains four Echo (E) bits, which echo the last D bit received from the TE.

The purpose of the echo is as follows: The D channel is a common channel shared by all TEs on the bus. It is used for signalling, in particular to allocate B channels to TEs. Thus there is no contention for B channels, since they are allocated in an orderly fashion, but there is contention for the D channel—two or more TEs may choose to seize the D channel at the same time.

Traffic on the D channel is in HDLC-like frames (see below) and as such has regular binary 0s inserted. Indeed, even the HDLC flag has no more than six consecutive 1s, so a would-be seizer of the D channel can always tell if it is active or not. If it is active 0s will be seen regularly; if not the idle state of continuous 1s exists. Thus the contention mechanism for seizing the D channel is for a TE firstly to 'listen' for eight or more continuous 1s; and then, if it desires to transmit, to start sending its own data in the D-bit positions of the frame of Fig. 5.26. Since the D channel data is carried in HDLC frames, the very first bit sent will be a 0 (the start of the HDLC flag 01111110), so other TEs can see the channel is taken, and reset their counts of continuous 1s to zero.

The TE which has started using the D channel now observes the returning E bits. If they are not what was sent, a collision has occurred— i.e. one or more other TEs have started transmission on the D channel. If collision is detected the sender should relinquish the D channel at once.

The procedure is more complicated than as described above. TEs can be of different priority classes, with some having stronger rights to the D channel than others. This is achieved by making the lower-priority TEs count more than eight (up to eleven) continuous 1s on the D channel, before making a bid for it. The priority of a TE is partly dynamic; in particular, a TE which has just used the D channel demotes itself temporarily.

The access mechanism for the D channel is reminiscent of Ethernet's carrier sensing multiple access with collision detection (CSMA-CD), but the backing off procedures in case of collision are rudimentary. This is because there is not the long 'loop delay' (in terms of bit positions) of Ethernet, and the number of TEs will always be small. However, it may be asked: What is the probability of repeated collisions on the D channel between two or more contending TEs?

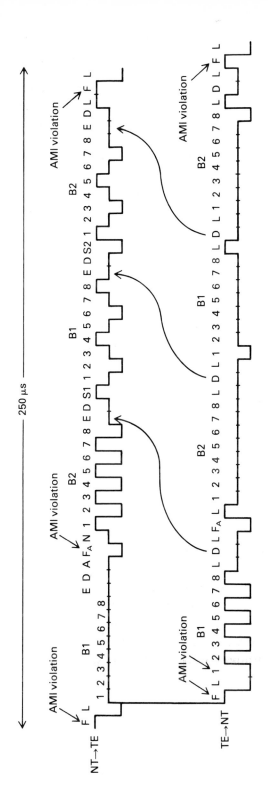

Fig. 5.26 Example of 48-bit frames on basic ISDN interface.
F = framing bit; F_A = auxiliary framing bit; L = DC balancing bit; B1 = octet from first B channel; B2 = octet from second B channel; D = bit from D channel; E = echo bit.

All D bits = 1
NT→TE B1 = 11111111, 10101010
        B2 = 0p0000000, 01010101
TE→NT B1 = 00000000, 01111111
        B2 = 11111111, 11111110

5.4.3 Use of the D channel

The D channel on ISDN interfaces is used for signalling. It can also be used for carrying packetized data. The LAP-D line procedure, a variant of HDLC, is used to carry the signalling messages securely across the interface; or to carry X.25 Level 3 packets for access to packet-switching services.

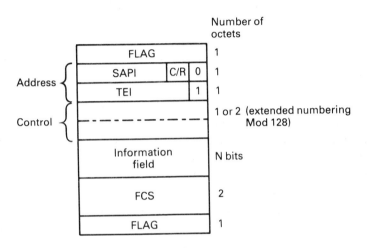

Fig. 5.27   Frame structure for LAP-D and addressing.

LAP-D supports the multidrop configuration of the basic physical interface, as well as point-to-point configurations. Addressing is at two levels. Each data link (i.e. LAP-D) connection is identified by a Service Access Point Identifier (SAPI) plus a Terminal Endpoint Identifier (TEI). The SAPI may be thought of as a point in the NT. For example, one SAPI could identify the access point to the service which handles signalling in the NT, another could identify the service handling packetized data. SAPIs are all distinct on a given physical interface. The TEIs identify specific connections within a terminal (TE), which may have more than one extant connection, and are, as it were, subaddresses within a SAPI. That is, for a given SAPI all TEIs are distinct, but TEIs can be the same if they belong to different SAPIs on the same physical interface. The address field in a LAP-D frame is shown in Fig. 5.27, where it will be noted that it also contains a Command/Response bit (set to 0 for commands from or responses to the TE, and 1 for

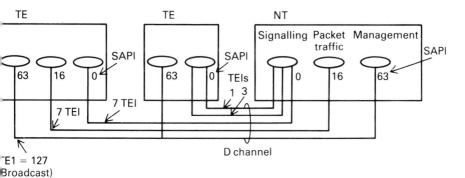

Fig. 5.28 Example of LAP-D SAPIs and TEIs.

commands from or responses to the NT). An example of an interface addressing scheme is shown in Fig. 5.28.

In order that the uniqueness of TEIs may be assured, LAP-D contains a procedure for allocating TEIs to terminal endpoints by the NT, or verifying their acceptability if they were pre-allocated, e.g. in the TE's hardware. This procedure uses a (new) Unnumbered Information (UI)-frame, which can carry 'managerial' information in agreed formats across the interface. The UI frame can also be used to carry higher level information across the interface where no acknowledgement is required, in particular for broadcasting commands within a SAPI. There are two further new commands called Sequenced Information 0 and Sequenced Information 1 (SI0, SI1) which can carry higher level information or acknowledge it, in an alternating fashion, frame by frame, as in old-fashioned procedures such as BSC.

Otherwise LAP-D is similar to LAP-B and other HDLC variants, using the flag (01111110), bit-stuffing, FCS, multiple-frame acknow-ledgement with N(S) and N(R), etc. Provision is also made for modulo 128, as opposed to the normal modulo 8, numbering of I frames. It is discussed in Recommendations I.440 and I.441.

Recommendations I.450 and I.451 cover the formidable subject of signalling on the D channel of the ISDN interface, for controlling B (and other) channels. They specify

(i) The procedures for establishing and clearing connections over the B channels of the interface, whether those connections be used for voice, circuit-switched or packet-switched data, or possibly other forms of traffic.

(ii) The messages employed by these procedures, and their formats. An example of a message is 'SETUP' which is used to request a connection to be set up on a B channel. All the messages are carried in LAP-D frames on the D channel.

(iii) The 'information elements' contained in a message and their formats. Examples of information elements (used in the SETUP message) are the 'destination address' of the connection which is to be set up, and the 'bearer capability' specifying the characteristics of the channel which is required for the connection, e.g. unrestricted 64 Kbps.

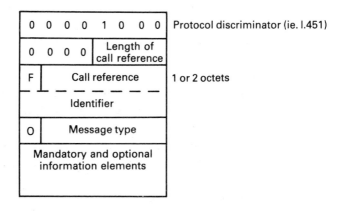

Fig. 5.29   Format of D channel messages for simple telephone call.

Figure 5.29 shows the general message format. The protocol discriminator effectively states that I.451 is in use. If the D channel is used to carry X.25 Level 3 packets then the X.25 protocol discriminator (QD01XXXX) is used. The call reference value identifies the call to which the signalling relates. The originating side of the interface sets the flag-bit to zero, the destination side sets it to 1. Thus if the TE originates a call and gives it reference 6 with Flag = 0, the NT will refer to it as 6 with Flag = 1; thus distinguishing this call from one originating at the NT and given the same reference 6, which the NT would refer to as 6 with Flag = 0, and the TE as 6 with Flag = 1. The 'call collision' problem is avoided. Reference values are unique within a given LAP-D data link, and normally one octet is allowed for them in the message header on the basic (192 Kbps) interface, two octets on a primary rate interface.

The next octet gives the message type. Some of the more important message types (with coding in parentheses) are listed below

Call establishment messages. SETUP (00000101). Used to request call establishment or initiate an incoming call. There is a SETUP ACKnowledgement (00001101) message which is a response to SETUP, requesting more information such as selection (dialling) information, if the SETUP message is not complete in itself.

CALL PROCeeding (00000010). Sent to state that call establishment is proceeding. ALERTing (00000001) is another message indicating that the called user is being alerted (e.g. his number is ringing).

CONNect (00000111). This states that the call has been set up. A CONNect ACKnowledge (00001111) also exists.

Call information phase messages. These are used when the call which is being controlled has been fully established

SUSPend (00100101). Used to suspend an existing call, maintaining its reference. For example, a user might suspend a call while it is being moved to a different physical terminal. SUSPend ACKnowledge (00101101) and SUSPend REJect (00100001) messages also exist.

RESume (00100110). Used to resume a suspended call. RESume ACKnowledge (00101110) and RESume REJect (00100010) messages also exist.

USER INFOrmation (00100000). Can carry messages, particularly end-to-end signalling messages, directly between users.

Call disestablishment messages. DISconnect (01000101). A request to release the controlled channel and its associated call reference.

RELease (01001101). Sent to indicate that the sender has disconnected the controlled channel and intends to release the call reference and that the receiver should do likewise. It is responded to by a RELease COMplete (01011010) message.

DETach (01000000). States that the controlled channel has been disconnected but the call reference still exists. This facility could be used when a user requires charging information about a call he has terminated. A DETach ACKnowledge (01001000) message exists.

Miscellaneous messages. These include FACility (01100010) used to request specific facilities such as reverse charging, call redirection, origination address required on incoming calls; and CANcel (01100000) to cancel a facility. Also included are REGister (01100100) to register user facilities (rather than to simply invoke them); STATus (01111101) which is used to report on unexpected events; and several other message types.

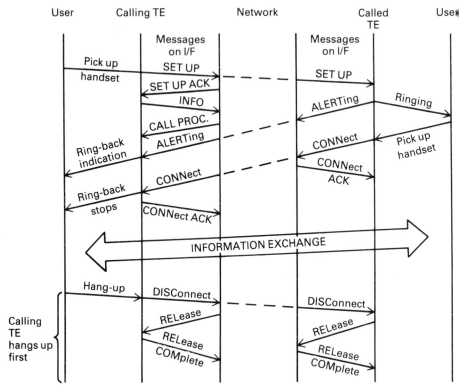

Fig. 5.30 Use of D channel messages for simple telephone call.

Figure 5.30 illustrates the use of these messages in the very simple case of establishing and clearing a circuit-switched call, e.g. a telephone call. In practice the complete procedures are much more complex. They must support various forms of call establishment, handle clearing at any stage, resolve problems as to *which* controlled B channel is to be used (including possible call collisions for a B channel), negotiate facilities, etc.

The rest of the message format (Fig. 5.29) contains the information elements which have the general format of Fig. 5.31. As an indication of the nature of information elements, some more common ones are listed below

(i) Channel identification. Identifies the controlled channel.

(ii) Destination address.

(iii) Origination address.

(iv) Cause (of error, of clearing).

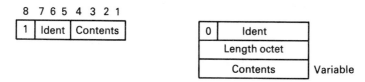

Fig. 5.31 Formats for information elements.

(v) Bearer capability. The type of bearer channel required by or offered to the call.

(vi) Keypad. Carries a message from a user's keypad (if present).

(vii) Display. Carries a message to a user's screen (if present).

(viii) CCITT standardized facilities. Identifies CCITT standardized facilities required or on offer.

(ix) Network-specific facilities. As above, but the facilities referred to are peculiar to this network.

It will be appreciated that I.451 is a fundamental recommendation which aims to permit many types of calls to be set up on B or other channels using a single set of procedures on the D channel. The terminals which do not comply with the physical interface required at point S or T of Fig. 5.22, where access is made to the network, can still be handled by this D channel signalling using Terminal Adaptors (TAs).

5.4.4 Examples of Terminal Adaptors (TAs)

Two simple examples of TAs may be outlined to show how existing user equipment may be interfaced to an ISDN.

The first example is that of interfacing X.21 equipment, see Chapter 2, which is done according to Recommendation I.461. In the 'minimum scenario' (Fig. 5.32), an Access Unit (AU) exists as well as TA1, both looking alike to the ISDN. Their functions are

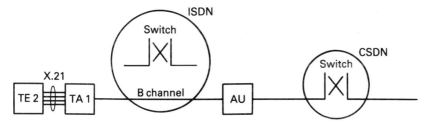

Fig. 5.32 'Minimum scenario' X.21 support.

(i) Rate adaption, or mapping the slower X.21 bit streams into the 64 Kbps stream. This can be done in two stages; for example by mapping a 2400 bps X.21 bit stream into 40-bit frames in an 8 Kbps bit stream; which itself is mapped into the first bit of each octet in the 64 Kbps bit stream. In this mapping the sampled states of the control and indication circuits of the X.21 interface are also put into the 40-bit frame.

(ii) Establishment between the TA1 and the AU of a B channel in response to the origination of an X.21 call by the user. This is 'hot-line' access. 'Semi-permanent' access does not even require this, since the B channel between TA1 and AU is permanently allocated.

In the 'maximum scenario' (Fig. 5.33) TA2 maps X.21 signalling into D channel signalling, including setting up a switched B channel through the ISDN using ISDN numbering schemes. An Interworking Unit (IU) between the ISDN and the CSDN will exist.

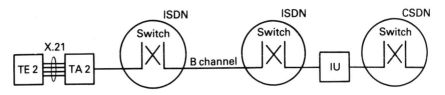

Fig. 5.33 'Maximum scenario' X.21 support.

The other example of a TA is that for equipment using the V-series interfaces, suitable for modems (see I.463). The TA will support full mapping of V-series interface signals into channel D signalling and rate adjustment of synchronous data into the 64 Kbps B channel. An IU to the PSTN will exist (if required). Interworking between V-series and X-series TEs over the ISDN will be possible, since both have ISDN-compatible TAs.

5.4.5 Support of X.25 by ISDNs

X.25 packet-switched access can be supported by ISDNs using

(i) The D channel, with LAP-D as Level 2, carrying X.25 Level 3 packets.

(ii) The B channel 'minimum scenario', in which X.25 packets are passed transparently through the ISDN on a B channel, apart from rate adaption. This should be done by inserting inter-frame HDLC flags. The B channel can be a semi-permanent connection, a 'hot line', or can be set up using D channel signalling, see Fig. 5.34.

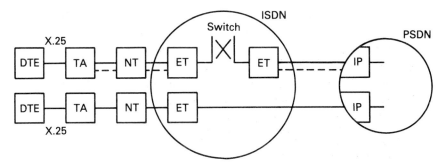

Fig. 5.34 'Minimum scenario' X.25 support.
ET = exchange terminal; ⟷ = B channel; ←-→ = D channel.

(iii) The B channel 'maximum scenario' in which case there is a Packet Handler (PH) in the ISDN which explicitly obeys X.25, and provides in effect a local node to the user (Fig. 5.35). In the maximum scenario there are questions about addressing. In particular incoming calls from an X.25 network could have to set up a B channel connection, if none already exists, before using it. Even if one already exists there may be more than one way of accessing a given destination TE, e.g. the D channel could be used. Recommendation I.462 addresses these problems.

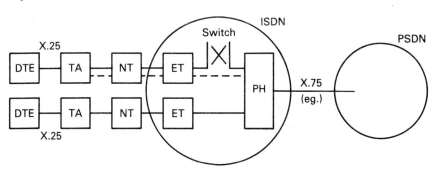

Fig. 5.35 'Maximum scenario' X.25 support.
⟷ = B channel; ←-→ = D channel.

5.5 SUMMARY OF ISDN INTERFACES

The I.400 Series of Recommendations are relatively new and ambitious in scope. The aim is to support all existing types of CCITT-approved terminals (telephones, packet-mode, X.21, etc.) on a single range of interfaces, using the three-layer D channel signalling to establish, maintain and clear connections.

Although the concept is bold the reader will no doubt detect certain limitations. The interface is already 'carved up' into channels. The user cannot divide up the bandwidth dynamically, but only at subscription time, i.e. the channels are 'semi-permanent'. It is true that a subscriber could lease, for example, a point-to-point H12 channel (1920 Kbps) between two of his sites and use this dynamically under his own control, for 64 Kbps voice or wideband data. He cannot however make external telephone calls to or from this channel. In effect the ISDN concept is firmly based on circuit-switching, and those who wish to do SAF-switching must use dedicated circuit-switched channels to carry the SAF data.

Note: The U-interface between NT1 and the ISDN switch (See Fig. 5.22) has not been discussed, since it awaits standardization. However, particular implementations exist. For example, a 160 Kbps U-interface for basic access has been developed providing full-duplex transmission on a *single* existing telephone pair, using echo-cancellation techniques.

REFERENCES

1 *Teletex: Recommendation F.200; Videotex: Recommendation F.300;* CCITT Red Book **II.5**, Geneva, 1985.
2 Message Handling Services: *Recommendations X.400* etc., CCITT Red Book, **VIII. 7**, Geneva, 1985.
3 The Ethernet, A Local Network, Data Link Layer and Physical Layer Specifications. Digital, Intel, Xerox, September 1980.
4 Wilkes M.V. and Wheeler D.I. (1979) *The Cambridge Digital Communication Ring* Proceedings of the LACN Symposium, Mitre and NBS.
5 *Data Communications Protocol for Providing the Connectionless Network Service* ISO DP8473, International Standards Organization.
6 *SL-1 PBX,* Northern Telecomm, Ottawa, Canada.
7 *MD-110—a Digital SPC PABX* Ericsson Review 1 & 2, 1982. Ericsson Telefonaktiebolaget, Stockholm.
8 Assam N. and Williams B. (1985) *The Meridian DV-1: System Architecture* Telesis No. 3 Bell Northern Research, Ottawa, Canada.
9 *Recommendations X.1, X.2, X.10* CCITT Red Book, **VIII. 2**, Geneva, 1985.
10 *Recommendations of the Series I* CCITT Red Book, **III. 5,** Geneva, 1985.

Chapter 6
The OSI Reference Model and Higher Level Protocols

In previous chapters we have discussed the standards and procedures for interfacing to networks. These procedures may conveniently be considered as 'layered'. There are lower layers which provide some basic service which is used by a higher layer. The higher layer enhances the basic service, by providing extra functions; so that it, in turn, offers a more comprehensive service to some still higher layer.

For example, the X.25 procedures are in three layers. The first layer defines the physical interface to a PSDN; the second layer defines procedures which will enable the establishment and maintenance of an error-free (thanks to error-detection and correction by retransmission) data link on top of the physical layer; the third layer specifies how transnetwork connections are set up, used and cleared, relying on the error-free interface provided by the second layer.

A similar three layer structure applies to the D channel of ISDN interfaces (see Section 5.4).

If we consider other types of networks we may, sometimes with some imagination, still identify the three layers. The telephone service has a physical layer, specified in terms of a pair of wires, with 600 ohm terminating resistors, etc. It has a link layer (not error-free!) which is concerned with the establishment and clearing of the link to the local exchange, and which uses off-hook 'seize', 'accept' and similar signals for that purpose. It has a 'network' layer defining procedures for transnetwork calls: selection (dialling), call progress signals, failure procedures (e.g. when the called number is busy), etc.

However, despite the complexities of signalling, routing and switching which have been discussed earlier, making the connection to and through the network is often the simpler part of communication. After all, the network imposes restrictions on users which lessen the possibility of incompatibilities. But 'end-to-end' communication *across* a network is wide open to every form of difficulty, ranging from low level problems such as the interworking of DTEs of different speeds (how can the faster one be prevented from overloading the slower one?) to complete incompatibility, e.g. when one speaker on the telephone network talks Portuguese and the other Russian.

It is possible to introduce some discipline into the analysis and solution of these 'end-to-end' problems. The approach is the layered one which has been discussed already. End-to-end communication service functions are identified which are, as it were, basic. These are gathered into a layer which is furnished with the additional protocols and other tools necessary to provide this basic service on top of the raw trans-network connection. On top of this basic service another layer may be built offering higher level end-to-end service functions, etc.

Thus a communication service at a given layer in this architecture is provided from two sources
(1) The service functions particular to the given layer (which might be mapping from one code to another, or end-to-end flow control, for example) and which have an associated protocol to enable them to be provided.
(2) The service functions provided by lower layers on which the enhancements of this layer are built.

In this chapter accordingly, we shall be discussing both these aspects of end-to-end communications: The protocols which provide the enhancements; and the services themselves on which the enhancements are built to offer higher level services.

6.1 THE OPEN SYSTEMS INTERCONNECTION REFERENCE MODEL (OSI/RM) [1], [2]

The famous Open Systems Interconnection Reference Model (OSI/RM) is a 'model' or an 'architecture', based on the principle of layering, for handling communications across networks. More specifically, the OSI/RM identifies seven layers (see Fig. 6.1) which provide progressively enhanced service functions to users. Each layer adds new service functions to those of the layers below and each layer is concerned with specific types of service functions. It is a fundamental aim of the model to identify clearly to which layer a given service function belongs.

The model is not immediately concerned with how a particular service function is provided. That is, in principle, an internal function of the layer in question. However, it is presumed that a layer consists of software modules running on the equipment between which the communication takes place, and which exchange commands and data accord-

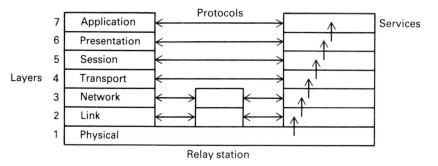

Fig. 6.1   OSI Reference Model.

ing to certain rules (the 'protocol') so that they may indeed provide the service function.

Thus the Nth layer might consist of two 'N-layer peer entities', i.e. software modules, running on two communicating computers. These N-layer peer entities rely on the service provide by the $(N-1)$-layer to exchange N-layer commands according to the N-layer protocol. The N-layer protocol must be rigidly defined if it is to serve as a standard for communication between different implementations of the N-layer on different computers.

The N-layer peer entities call on the service of the $(N-1)$-layer using 'primitives'. These primitives are internal to the computers at each end of the communication path, so that, while they should perform similar functions in each implementation, the details of formats, calling mechanisms, etc. may be local, i.e. non-standard. In turn, the $(N+1)$-layer is provided with 'primitives' by the N-layer, so that it may use the service of the N-layer. See Fig. 6.2.

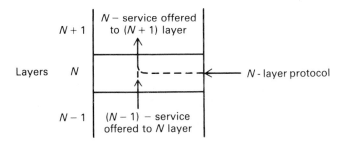

Fig. 6.2   Layers, services and protocols.

The seven layers of the OSI/RM, and their service functions, are as follows

Layer 1—physical layer. The physical layer provides a physical path linking communicating entities. In most applications of the model the physical layer is point-to-point, so that only two communicating entities are supported. However, this is not necessarily so. The physical layer may support the serial establishment of multipoint connections, or indeed the simultaneous use of multipoint connections, as in broadcasting. The physical layer of a given connection may involve several concatenated physical links interconnected by 'relay' functions. It is also a function of the physical layer to ensure that bits are delivered in the same order in which they are transmitted ('Sequencing'). The physical layer may have certain specific characteristics in any given instance, e.g. a bit error rate.

Layer 2—data link layer. The data link layer supports the establishment, use and clearing of data link connections between network entities such as nodes, or a DTE and its local node. In use, the data link layer is primarily concerned with the correct transmission and reception of blocks of data ('data-link-service-data-units') across the underlying physical layer. The data link layer can, in principle, handle parallel physical paths (cf. X.75) as though they were a single physical path. Error-detection and correction, if required (as they usually are), is a prime function of the data link service. A transnetwork connection may be made up of several concatenated data links.

Layer 3—network layer. The network layer provides connections between user-equipment, i.e. DTEs, across a network. As such, it obviously supports addressing and routing functions. Normally it only handles point-to-point connections. The network layer should report unrecoverable errors to the user, or more precisely, to the next higher layer—the transport layer. Optional functions of the network layer are multiplexing of many network connections on to a single data link; flow control, to protect the network, or DTEs (or both) from overload; sequencing, if the routing used could cause loss of sequence (e.g. if X.25 is built on top of a datagram network); and possibly relaying across concatenated subnetworks, for example if a DTE is connected to a LAN which is in turn connected to a public data network.

Layer 4—transport layer. The transport layer is the first proper 'end-to-end' layer. Its objective is, in broad terms, to optimize the use of the network layer underlying it and to provide an adequate end-to-end communication facility for use by higher levels. This means that a central aim of the transport layer is the 'masking' of the peculiarities and deficiencies of the network in use. It should map transport addresses (known to users) on to network addresses (not necessarily known to users). It should provide: end-to-end sequence control; end-to-end error detection and recovery, if required; end-to-end flow control. It should also segment and re-block data units, for example to fit large blocks of data into a sequence of smaller packets on a PSDN. The transport layer can also multiplex user connections on to a single network layer connection, although this is seldom used.

The transport layer service may be regarded as a 'platform' on which higher layer services are built. Below this platform there may exist a variety of networks with different characteristics. Above this platform there may exist a variety of services. But at the transport layer the aim is to provide a uniform, basic, end-to-end service.

Layer 5—session layer. The session layer is, as its name suggests, concerned with sessions established between processes (whether computer programs or persons) across a network. As such, a central objective is the control of the dialogue: who has the right to send data and how is that right transferred to the other end? The session layer also allows processes which are communicating to synchronize their activities; so that a receiving process may, for example, know when it has received some complete command stream from a sender, act on it, and then advise the sender of the result. 'Quarantining', by which is meant the delivery of information to the receiving user of a session only when it has been completely received by the receiving session-entity and authorized by the sending session-entity, is also a session layer function.

Layer 6—presentation layer. The presentation layer is concerned with the syntax, i.e. the representation, of end-to-end data. As such it is responsible for agreeing on codes and formats to be used in the exchange of application data during a session. The presentation layer could be responsible for formatting data streams for correct output on a given line printer or a VDU screen. It could also perform compression and decompression. As will be seen, presentation layer functions are frequently handled in practice by user applications, and the presentation layer is in fact often void. Encryption is now also regarded as essentially a presentation layer function (see Section 7.5).

Layer 7—application layer. The application layer contains all user applications. Since there are thousands of applications running over networks it is hardly useful to attempt to classify them. However, some typical applications are: file transfer; remote job entry (a special case of file transfer); messaging, or the exchange of mail files, etc.

The above brief overview of the OSI/RM should help to understand the scope of the concept. The general objective is to enable open systems interconnection; that is, any computer should be able to interwork with any other computer over a network (which offers the possibility of physical interconnection). The key-word is 'open'—all entities connected to a network should be able to communicate. The reference model gives a systematic architecture for discussing the many areas where incompatibilities can arise, and for resolving these incompatibilities, so that true open systems interconnection is possible.

It would be idle to pretend that the model itself, and the protocols built in accordance with the model, have removed all difficulties of interworking across networks. There are many anomalies, not only in theory but in practice. Consider, for example, a network in which bulk data are sent over a satellite channel in one direction, while a terrestrial X.25 connection is used for their acknowledgement and for error-recovery in the reverse direction (Fig. 6.3). This function is that of the data link layer between the sender (the computer at the transmitting earth station) and the receiver (the computer at the receiving earth station). But data link layer acknowledgements are to be sent *on top of* network layer (X.25) services on the reverse path! One could pretend this data link layer was a kind of transport layer, but this would be distorting the facts—the functions are those of the data link layer.

Thus the OSI/RM is not a panacea which will solve all problems. It scarcely addresses multipoint connections. It suffers from considerable confusion at the presentation/application layers. The literature it has generated is enormous, and yet when one reads the session layer service specifications, for example, one wonders why so many pages and such verbose terminology are required merely to state that sessions can be established and cleared (the additional functions of dialogue control are really very straightforward and often redundant). Nevertheless, as a framework for discussion there is no doubt that the OSI/RM is of fundamental importance. We shall try to adhere to it for the remainder of this book.

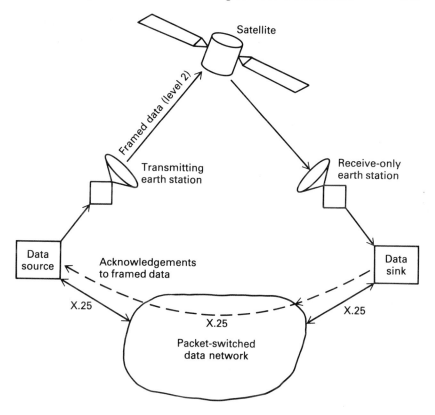

Fig. 6.3 A level 2 service, carried by level 3.

6.1.1 Some Additional Comments on the OSI/RM

The OSI/RM has its origins in standardization work within the International Standards Organisation (ISO). The original concept, due largely to H. Zimmerman, appeared as the ISO standard 7498 [1]. Since then the model has been widely accepted and appears in many fields ranging from the architecture for ISDNs, LANs and satellite networks to the design of distributed data bases, security mechanisms and even computer operating systems—far beyond the original area of application which was essentially confined to conventional wide area networks, with a particular emphasis on packet-switching.

Standardization work associated with the model is still centred on ISO, but many other bodies have actively contributed. For example the

European Computer Manufacturers Association (ECMA), has submitted many OSI proposals to ISO, some of which have been incorporated into standards. Other groups, for example the UK Joint Network Team (JNT), have produced protocol specifications conforming to the OSI/ RM. JNT, in particular, developed the 'coloured books' series of protocols for the support of end-to-end services on networks [9]. The best known of these is perhaps the 'blue book' file transfer protocol which has been widely used outside as well as within the UK.

However, the most important recognition to be given to the OSI/RM comes from CCITT. In the X.200 series Recommendations CCITT [2] had adopted the concepts as its own, starting with the model itself (X.200); and following with a series of other Recommendations such as X.213 (Network Service Definition), X.214 (Transport Service), X.215 (Session Service), X.224 (Transport Protocol Specification) and X.225 (Session Protocol). Moreover, CCITT has extended the use of the OSI/ RM to fields other than that of traditional data communications. For example the telematic services (T-Series Recommendations), the message handling systems (X.400 Recommendations), and the ISDN (I-Series Recommendations) are all presented within the general OSI layered framework. These Recommendations are discussed later in this chapter.

Nevertheless, despite the wide acceptance of the OSI *concept* it must be emphasized that there is a considerable way to go before there are universally accepted *standards* applicable to all the layers of the model. For example, the JNT 'coloured book' standards agree very largely with the OSI architecture, but the protocols they specify for use between peer entities at the different layers are not compatible with those put forward by ISO and/or CCITT. Again, IBM's Systems Network Architecture (SNA) is a layered structure, within which several of the layers correspond more or less directly with the OSI model with regard to their functional capabilities. The protocols, however, are IBM's own. In certain circumstances, due to functional compatibility, it is possible to envisage mapping one N-layer protocol directly into another in some interfacing gateway (see Fig. 6.4); but this is by no means always the case.

Finally, a particular unresolved problem area is that of network management. The original OSI model concentrates on user traffic, but in any real network there is a significant amount of traffic carrying management information such as statistics, event reports and operator commands (see Section 5.1). The scope and nature of such management

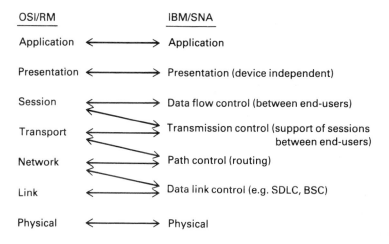

Fig. 6.4 Putative relationships between OSI/RM and SNA.

functions is hardly touched on in the 'classical' OSI concept—although the ISDN Recommendations do take them seriously.

6.2 NETWORK, TRANSPORT AND SESSION LAYERS

6.2.1 The Network Layer

Examples of network layer services providing connections between end-users have been discussed in Chapters 2 and 3 under X.21 and X.25. X.21 and X.25 are of course *protocols* for establishing, using and clearing connections on circuit-switched and packet-switched networks, respectively. The *services* provided by X.21 and X.25 are implied rather than stated, in those Recommendations.

In Recommendation X.213 [2], CCITT attempts to define a network layer *service* explicitly in terms of the primitives it offers to the higher transport layer, together with their associated parameters, and the interaction between primitives and network events. In this Recommendation use is made of a queue model—i.e. between two connected network service users queues of data in transit may exist, on which a flow control function operates. The primitives offered to the user also strongly relate to X.25, with the addition of a network data acknowledge primitive which is used to provide end-to-end acknowledgement (as could be implemented using the D-bit of X.25).

The only other points of interest in X.213 are the quality of service parameters including: connection establishment and clearing delays; data transfer throughput and transnetwork transfer delays; probabilities of failure of set-up or clear; probability of network errors (loss, corruption, duplication of data); protection (i.e. privacy), priority and maximum acceptable cost. Values for these parameters should be known to subscribers to the network; indeed they are the basis for a potential user deciding whether he will become a subscriber or not, and if so, for determining which protocols he will use (if there is a choice), with which special facilities. Two of the parameters—data transfer throughput and delay—are supposedly negotiable at the start of each call, rather than simply at the time of subscription.

X.213 is a tidying-up operation, being a rationalization of existing network services as implied by (for example) X.25, and available in reality on networks throughout the world. It remains to be seen if X.213 will develop into a standard with which network service providers will consciously aim to comply.

6.2.2 The Transport Layer

By contrast with the Network Service Definition, the Transport Service Definition (X.214) and the Transport Protocol Specification (X.224) are important documents of wide application [2].

The Transport Service (TS) provides to end-to-end users transparent connections (i.e. on which arbitrary data may be sent), with a user-selectable quality of service, which hides any differences in quality which might exist between different underlying networks. In practice, quality

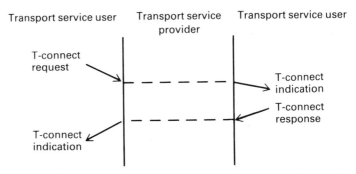

Fig. 6.5 Successful establishment of a transport connection using the T-connect primitive.

of service is agreed, very largely, at subscription time and in effect specifies which Class (0 to 4) of the Transport Protocol (TP) will be used. The primitives provided to the TS user are

(i) T-CONNECT (Request, Indication, Response, Confirm) which is illustrated in Fig. 6.5. Parameters are: called and calling addresses, expedited data option (i.e. the optional capability to send data not subject to flow control), quality of service (if negotiable) and TS user data (restricted in size during the connection phase).

(ii) T-DATA and T-EXPEDITED DATA (Request, Indication) with TS-data as a parameter.

(iii) T-DISCONNECT (Request, Indication) also with TS-data as a parameter. Additionally the T-DISCONNECT indication can carry a 'Disconnect Reason' as a parameter.

The protocol between the communicating transport 'peer-entities', which ensures that the TS is properly provided, is discussed in Recommendation X.224. It exists in five forms or classes (Classes 0 to 4), designed to give progressively more powerful functions, to compensate for underlying networks of progressively lesser reliability. The Classes are

(i) Class 0. (Simple class). This is designed for use over a high quality network; that is, one which has a low level of errors (such as X.25 resets) signalled to the user and a low level of unsignalled errors (such as loss of data within a switching node). The Class 0 protocol provides for no error recovery when an error is signalled, but simply closes down the connection. Also, in Class 0, only one Transport-connection (T-connection) can exist on a Network-connection (N-connection)—there is no multiplexing. Class 0 is compatible with the Telematic T.70 protocol (see Section 6.4) [3].

(ii) Class 1. (Basic error recovery class). This class enables recovery from signalled network errors such as a reset or a disconnection. The errors are hidden from the TS user thanks to the recovery mechanism. Class 1 is designed for use with less reliable networks than those required by Class 0.

(iii) Class 2. (Multiplexing class). This class, which provides no error recovery and so is designed for use with high quality networks, does permit multiplexing of several T-connections on to a single network connection. This is obviously an attractive facility for users of circuit-switched data networks, or of leased circuit connections, where the network layer performs no multiplexing, or perhaps is absent altogether.

Because several T-connections may share the one N-connection, a flow control option is provided within Class 2, enabling the data rate of each individual T-connection to be separately controlled by means of a credit mechanism.

(iv) Class 3. (Error recovery and multiplexing class). This is identical to Class 2 except that a mechanism (as in Class 1) is introduced to enable recovery from errors signalled by the network service.

(v) Class 4. (Error detection and recovery class). This class is for use with 'unreliable' networks, in particular with datagram packet-switching in which functions such as packet sequencing may not be guaranteed. Class 4 has all the functions of Class 3 plus the capability to *detect* and recover from network service errors, such as loss, corruption, duplication or delivery out of sequence of a Transport Protocol Data Unit (TPDU).

The transport protocol is perhaps best explained by discussing the TPDUs and their functions. The general format for a TPDU is shown in Fig. 6.6. A one-octet length indicator (maximum value 254) defines the combined length of the fixed and variable parts of the header in octets.

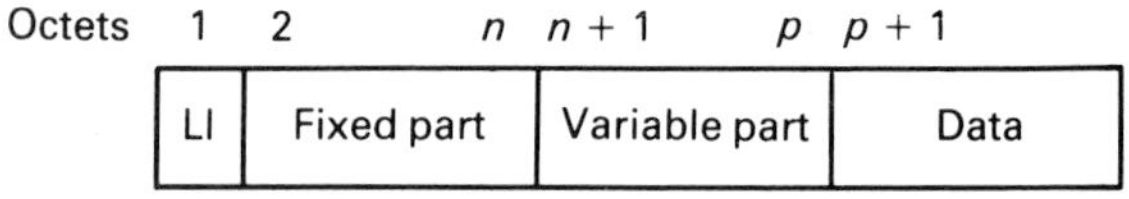

Octets   1   2 n $n+1$ p $p+1$

LI	Fixed part	Variable part	Data

Fig. 6.6   General format of a Transport Protocol Data Unit.

The fixed part of the header contains one octet defining the type of TPDU, followed by some more octets of necessary control information, depending on the type. The types of TPDU, and the corresponding coding of the first octet of the fixed part of the header, are

Connection Request (CR)	1110 xxxx
Connection Confirm (CC)	1101 xxxx
Disconnect Request (DR)	1000 0000
Disconnect Confirm (DC)	1100 0000
Data (DT)	1111 0000
Expedited Data (ED)	0001 0000
Data Acknowledgement (AK)	0110 zzzz
Expedited Data Acknowledgement (EA)	0010 0000
Reject (RJ)	0101 zzzz
TPDU Error (ER)	0111 0000
Transport Protocol Identifier (PI)	0000 0001

where xxxx and zzzz are used to carry Flow Control Credits, where applicable.

The variable part of the header carries parameters, typically those associated with negotiating facilities when setting up a T-connection. Each parameter is conveyed as a three-part unit: one octet identifying the parameter type, the second octet identifying the length of the parameter value and the third part (one or more octets) carrying the value itself. A range of valid parameters is defined in the X.224 Recommendation. It should also be noted that, in Class 4, a checksum parameter may be carried in the variable part of the header, the check being performed on the entire TPDU.

The different types of TPDU and their uses will now be presented.

CR and CC. Figures 6.7a and 6.7b illustrate the formats for the Connection Request (CR) and Connection Confirm (CC) TPDUs. The CR is sent from the source to the destination over the network connection.

Octets

1	2	3	4	5	6	7	8	p	p + 1	
LI	CR 1110 CDT	00000000	00000000	SRC-REF		Class, options	Variable part	Data		**(a)**
		DST-REF								

1	2	3	4	5	6	7	8	p	p + 1	
LI	CC 1101 CDT	DST-REF		SRC-REF		Class, options	Variable part	Data		**(b)**

Fig. 6.7a   CR TPDU.

Fig. 6.7b   CC TPDU.

The destination should reply with CC if the request is accepted; or with Disconnect Request (DR) if it is rejected, for example because the requester specified a class not supported by the destination. (An ER could also be sent in response, if CR formats were wrong.) If the source receives CC the T-connection is established. If it receives DR or ER the T-connection is completely cleared.

The CR and CC exchange credits (CDT) in the lower half of octet 2. A credit is the right to send up to the specified number of DTs (Data TPDUs). The right is given by a receiver of DTs to a sender. The credit extends upwards from an acknowledgement number (YR-TU-NR) sent in AKs, see below. Credits only apply to Classes 2, 3 and 4 which support multiplexing.

The CR and CC also exchange identifiers for the T-connection in the fields SRC-REF and DST-REF. The values of these identifiers are the concern only of the communicating peer entities. The value given by an entity (e.g. DST-REF given by a destination) should be unique and independent of the network connection, which may fail without bringing down the T-connection. Once identifiers are exchanged a sender always uses the (single) remote entity's reference, i.e. DST-REF to identify the T-connection. Identifiers are principally of use when multiplexing takes place, so, for example, DT TPDUs in Classes 0 and 1 do not include a DST-REF field.

In octet 7 of the header the first four bits specify the class requested (CR) or allocated (CC). In CR, the class bits of octet 7 are the first choice for a class; second and other preferences may be included in the variable part of the header. A destination will try to match the requested class in order of preference. If it cannot do so it will disconnect the T-connection. The lower bits of octet 7 can be used to select explicit flow control (or not) in Class 2 and the use of extended formats for numbering DT TPDUs in Classes 2, 3 and 4 (see below).

In the variable part of the header CR carries desired values for optional parameters such as

(i) Proposed maximum TPDU size
(ii) Security parameters (user defined)
(iii) Checksum (Class 4 only)
(iv) Throughput desired (not Class 0)
(v) Priority desired (not Class 0).

In the variable part of the header CC carries responses to CR's parameter proposals. Essentially, valid responses are more restrictive. A CC may respond with a smaller TPDU maximum size than that proposed in the CR, but not a larger size. It may reject the use of the checksum if proposed, but not accept it if it was not proposed.

In the user data portion of the CR and CC TPDUs up to 32 octets of user data may be conveyed. This field is not valid in Class 0.

DR and DC. Figures 6.8a and 6.8b illustrate the Disconnect Request (DR) and Disconnect Confirm (DC) TPDUs. Either end of a T-connection can send a DR whenever it desires to release the T-connection. The correct response from the far end is DC. However, if a DR is received as a response (both ends decide to clear the T-connection at once), the effect is the same and the connection is released. As discussed above, a DR may be sent to clear a connection which has not been fully established (no CC yet sent). Such a DR requires no DC response.

In Class 0, there is no need to perform the DR/DC sequence; clearing

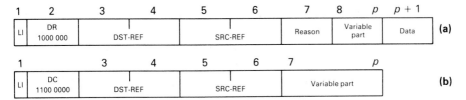

Fig. 6.8a   DR TPDU.

Fig. 6.8b   DC TPDU.

the network-connection automatically clears the T-connection. By contrast, in Classes 1 and 3 an explicit procedure exists for re-establishing a failed N-connection used by the T-connection, followed by a resynchronizing procedure.

The DR TPDU octet 7 contains the reasons for disconnection, e.g. normal disconnection because the higher level session has ended; protocol error; congestion (no buffer space), etc. In the variable part of the header a parameter, whose value conveys additional information about the clearing of the T-connection, may be placed. The DC TPDU is self-explanatory.

DT and ED. Figures 6.9a, 6.9b, 6.9c illustrate the formats for Data (DT) TPDUs and 6.9d, 6.9e for Expedited Data (ED) TPDUs.

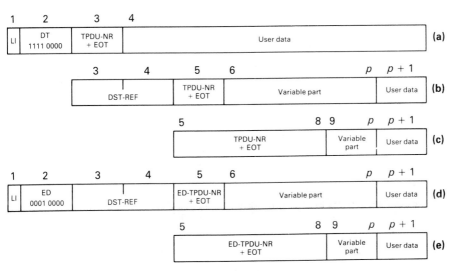

Fig. 6.9   DT and ED TPDUs.

For Classes 0 and 1 (Fig. 6.9a) the fixed part of the DT header is only two octets (besides LI): One to identify DT; one to carry the TPDU number (TPDU-NR), which is essentially a sequence number incremented by one each time a DT TPDU is sent. However, in Class 0 this number is not used, so it is always set to zero. The most significant bit (bit 8) of this TPDU-NR field is reserved for an 'end of TSDU' indicator, EOT. EOT signifies that this DT TPDU carries the last part of a transport *service* data unit (i.e. a unit of data given to the transport service by a higher layer), which was segmented into several TPDUs.

For Classes 2, 3 and 4, where multiplexing may apply, octets 3 and 4 carry the DST-REF of the T-connection, and the TPDU-NR is in octet 5 (Fig. 6.9b). For Class 4, there may also be a variable part in the header, used to hold the checksum.

There also exists an extended numbering scheme for Classes 2, 3 and 4; in which TPDU-NR is not restricted to 7 bits (cyclic), but uses 31 bits of octets 5, 6, 7 and 8 (Fig. 6.9c). This is suitable for connections with long loop delays, such as satellite channels.

The purpose of the TPDU-NR is to enable flow control, recovery from error conditions and resequencing of DT TPDUs (Class 4) to take place. Flow control uses a 'window mechanism'. A sender may transmit DT TPDUs with increasing TPDU-NRs subject to the constraint

Lower window-edge $\leq$ TPDU-NR $<$ Lower window-edge+CDT (Modulo

where $N = 2^7$, or 2^{31} for the extended numbering scheme.

The value of the lower window-edge is that of YR-TU-NR as received in AK and RJ TPDUs, see below.

The ED TPDUs (Figs 6.9d, 6.9e) are not subject to the window flow-control mechanism. However only one may be sent at a time; i.e. until it has been explicitly acknowledged by the remote peer entity no further ED may be sent. ED TPDUs carry an ED-TPDU-NR for acknowledgement and error recovery purposes and both the normal and extended numbering schemes are permitted. The variable part of the header can carry the checksum, in Class 4 only.

AK, EA and RJ. The AK TPDU, illustrated in Figs 6.10a (normal numbering) and 6.10b (extended numbering) is a positive confirmation sent from a receiver of DT TPDUs. (Obviously, both ends of a T-connection can be simultaneously senders and receivers of DT TPDUs). As previously mentioned, the YR-TU-NR field in AK becomes the

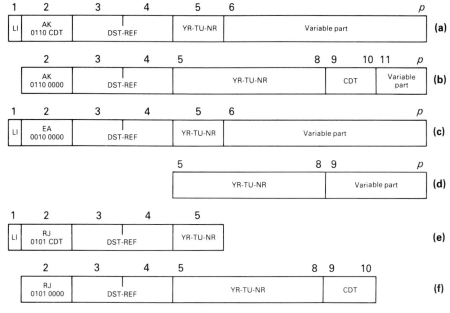

Fig. 6.10 AK, EA and RJ TPDUs.

remote DT-sender's lower window-edge: All previously sent DTs, with TPDU-NRs less than this YR-TU-NR, are explicitly acknowledged by receipt of the AK. The CDT, for the remote sender, is carried in the lower half of octet 2 (normal numbering) or in octets 9 and 10 (extended numbering).

The flow control procedures are more complex than indicated. For example, a receiver of DT TPDUs may *withdraw* credit, or send CDT = 0; provision is made for handling duplicate DTs and AKs, etc. In particular, in Class 4, a series of timers are defined for handling the situation when either end of a T-connection fails to respond; and additional sequencing and flow control information are carried in the variable part of the AK TPDU.

The EA TPDU is self-explanatory (see Figs 6.10c,d). It acknowledges received ED TPDUs.

The RJ TPDU is used to demand retransmission of DT TPDUs, following an error (in particular, a signalled network error such as an X.25 Reset) beginning at the lower window-edge specified by YR-TU-NR (see Figs 6.10e,f).

ER and PI. The main purpose of the ER TPDU (Fig. 6.11) is to reject

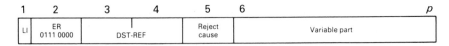

Fig. 6.11   ER TPDU.

invalid connection requests and invalid TP DUs in general. The cause
of rejection is placed in octet 5.

The PI TPDU, Fig. 6.12, is sent by the initiator of a *network* connection to state what Transport Protocol he intends to use. The PI can be
sent with the network connection request (e.g. in the Call User Data
Field of an X.25 call request packet), or it can be sent as data following
the establishment of the network connection. The PRT-ID field identifies
the transport protocol and the value 0000 0001 specifies the protocol
discussed here. The SHARE field handles the possible sharing of the
N-connection by *different* transport protocols, and the variable part
specifies the corresponding details—if sharing is possible.

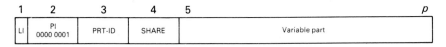

Fig. 6.12   PI TPDU.

6.2.2.1 *Some Comments on the Transport Layer*

The X.214 and X.224 transport layer has been discussed at some length
because it is reasonably well defined and is important, being the first
end-to-end layer on which all other end-to-end layers are built. Some
further comments on it are appropriate.

The natural question arises: Which class(es) and options of the transport layer should a user support, i.e. have implemented or installed as
a software module, on his computers attached to networks?

As discussed, the distinct classes aim to address networks of different
'reliability'. In practice, most of the world's public networks are based
on X.25, and since OSI protocols are aimed at public or 'open' systems,
the question essentially becomes: what classes and options in the T-layer
should be used with an X.25 N-layer?

The immediate answer is that, since X.25 provides a low residual
error rate, but nevertheless can produce signalled N-layer errors such

as reset, the indicated class is Class 1 (Basic Error Recovery). There should be no need for multiplexing at the T-layer since multiplexing at the N-layer is possible. A computer which wishes to have several *simultaneous* calls, to the same physical destination DTE, can do so by establishing parallel X.25 connections, with one T-connection per X.25 connection. In most networks, where volume charges predominate, the impact on cost of having several, instead of only one, X.25 call is negligible; it may even be cheaper, since the overheads in the transport protocol header are less in Class 1.

But the argument in favour of Class 1 is not quite so simple. Class 1 has no multiplexing and therefore no flow control. X.25, however, does have a flow mechanism; is it sufficient?

The X.25 flow control (see Chapter 3) consists of controlling the flow of packets out of the network into a receiving DTE, thus building up a queue of packets in the network. This queue can stretch back to control the flow of packets out of the sending DTE into the network. In principle, a receiver who restricts the incoming flow from an X.25 network effectively performs end-to-end flow control—albeit with a queue of unknown size within the network. Moreover, if the D-bit is supported, X.25 flow control can be turned into proper end-to-end flow control. The real question is then: When does the X.25 Network entity within the receiving DTE send 'credit' (or window-edge updates) to the network, and hence to the remote transmitter?

The answer usually is: As soon as it has found a buffer in which to place the contents of a received data packet, a TPDU. See Fig. 6.13.

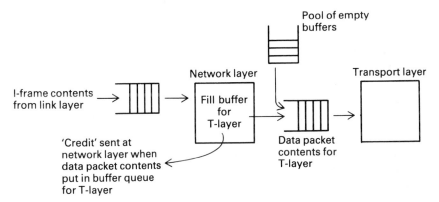

Fig. 6.13 A flow control problem: T-layer does not control N-layer flow control mechanism.

In effect, the higher transport layer has no control over the rate at which the network service delivers TPDUs to it. Without a *local* flow control mechanism on the service interface between layers of the OSI model in the same computer, the flow control provided by a lower layer is outside the control of a higher layer user.

Only in the case of Class 1 does the transport protocol definition attempt to address this problem, by allowing one of two options for confirmation of receipt to be selected, using a parameter in the variable part of the CR TPDU. These options refer to the retention of TPDUs at the remote end for possible retransmission. As an alternative to the normal AK mechanism, which carries the YR-TU-NR for acknowledgement but no CDT (CDT is set = 1111) in Class 1, the user can employ a N(network)-Data Acknowledge primitive on the interface to the N-layer, which should result in an acknowledgement of receipt *at the network layer* being sent to the remote sender. In the case of X.25 this would presumably be done using the D-bit mechanism, and the effect would (probably) be to update the remote N-layer's window edge; thereby giving the receiving T-layer entity a somewhat indirect control over flow towards it at the N-layer. But these N-Data acknowledgements primitives are in response to received N-data (although no numbering scheme exists to correlate them), which implies a 'synchronous' interface (such as a subroutine call mechanism) between T- and N-layers at the receiver, rather than a buffered interface.

A similar comment applies to the session layer interface to the transport layer. If a buffered interface exists between these layers (as would be normal) then the session layer has no control over the transport layer's flow control mechanism. The transport layer can continue to give credit to its remote peer entity until it has run out of buffers in which to put session layer data units.

The peer-to-peer flow control mechanisms of OSI, and the almost complete absence of flow control mechanisms on local service interfaces, can result in huge queues building up, both in the network and between layers in the computer.

To remedy this defect either (as is frequently done) the implementor invents flow control primitives for the inter-layer interfaces, which are used by higher layer receivers; or buffered inter-layer interfaces are not used. For example, if the network layer is, as it were, a series of sub-routines called by the transport layer, then the act of reading a TPDU from the network layer may be taken as authorizing the sending of a window-edge update to the far end. In turn the transport layer could be a set of subroutines used by the session layer. The reader will readily appreciate that such structures could become very confused.

A third approach to the flow control problem is to pre-allocate strictly limited numbers of buffers to well-defined and limited areas of use. Flow control will be exercised when buffers allocated to that particular area become scarce. There is no fear that system-wide buffers will be consumed by the hundred.

The above discussion serves to point out that, with regard to flow control, before making a decision as to whether Class 1 or Class 3 (probably without multiplexing but with flow control—i.e. a single T-connection) be used over an X.25 network, the local internal software structure should be examined. With an adequate software structure for local internal flow control, Class 1 is sufficient. With a poor structure Class 3 is insufficient since the application cannot use the flow control mechanisms it provides. (The structure should also enable the parallel operation of multiplexed N- or T-connections.)

A final comment on buffering problems may be made with regard to resequencing of DT TPDUs in Class 4. If there are N simultaneous T-connections, and each can give credit up to C, then the number of buffers available for holding received DT TPDUs for resequencing must exceed $N(C-1)$. This is because out-of-sequence TPDUs may not be delivered to the session layer, and if C are sent the last $(C-1)$ could arrive before the first (Fig. 6.14). If this happens on all T-connections, and there are only $N(C-1)$ buffers available, then the classic deadly embrace problem has arisen. No buffers may be released until another TPDU arrives; no TPDU can arrive until a buffer is released. There

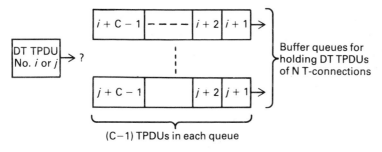

Fig. 6.14 The 'deadly embrace': there is no space to receive DT TPDU no. i or j, but space can not be created until it is received.

are other means of avoiding this problem, apart from supplying more than $N(C\text{-}1)$ buffers [4].

With regard to options to be used with the transport layer over an X.25 network, probably only one is of importance: the maximum TPDU size. The default value is 128 octets which, although it fits in a packet, is probably far too small in most applications. An implementation should be capable of supporting at least up to 2048-octet TPDUs, even if all users do not need it.

In the specific case of Class 1, used over X.25, the use of the expedited data service would appear to be unnecessary; while the choice between AK and N-data acknowledgement for remote acknowledgement is subject to the rather complex, but nonetheless important, considerations reviewed above.

6.2.3 The Session Layer

The CCITT session layer service is described in X.215 and the protocol in X.225 [2].

The Session Service may be summarized in terms of various components of that service, as follows

(i) Session connection, including identification of the session and negotiation of parameters.

(ii) Data transfer. Four data transfer services are identified—Normal, Expedited, Typed and Capability. Normal data transfer is flow controlled and subject to a 'right-to-transmit token', e.g. for a half-duplex conversation. Mechanisms exist for transferring this token from one end of the session to the other. Expedited data transfer is not subject to these constraints. Typed data transfer is subject to flow control, but not the token. Capability data exchange allows exchange of data without the 'Activity' structure, see point (vi) below.

(iii) Token management, including Give Token, Please Token and Give Control (which gives all, rather than just a specific token to the remote session entity).

(iv) Synchronization and Resynchronization. Three services exist: Minor synchronization allowing synchronization points or markers to be introduced into the session data stream for the purposes of recovery; Major synchronization, or the introduction of complete breaks in the data exchange between one conversation ('dialogue unit') and the next;

Resynchronization, or the ability to restart communication at an agreed synchronization point.

(v) Error reporting, including from the service to the user and vice versa.

(vi) Activity support. An activity is a logical piece of work, which may span several sessions; or conversely, several serial (not parallel) activities may exist in a single session. An activity could be, for example, a search of a data base by a user. There are five activity services: Start, Interrupt, Resume, Discard (i.e. Abort) and End (normally).

(vii) Session release, including orderly release, and session user or session provider initiated abort.

The session service is regarded as being composed of 'functional units' or logical groupings of the above services, since they are not all necessarily supported on any given equipment or occasion. For example the 'Kernel' functional unit supports session connection ((i) above), normal data transfer (the first of (ii)), and the three session release services (vii); the 'half-duplex' functional unit handles Give and Please for tokens; the activity management unit supports all the token management (iii) and activity (vi) services.

On session establishment, the appropriate functional units are selected. (Predefined groupings of functional units called 'subsets' also exist, essentially as guides for implementation.) Also on session establishment parameters allow references to be allocated to the S-connection. These references are up to 64 octets in length, so that text references are envisaged. Further parameters permit the initial assignments of tokens and synchronization point serial numbers to be made, and (hopefully) quality of service features to be agreed.

The protocol itself (X.225) maps the session service primitives such as S-connect (plus parameters), S-data, S-token-please, S-sync-major, S-activity-start on to Session Protocol Data Units (SPDUs)—respectively Connect SPDU, Data Transfer SPDU, Please Tokens SPDU, Major Sync Point SPDU, Activity Start SPDU, for those listed above. The SPDUs are carried in Transport Protocol DT-TPDUs. There is only *one* session allowed per T-connection; there is no multiplexing.

There are rules about segmenting an SPDU into several TPDUs, or concatenating several SPDUs into one TPDU. (Strictly speaking we should talk of Transport *Service* Data Units, TSDUs, but it is sometimes helpful to envisage blocks of data and commands on the actual communication channels.)

The format for an SPDU is illustrated in Fig. 6.15. The one octet SI field identifies the type of the SPDU. The LI field, 1 or 3 octets in length, specifies the size in octets of the following parameter field, (0 to 254) or (255 to 65 535) respectively. The parameter field contains either Parameter Group Identifier (PGI) units or Parameter Identifier (PI) units. A PI unit consists of three items: the PI itself, an LI specifying the length of the parameter value (PV) and the PV itself. A PGI unit consists of the PGI itself, a length indicator and one or more contained PI units. (The existence of PGIs is to ensure compatibility with the telematic protocol T.62 [3], see Section 6.4.) The user information field is for user data.

| SI | LI | Parameter field | User information field |

Fig. 6.15   General SPDU structure.

Some thirty-four(!) SPDU types are defined and it would be tedious to discuss them when they can be studied directly in the X.225 Recommendation. X.225 also, of course, specifies the procedures for their use: When and how is an SPDU generated? What is done on its reception?, etc. State tables are used to define the procedures, which are far from self-explanatory. One of the objectives in this state-machine approach to defining the protocol is that it should be more susceptible to mechanized proofs of correctness. Nevertheless, only time will show how correct, and useful, such relatively complex procedures are.

6.3 VIRTUAL TERMINALS AND FILE TRANSFERS

The discussion in this and earlier chapters of layers 1 to 5 of the OSI/RM has been based on 'standard' services and protocols, with particular reference to CCITT standards, although similar ISO, ECMA and other standards exist of varying degrees of compatibility.

For layers 6 and 7, presentation and application, a slightly different approach is adopted, partly because standards are not so well defined or accepted and partly to alleviate the monotony of detail and to give a wider vision of the scope of the OSI idea.

6.3.1 Virtual Terminals

The presentation layer is concerned with the syntax or format of application data exchanged during sessions. In many cases the layer is unnecessary, since it is known in advance that all application data are in the form of ASCII character strings, for example. However, when one application entity is a human user, then the presentation layer has a very practical task: Ensuring that the syntax is adequate for formatting the data on the device employed by the user; be it printer, VDU screen or graphics terminal.

As an example, consider a typical commercial application such as order entry, in which a user is presented with a formatted screen complete with protected prompts (which he cannot overwrite) and fields into which he can directly enter data such as the identification of the ordered item, the number ordered, cost, purchase identification, discount applicable, etc. The remote computer handling the application must be able to create the screen, including the prompts with their attributes such as 'protected', 'high-lighted' (e.g. blinking or reverse video); and recognize the user input to each entrable field, including checking the correct length and format (e.g. only alpha, or alphanumeric) of the contents. Agreement is required on commands to say input is complete, to request a new screen of the same or a different type, etc.

In general each manufacturer of VDUs having this 'page-mode' capability, in which a page of prompts is presented as a unit on the screen and the user can enter data into fields at will (and in principle in any sequence, although there will normally be a natural sequence for entry), will have specified special control characters for moving the cursor, protecting a field, tabulating to the next one, etc. These special characters will not be identical between one manufacturer's VDU and another's.

If the communication medium between such VDUs and the host computers is a data network, and the OSI ideal is accepted, then every VDU should be capable of being used with every computer. But if there are M types of computers and N types of VDUs, each computer will require N distinct software modules to handle the distinct VDUs, making NM software modules in all. In such a set-up a basic task of the presentation layer would be to identify the type of VDU at the earliest opportunity to a host, so that the host could bring into play the appropriate software module.

A more attractive approach is to define a standard or 'virtual' terminal (VT) for which only M software modules would exist (one per host computer type), and which the host then drives with the appropriate commands of the protocol for this VT. Such a protocol is called a Virtual Terminal Protocol or VTP. *Real* terminals would then either be fully compatible with this VTP or would map the VTP commands and responses to or from those used by the terminal hardware itself. There could be up to N mappings required in the (assumed programmable) terminals, but $(M+N)$ software modules is still less than MN. The idea is illustrated in Fig. 6.16.

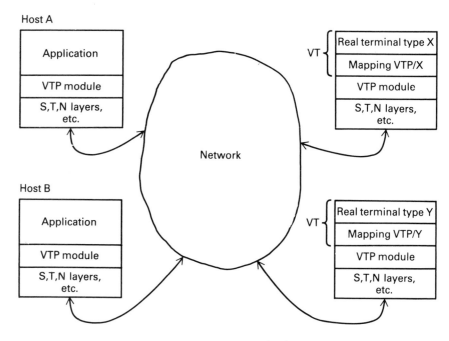

Fig. 6.16 The virtual terminal (VT) concept.

The VTP concept first arose in the context of early packet-switching projects such as EIN [5], Cyclades [6] and Euronet [7], the international European network for information retrieval from bibliographic data bases. We shall use such VTPs as a basis for discussion, since, although dated, they provide as good an example of the concept as any other. The VT itself is to be considered as composed of
(i) A presentation device (e.g. a screen).

(ii) A keyboard.

(iii) A control unit in which the VTP software runs; and in which also exists all the software necessary to provide an adequate session service to the VTP for communication with the remote host.

(iv) Possible ancillary devices such as a hard-copy printer or diskette, which are not further considered here.

In a typical VTP (e.g. that used on the Danish Centernet [8] packet-switched network) four types of protocol primitives are supported

(1) Interrupts, carried by some form of lower layer expedited service, and used to clear the screen, resynchronize the presentation dialogue, etc.

(2) Text-blocks which carry formatted text in either direction.

(3) Control-blocks, used to control ancillary devices, etc.

(4) Parameter negotiation commands, used to agree on the terminal's mode of operation and characteristic, at the start of a session.

The last three primitive types are carried in VTP blocks, illustrated in Fig. 6.17, whose block code header indicates the type and whose body carries the text, control or parameter items.

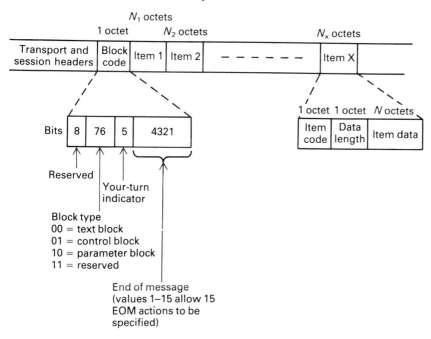

Fig. 6.17 An example (Centernet) of a VTP block structure.

The VTP proceeds through various phases during the session. Initially, agreement must be reached between host and terminal as to how the terminal is to be driven. A physical terminal could, for example, be capable of operating in three modes: ordinary scroll-mode, i.e. X.28 compatible; its own native mode as designed by its manufacturer, so that it must be driven from the remote host by specific manufacturer-dependent commands; or VT page mode, using the VTP to the remote host, with appropriate internal mapping of VTP commands to native commands. The host may be capable of supporting all or none of these modes, so the first phase involves one party proposing a mode and the other accepting it, or proposing an alternative mode, or rejecting communication, etc., using the parameter negotiation primitives.

Suppose it has been agreed that the VT page mode will be used, then the next phase requires agreement on the terminal's physical characteristics. How many rows and columns fit on the screen? Are double-height characters supported? What attributes are available for characterizing fields on the screen; e.g. high intensity or reverse video, non-entrable or protected, entrable but without echo, etc?

Once the host has determined these characteristics (which it will presumably use to format its application output—although this clearly implies a more sensitive application than would typically exist) the user dialogue can begin. Generally this is half-duplex, question and answer, but the user will always be given an attention or similar interrupt facility to allow him to get the attention of the host at any time, irrespective of the current state of the dialogue. (This sort of dialogue control properly belongs to the session layer, but the older VTPs which were used without a proper session layer incorporated their own dialogue control.)

Text transfers take place to or from the 'data structure' in the VT. This is illustrated in Fig. 6.18 and represents a screen divided into fields, each field being preceded by an attribute characterizing the field, and which in principle occupies a character position—as is physically the case in many terminals. (If an attribute, such as 'protected', does not occupy a physical screen position it may be positioned on top of the last character of the preceding field.) A pointer or cursor is maintained for the data structure, indicating the location into which the next character will be written. It is advanced each time a character is written, and can be moved explicitly to a different place on the screen using X-Y addressing. The text primitives, or items which may be carried in a text block are, for example

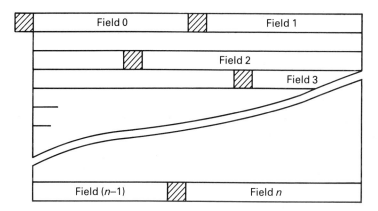

Fig. 6.18   A possible screen layout for a VT. ▨ indicates that an attribute has been associated with the character position.

(i) Text segment, a string of characters.

(ii) New line, a command to move the cursor to the start of the next line.

(iii) Carriage return.

(iv) Position, a command to move the cursor to the specified X-Y co-ordinate position.

(v) Next unprotected field, a command to move the cursor to the start of the next unprotected (i.e. user-entrable) field.

(vi) Attribute, a command from the host to define an attribute applying to the current cursor position, and the following character positions up to the next attribute (or the end of the structure).

(vii) Hide, a command from the host to make the VT hide (i.e. not echo) the next input from the keyboard, such as a password.

(viii) Delete attribute, delete that attribute applying to the current cursor position.

(ix) Erase (all) unprotected fields, used by the application to permit new entries to be made by the user.

(x) Delete all. Fully clears the data structure of characters and attributes.

In page mode operation the host application starts the half-duplex dialogue by sending a formatted screen, using the appropriate text primitives, to the VT; and giving the turn-to-speak to the user at the terminal. Using the keyboard and local editing facilities, which are outside the scope of the VTP, the user can fill the unprotected fields of the data structure as he wishes—the entries appearing on the screen as they are made. When the user wishes to send the entered data to the host he depresses a 'transmit' key, and the unprotected fields are sent to the host in the format:

⟨Text Block Code⟩ ⟨Next U-Field item⟩
⟨Text Segment Item⟩ . . ⟨Next U field item⟩
⟨Text segment item⟩

All unprotected fields are sent, empty or not, but empty fields are identified by having special null characters in them. The ⟨Next U-Field Item⟩ is in effect an identifier of and a delimiter between logical text segments, rather than a mover of the cursor, in this instance. A more refined arrangement could be envisaged in which a subset of all entrable fields is sent, either explicitly selected by the user or perhaps only those which have been accessed by him. This would speed response and save money on, for example, public packet-switched networks.

The VT and VTP approach illustrates a particular aspect of the presentation layer, where it is used to address the formatting conventions of input/output devices such as a VDU or a printer. In direct computer-to-computer communication there is often hardly any need for a presentation layer below the application, but the application may have formatting requirements within it. For example, the so-called telematic services, which handle the exchange of text, facsimile or other types of electronic documents (see Section 6.4), may be viewed as document-handling applications at Layer 7. On top of, and within, those applications formatting procedures are obeyed. Thus there is some confusion as to the scope and exact location of the presentation layer.

6.3.2 File transfers

Perhaps the most typical of end-to-end applications is that of the transfer of files between two DTEs, across a network. This is clearly an application layer function, concerned as it is with considerations such as filenames; access rights to files; creation, deletion, replacement of or extension to existing files, etc. Nevertheless, file transfers also have an anomalous position with regard to the presentation layer, as discussed at the end of Section 6.3.1. For example, a major concern in any file transfer could be the definition and preservation of the file's record structure (which has many similarities with the fields of the VT's data structure). Is the support of a file's record structure a presentation layer function, and if so why is the presentation layer below the application in the OSI/RM? Suitable casuistry may, no doubt, answer this question, but there are clearly grounds for wondering whether the OSI/RM is correct in its identification of Layers 6 and 7.

One of the most long-established and widely accepted File Transfer Protocols (FTPs) is the 'Blue book' of the UK's Joint Network Team; although newer procedures such as ISO's File Transfer Access Method (FTAM) are now available. In a sense, given adequate lower layer services, the data transfer portion of an FTP is non-existent—i.e. the FTP need provide no facilities over and above those given to it by the lower layer services. For example, the Blue book FTP is structured into three levels

(1) Level 0. The procedures for starting and stopping file transfers.
(2) Level 1. The procedures for synchronizing the file transfer, including acknowledgements, temporary halts, etc; and the procedures for selecting previously agreed data formats (e.g. ASCII or binary) for subsequent Level 2 traffic.
(3) Level 2. The procedures for transferring the data of the file.

All file data are divided into records (of significance only to the users), which are in turn divided into subrecords by FTP. Each subrecord, of maximum length 63 octets, has a subrecord header of one octet (see Fig. 6.19), which either specifies the length of the subrecord explicitly, or provides a compression mechanism using a repetition count applicable to the next data character. Level 1 commands are always of two octets in length, and are introduced by an all-zero subrecord header, see Fig. 6.20.

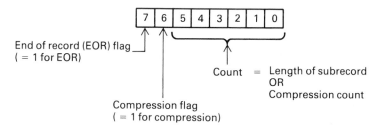

Fig. 6.19   A 'Blue book' FTP sub-record header.

Thus the Level 1 procedures and the subrecord structure of the Blue book may be considered to provide functions more properly provided by the session (synchronization) and presentation (format identification,

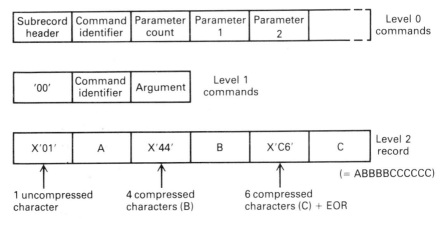

Fig. 6.20 'Blue book' FTP command formats.

compression) layers. One could imagine the file transfer application simply delivering and receiving data records to or from the lower layer services using basic primitives; so that the FTP would be reduced to the end-to-end Level 0 commands, which are concerned with specifying the file(s) to be transferred, and the access procedures to be used. Hence the name FT 'Access Method' or FTAM.

The Level 0 commands of the Blue book FTP are only six in number, although with some of the commands a wide range of parameters may be used. FTP distinguishes the File Transfer Initiator (P) from the Responder (Q). The initiator is not necessarily the Sender (S), but can also be the Receiver (R) of the transfer. Thus a station can be in one of four states (PS, PR, QS, QR). The sequence of FTP Level 0 commands is shown in Fig. 6.21 for these states. The six commands are

(1) SFT (Start File Transfer). Sent by P to propose the transfer. The parameters which can be used with this command include

(i) Mode of access for the transfer (e.g. make a new file, append to old file, replace an old file, read, read and remove, etc. plus various values for the parameter specifically designed for handling job input and output).

(ii) Code specifier (e.g. ASCII, Binary, EBCDIC).

(iii) Format effector (the value of this parameter can be used to indicate that each record represents a new line for printing, or that the first character of each record is a Fortran format code, etc.).

(iv) Binary mapping (defines how binary codes, if used, are mapped onto the octet-based data stream).

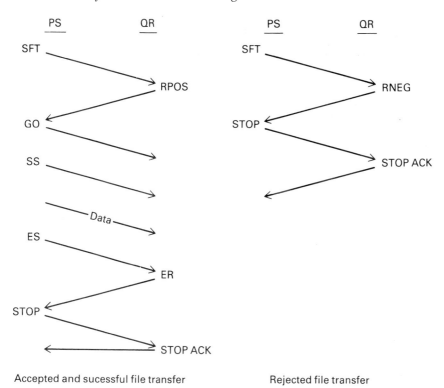

Fig. 6.21 'Blue book' FTP command exchanges.

(v) Maximum record size.
(vi) Facilities (e.g. compression allowed, restarts permitted within this transfer).
(vii) Filename.
(viii) Username, identifying the file's owner.
(ix) User password, for the owner's directory.
(x) File password, or key to access the particular file.
(xi) Account number, to be charged for the transfer.
(xii) Account password.
(xiii) File Size (to reserve storage at R).
(xiv) Operator Message (The value of this parameter is a text message conveyed to the remote operator.)
(2) RPOS Reply Positively to SFT, agreeing that the transfer will take place. RPOS can also carry parameters, with values different from those

proposed in SFT. For example Q might accept all P's suggestions for parameter values except the use of compression, in the facilities.

(3) GOP. Sends the GO command, if it agrees with Q's RPOS.

(4) RNEG. If Q cannot accept P's proposed transfer it sends Reply Negatively, with parameters defining the reasons for non-acceptance.

(5) STOP. Sent by P to stop the transfer: When it is complete; In response to Q's RNEG; In response to Q's RPOS if parameter values are unacceptable; Or when the transfer has been aborted using Level 1 commands.

(6) STOPACK. Q's acknowledgement to P's STOP. It is usually desirable to have explicit confirmation of the termination of any protocol session.

In Fig. 6.22 the course of a typical successful file transfer using the Blue book FTPB is indicated. Level 1 commands Start-Sender (SS), End-Sender (ES) and End-Receiver (ER) are also shown with the Level 0 commands. The figures represent delays in seconds as measured at one end of the transfer between sending a command and receiving the response to it. They were acquired over a link incorporating three concatenated packet-switched networks between Ireland and Denmark, in

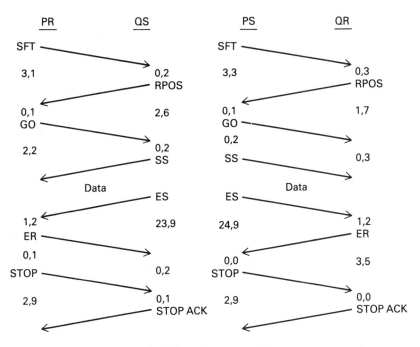

Fig. 6.22 'Blue book' FTP performance (delays are in seconds).

which the slowest link was 2400 bps [10]. It is worth noting how relatively long the time intervals are, and how great is the combined buffering capacity of the software and of the network—as seen by the time interval between sending ES and receiving the ER reply.

With the 2400 bps limitation, 300 characters per second is nominally attainable. However, taking into account the overheads involved with all the headers of the various layers, and competition for channel capacity by acknowledgement traffic at lower layers (e.g. a T-layer ACK requires an N-layer RR in the reverse direction), the theoretical maximum throughput was calculated to be 254 characters per second. The maximum throughput ever achieved was less than 90% of this, or about 75% of the nominal throughput.

In this particular case, it was also calculated that there was an 18% increase in the volume charge over the (public) packet-switched network, due to the use of protocols above the N-layer, i.e. above X.25.

These figures for overheads are modest. The transport and session layers used in this FTP test were not ISO or CCITT standards, and were relatively compact. Using internationally agreed standards, it is to be feared that overheads in cost and decrease in nominal throughput are likely to be worse than the 20 to 25% found here. Additionally, no reckoning of the overheads associated with the FT, session and T-connection establishment and clearing phases has been made. These overheads are undoubtedly significant, particularly if the transfer is a short one.

6.4 TELEMATIC AND MESSAGE HANDLING SERVICES

In our discussion of the OSI Reference Model it should be abundantly clear why the international standardization of protocols, which will provide the services pertaining to the different layers of the model, is necessary. If networking is to be 'open', then users of networks must be compatible with each other end-to-end, and the necessary standardization to achieve this is obviously an important topic for the International Standards Organisation, ISO. The lower layer problem of providing standards for interfacing to (and between) networks is also clearly a topic of interest to CCITT, which essentially represents network operators.

But it has been seen that, in the X.200 Series of Recommendations, CCITT has also concerned itself with end-to-end standardization. Why?

Is this not an area of concern only to users and to ISO?

The reason for CCITT's concern with end-to-end protocols, is that network operators are planning, and in some cases already provide, a range of *application* services supported on specialized terminals attached to the network, or on computers within the network. These application services require end-to-end protocols—hence Recommendations X.200. Thus CCITT does not concern itself only with infrastructure, but also produces recommendations and standards for end-user services. Two important classes of such services are the Telematic and the Message Handling Services.

6.4.1 Telematic Services [11]

The term 'telematic' does not have a universally accepted meaning, but when employed by CCITT a 'telematic service' is a service for the direct exchange of text between users. 'Text' means information presented on a page to be read, and includes both ordinary characters, coded as such, and 'photographic' data, coded using facsimile procedures. A telematic service is usually considered to include a user-machine, such as a facsimile transceiver or a Teletex terminal. Thus a telematic service is an application, based on specific user-machines, for the point-to-point exchange of text over a variety of networks, using the supporting services provided by lower layers of the OSI model.

Teletex, Videotex and Facsimile services are telematic services. Message handling services (MHS), although closely related, are not classed as telematic services; because an MHS is a service for switching, holding and delivering messages in electronic form, which specifies how users may connect to it, but does not define or include standard user-machines.

6.4.1.1 The Teletex Service [11], [3]

The Teletex service may be viewed as upgraded Telex at 2400 bps. Teletex terminals are equipped with memories (e.g. diskettes, between which the text transfers take place); an extensive graphic character set, supporting capital and small Latin letters, and a wide range of diacritical marks (accents, cedillas, umlauts, etc.); characters for format control, such as 'backspace', including the support of subscripts and superscripts; a keyboard for the generation of text and commands; a printer with facilities for handling pages of paper, rather than continuous stationery; and a small screen for viewing the status of messages, etc.

The service is specified in CCITT Recommendation F.200 [11]. It is a page-handling service, in which the basic unit of transmission is a page of a document, within which the text is laid out using the format effectors. It is possible to select from different options for character pitch and vertical spacing at the beginning of each new page. It is also possible to change from one subset (i.e. standard or national selection) of the graphic characters to another at any time. Recommendation T.60 defines a Teletex terminal, and T.61 defines the character set [3].

The Teletex service is available in various countries, and is familiar to many, so it will not be described further here. However, in the context of the OSI Reference Model, it is worth looking at the network aspects of Teletex briefly.

Teletex uses 'control procedures' specified in Recommendation T.62 [3], which may be considered equivalent to the session layer. The extent of the compatibility between T.62 and X.215 and X.225 is, however, uncertain. Teletex also uses a transport layer protocol, T.70 [3], with which Class 0 of X.224 is intended to be fully compatible. Thus the Teletex service is an application with a well-defined presentation layer, in terms of character sets and format effectors, even if there are no conversion facilities and almost no negotiation is supported. It also has its session and transport layers (Fig. 6.23).

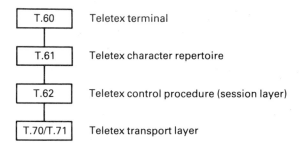

Fig. 6.23 Relationships between Teletex standards.

At the network level, Teletex is supposed to be able to work over a variety of networks—telephone, circuit-switched data and packet-switched data. A coherent numbering system is needed so that one

Teletex terminal on one network may be contacted from any Teletex terminals on other networks. The interfacing between networks is in principle not complex, and once a call is established data transfer is transparent. However, since different networks offer different Grades of Service, this use of Teletex over mixed networks is not altogether straightforward. For example, if half the circuit used by a Teletex call is provided by the telephone network, and the other half by a PSDN, the user will experience telephone circuit, not PSDN, residual error rates. (An interim T.71 Recommendation [3], based on HDLC, exists to tackle this problem when Teletex calls are entirely on the telephone network.)

Teletex is also designed to be capable of interworking with Telex. That is, a Telex and a Teletex terminal can communicate (using restricted Teletex facilities over a suitable interconnecting channel, at 50 bps).

In practice Teletex, though well-established, is not as widely used as was originally foreseen. Part of the reason for this is the networking problem discussed (On what networks, with what numbering scheme, shall we support Teletex?); part is due to the fact that Teletex has been overtaken by MHS.

6.4.1.2 Videotex

Videotex is another telematic service. It is also familiar to the general public in various forms both public, e.g. Prestel or Bildschirmtext, and private. Basic Videotex services are based on the telephone network using low speed (e.g. 1200 bps) modems; and cheap user terminals, consisting of a rudimentary keyboard plus controller for user input, and a domestic television monitor for output. From such a terminal the user can access Videotex data bases across the network, and perform searches for semi-permanent or transient information, such as airline flight time-tables or stock exchange prices (Fig. 6.24). The Videotex service is described in CCITT Recommendation F.300 [11].

Besides support of a character set based on the Latin alphabet the service permits the display of pictorial information, both in black-and-white and colour. Pictures may be made up from basic 2×3 dot matrices; by drawing lines, arcs, rectangles, etc.; by downloading a dot-matrix definition of a character set to the terminal at the start of a call, and invoking it during output to the screen when required; or by simply treating the screen as made up of areas of pixels (as in facsimile). Output

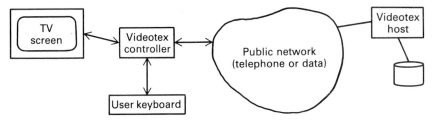

Fig. 6.24 The Videotex system.

to the screen is a page at a time, under user control. A simple menu-driven search procedure allows users to select pages. In addition to the information retrieval service of Videotex, many Videotex hosts support conventional electronic mailboxes for subscribers, so that one subscriber may create a text message and send it to a second subscriber's mailbox file—whence it may be read later by the second subscriber.

From the OSI/RM viewpoint, Videotex is an application with a presentation layer defining character sets and pictorial modes, and procedures for selecting them. The session and transport layers are subsumed into the network layer, which in the case of the telephone network is susceptible to errors. However, if a packet-switched data network is used for interconnecting the Videotex terminal and the host, then error-free communications are possible. Videotex terminals are not X.28 compatible, being page-mode rather than scroll-mode. Nevertheless, with suitable minor adjustments and judicious X.3 parameter settings, the Videotex service can indeed operate over a PSDN.

6.4.1.3 *Facsimile Services (Telefax)* [11], [3]

Facsimile transmission consists in sending picture elements, 'pixels', obtained from scanning a document along a series of parallel lines, for reproduction by a synchronized printer at the remote receiver. Typical scan resolutions are 8 or 12 samples per mm; and normally a single bit represents a pixel: 1 = Black, 0 = White. However, various shades of grey, and also colour, can be supported by allocating more bits per pixel. Groups 1 and 2 facsimile services directly encode pixels in analogue form for transmission over voice-grade circuits. Group 3 facsimile performs digital encoding and compression, for use with modems (2400 bps) on the telephone network, or possibly over a data network.

Facsimile can clearly handle characters, graphs, or pictures indiscriminately and is particularly suited to the transmission, in electronic form, of documents containing difficult character sets such as Japanese or Chinese. However this flexibility is achieved at the cost of a huge increase in data volumes. An A4 page of text treated as coded characters might contain 4000 characters, or 32 Kbits. Coded by the facsimile technique, this could rise to 4 Mbits using only black and white and 8 pixels per mm—plus synchronizing, end-of-line, end-of-page bits and other similar overheads.

Given that many pages of documents are largely white, and have a strong vertical correlation as progressive 'slices' across the page are sampled, it is obvious that facsimile encoded documents should be amenable to compression techniques. Group 3 facsimile uses both horizontal mode compression, in which 'runs' of black or white bits are Huffman-coded using a lookup table; and vertical mode compression, in which the current line is coded with reference to the previous line. Such compression can reduce typical A4 documents to 1 Mbit or even 500 Kbits in volume, depending on the contents. But a compression procedure which results in symbols of variable lengths to represent the 'runs', and with a variable number of symbols per line, is highly susceptible to error. A bit error can cause loss of symbol synchronization. In Group 3 facsimile this problem is minimized by special resynchronizing at the end of each line, and by prohibiting vertical mode compression coding for more than two consecutive lines—thereby avoiding perpetuation of errors in the initial reference line.

The facsimile services, called Telefax, offered by the PTTs according to CCITT standards, are thus based on terminals containing a scanner, a printer, paper-handling and control functions, supporting various standard paper dimensions and scanning densities and using standardized compression and encoding techniques. For example, for Group 3 facsimile, CCITT Recommendations F.180, T.4 (the specific Group 3 apparatus and compression techniques), T.10 bis, T.21 and T.30 apply [3].

A more advanced approach to solving the problem of transmission errors is that of Group 4 facsimile (Recommendations T.5 and T.6) [3]. It is based on the use of an error-free network infrastructure, as provided by circuit-switched data networks plus LAP-B, packet-switched data networks using X.25, or the telephone network with the T.71 link-plus-transport protocol. On top of these the T.70 transport protocol (where applicable), and the T.62 'session layer' protocol, are used. Moreover, the T.73 document interchange protocol is also employed as a supplement to the basic presentation layer functions inherent in the coding and compression procedures. T.73 is discussed in the next section [3].

Using these higher layer protocols, and assuming they guarantee error-free transmission, it is possible to make the Group 4 compression more efficient than that of Group 3. Specifically, in Group 4, the restriction on the use of vertical mode compression to only two consecutive lines is removed. Moreover, there is no need to maintain a continuous bit stream across the network. The higher level protocols can recognize blocks of facsimile data, and a receiver can in principle buffer or store them, for later use in driving the printer, continuously or in bursts. Facsimile transfers can be off-line, or spooled.

6.4.1.4 *Document Architecture and T.73* [3], [12]

Anyone familiar with word-processing will understand the concept of, and the need for, a document architecture. A document may be regarded as being composed of

(i) A document profile describing the document as a whole, its identifier, title, author, characteristics (e.g. final version, not revisable), etc.

(ii) The document content, which is made up of a number of content portions consisting of 'text' in its widest sense.

(iii) A logical structure identifying sections, paragraphs, footnotes, headings, figures, etc.; and relating these elements to content portions and to each other.

(iv) A layout structure relating content portions to pages (or sets of pages), to areas within a page, to subareas within areas, etc.

Each element of the document will have appropriate 'attributes' defining its characteristics. For example, a portion of the document contents, a piece of text, could be in the Teletex T.61-coded character representation; or it could be a portion of facsimile encoded information. The attributes associated with this content portion would define the coding used by it. The attributes of a layout element could define on which page, and where within the page, it is to be located (possibly using a reducing or magnifying scale); and, if the element were to overlay another element, what the effect should be (obliterate one, the other, both or neither of the overlayed portions).

Using these types of elements and attributes arranged in some suitable order, which constitute the 'architecture', it is possible to describe a document fully. The description can be transmitted to a remote site—and then one has the central portion of a document interchange protocol. The protocol would, of course, need to be supplemented with procedures for negotiating the acceptability of certain attributes, such as paper size or the use of facsimile encoding, before transmission; and with other procedures for dealing with errors and abnormal situations.

Such a document architecture would allow the mixing of blocks of 'text' encoded in different forms, such as facsimile or Teletex, within the one page (see Fig. 6.25). Frequently small blocks of pictorial information, such as a company's 'logo', or of characters, such as a heading or a copyright notice, appear on every page of a document. The architecture should also permit the specification of these 'generic' logical or layout objects; which then may be referred to, for example within a *specific* page, to ensure that they are included, without the need for defining them each time.

Finally, the *logical* structure of a document is of little importance unless the document is likely to be revised. An architecture which defined the content portions and the layout structure of the document, but omitted the logical structure, would be quite sufficient for handling documents in their final form. However, if a document is to be revised it must permit operations such as removing a paragraph from one section and relocating it in another. This must of course be followed by a corresponding change in the layout structure, which would normally be automatic, subject to minor human adjustments.

Thus the document is composed by creating content portions and building them into a logical structure, which is edited and adjusted as required. This is then submitted to a layout procedure which allocates content portions to pages and positions within a page semi-automatically. If the result is satisfactory and final, the document profile, contents, and layout structure may be sent to a remote site for reproduction. If the result is not final, but revisable, the logical structure should also be sent to the remote site for editing and review. Indeed the layout structure might be omitted, on the assumption that if the remote site can edit the document it must be able to perform its own layout, so there is no need to send it.

The above discussion has covered topics familiar to many people, but they serve to explain the concepts behind CCITT's Document Interchange Protocol, T.73. T.73 is intended to allow the exchange of docu-

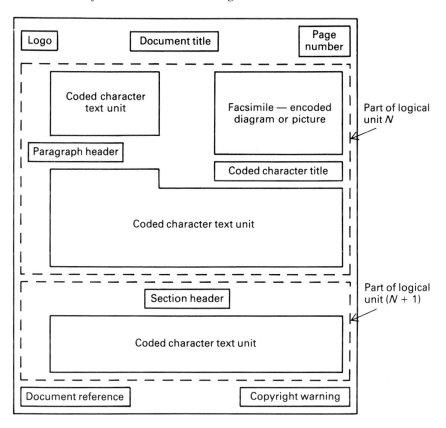

Fig. 6.25 A possible page of a document, showing different physical and logical units.

ments across a network both in their final form (i.e. contents and layout) and in processable form (i.e. also with a logical structure). However the latest (1984) version of T.73 still leaves the functions for the interchange of text in processable form 'for further study'. The 'text' included in a T.73 document may be in Teletex of facsimile coding, but these codings can refer to a sub-unit of a page called a 'block'. A given block can only have one type of coding. Blocks may be grouped into, and laid out within, frames; and frames may be laid out on a page. Blocks and frames may be overlaid.

The OSI architecture into which T.73 fits, as a presentation layer entity, is illustrated in Fig. 6.26. It uses the T.62 session layer and the

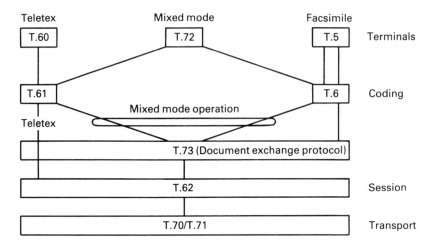

Fig. 6.26   T.73 document exchange in OSI architecture.

T.70 transport layer. It supports various types of documents: Pure Teletex (by-passing T.73); structured Teletex, in which the text units are
solely in Teletex code, but may be organized in blocks and frames *within*
a page; pure Group 4 facsimile a page at a time; structured facsimile in
blocks and frames within a page; and mixed mode Teletex and facsimile.
The negotiation as to which type of document will be used in a transfer
is done using functions provided by the T.62 session layer. More than
one document type may be handled during a session, but only one type
is invoked at a time. In the initial version of T.73 pure Group 4 facsimile,
and basic mixed-mode Teletex and facsimile, are supported using the
respective text interchange formats TIF.0 and TIF.1.

   It will be appreciated, assuming T.73-compatible terminals become
readily available, that an end-to-end inter-terminal service for the transfer of documents can be provided over any suitable underlying network
(including ISDN). Future upgrades of T.73 may be imagined, such as
the support of coloured text, or digitized voice in a document; and the
inclusion of facilities for remote editing of a document, editing being
currently a local function which is supposed to use the text's logical
structure, although the editing function itself is outside the scope of
T.73. It remains to be seen how acceptable T.73 becomes; and, in particular, whether the manufacturers of word-processors will implement
interchange protocols compatible with it, so that the number of terminals

which may use the service becomes sufficiently large to make the service attractive to the general public. It should also be noted that other 'standards' for document architectures exist [12].

6.4.2 Message Handling Services (MHS)

The telematic services of Section 6.4.1 provide direct end-to-end exchange of text, in various formats, between compatible terminals. They are based on an unintelligent network, whose only function it is to allow a channel to be established and used. The terminals remedy the defects and limitations of the network by using transnetwork protocols such as T.70 and T.62.

Another form of messaging service available on networks, both private and public, is based on intelligence within the network, or at least on specialized hosts operated by the network administration. Most large commercial services of this sort have grown from a mailbox service originally made available on the host computer of a time-sharing system, as mentioned in the discussion of Videotex (see Section 6.4.1.2). In these systems the owner of a mailbox is usually advised of the arrival of new mail when he logs into the host; he can display or print his received mail; he can delete it selectively; he can reply to specific messages explicitly, or copy them to other subscribers' mailboxes; he can generate new mail and send it, etc.

As the time-sharing systems grew from a single host accessed by a star network, to multiple hosts accessed by a switching (usually packet-switching) network, so the mail service has typically grown to be distributed over the multiple hosts. The owner of a mailbox on one host can send messages to or receive messages from mailboxes on other hosts. He does not have to know the physical addresses, but only the name of the mailbox. The system contains a 'name-server' which, given a name, will find a physical address and put it to use.

The messaging services provided by such systems are frequently further extended by interfaces to other networks or services. For example, an interface often exists to the Telex network, so that the owner of a Telex terminal may use the system (Fig. 6.27). To send a message, he makes a Telex call to a host and sends his message in the correct format, i.e. with 'To: ⟨Destination Mailbox⟩' and similar elements clearly identifiable in the message. The host receives the Telex call, analyses the message and posts it to the correct mailbox. Conversely, a normal

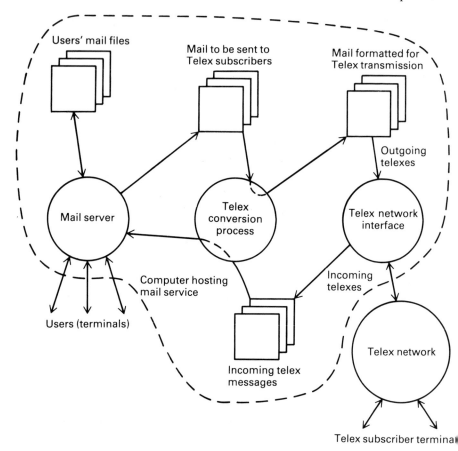

Fig. 6.27 Adding telex access to a conventional mail service on a computer.

user of the messaging service may specify a Telex number as a destination, instead of a mailbox identifier and the system will make an outgoing Telex call. In some systems express or courier postal services may be interfaced. For example, a message might be sent from a European subscriber to a non-subscriber in Hong Kong. Instead of being held in a (non-existent) electronic mailbox, the message would be printed in Hong Kong as soon as sent and taken for physical delivery by a courier.

Further radical extensions of mailboxing services support group communications and teleconferencing; but this topic is deferred to Chapter 7.

In contrast to the Telematic services, these messaging services are usually accessed by simple scroll-mode unintelligent terminals; and frequently between an X.28-like protocol and the application itself there are no intermediate layers. The presentation layer is merely represented by the convention that standard ASCII coded-character strings will be used.

Thus one may categorize the two approaches to text interchange, discussed so far, as follows
(1) Telematic Services—end-to-end direct exchange of structured and formatted documents, between simultaneously on-line user terminals.
(2) Mailbox Services—non-real-time, unformatted and unstructured, document exchange, dependent on a designated recipient logging in to the system; but with intelligent facilities for copying, replying, addressing, multi-destinations, etc.

One might make more ambitious demands on such text services and on the network. For example, one might submit to the network a piece of text—a message—to be delivered to a list of persons identified by name or job title and address. The message could be for immediate delivery to some in the list, and for deferred delivery (e.g. wait 24 hours) to others. If the remote receiver's terminal equipment is inoperative, one might ask the network to hold the message until the terminal is available—or this function could be implicit. One might also request explicit confirmation of delivery of the message.

Such a service would be a Message Handling Service (MHS) of the sort proposed by CCITT in the X.400 Series Recommendations.

6.4.2.1 The X.400 MHS [13]

The MHS recommended by CCITT is based on two major components: The Message Transfer Agent (MTA) and the User Agent (UA). MTAs are message-switching (i.e. store-and-forward) nodes which route, forward, copy, hold and account for messages given to them. UAs represent the user and are intelligent terminals (or similar) which act as sources and sinks of messages. As seen from the inside of an MHS a UA is a well-defined object, with specified behaviour. As seen by the user a UA is undefined, this external interface being outside the scope of X.400; but it may be presumed that a UA has a keyboard, screen and/or printer, editing facilities, accounting facilities and storage for holding received messages and possibly copies of transmitted messages.

An important point to note is that UAs, unlike telematic terminals, need not be permanently connected to the MHS. If a UA is connected it will receive messages sent to it. If it is not connected, the MHS, or rather one or more MTAs in the MHS, will hold messages for that UA, until it connects to the MHS. Because a UA is not necessarily permanently connected, it does not necessarily have a physical address. Indeed a UA could be mobile. For example, a diskette representing user A's UA could be taken to user B's physical terminal, so that B's terminal is converted into A's UA.

MTAs are connected to each other, and to UAs by a Reliable Transfer Service (RTS) which would very probably be built from Layers 1 to 6 of the OSI Model (see X.410). Typically, MTAs in an MHS may be regarded as forming a fully connected system, even though the connections may pass through many intermediate network-layer nodes (Fig. 6.28). Typically also, a given UA will 'belong' to one particular MTA, to simplify the problem of handling mobile UAs. More precisely, messages sent to any given UA will always be sent to its owning MTA, which will deliver or hold them, depending on the circumstances. An

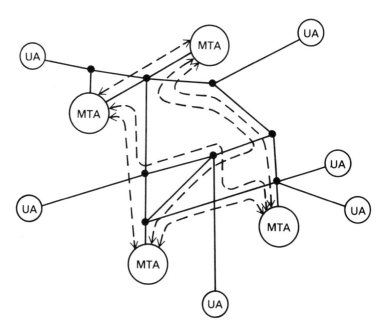

Fig. 6.28   MTAs and UAs, effectively fully connected by underlying network.

unconnected UA must always connect to its own MTA to use MHS, even if remote from it—which presents no problems assuming the existence of a wide-coverage low level network, over which the RTS between UA and MTA can operate as a point-to-point session. (The concepts of a fully connected MTA network and of UAs having owning MTAs are *not* part of X.400, but are rather a natural way to implement X.400 without duplicating lower level routing and switching functions.)

MTAs forward messages to each other using the P1 protocol, and MTAs exchange messages with UAs using the P3 protocol (see Recommendation X.411). Different sorts of end-to-end, but not interactive, protocols may exist between UAs; and one particular one, P2 (X.420 Interpersonal Messaging Protocol) is defined. The X.400 OSI-compatible architecture is illustrated in Fig. 6.29. For all practical purposes it may be stated that there is no presentation layer required by MHS at Layer 6 of the OSI hierarchy. Obviously, if formatted or mixed-mode documents are to be exchanged using MHS, extensive presentation protocols (non-interactive) are required—but these are on top of the application, not below it! (However X.409 does describe at some length the formats and syntax of the application protocol commands themselves.)

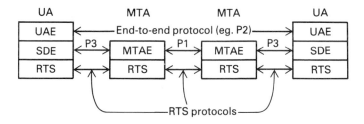

Fig. 6.29 X.400 MHS protocol architecture.
UAE = user agent entity; SDE = submission and delivery entity; MTAE = message transfer agent entity; RTS = reliable transfer server.

The contents of the messages handled by an MHS must be encoded according to some standards if they are to be reproducible on reception. In Recommendation X.408 the following methods of representing text in coded form are defined as permissible
(i) Telex.
(ii) IA5 (V.3).
(iii) Teletex (T.60 and T.61). Recommendation X.430 also describes how Teletex terminals may access an MHS.

(iv) Group 3 Facsimile (T.4, T.30).

(v) TIF.0 and TIF.1 (see Section 6.4.1 on T.73).

(vi) Videotex (T.100).

(vii) SFD or Simple Formattable Document, as defined for the Interpersonal messaging service, using Teletex coding.

(viii) Possibly encoded voice.

Between these formats conversions may take place, so that, for example, a UA which uses Teletex formats and codes may exchange messages with an IA5-compatible UA. Not all conversions are practicable. The conversion service is one of the service elements provided by the Message Transfer Service, MTS, which is the network of MTAs comprising the core of an MHS.

A major feature of the X.400 MHS is that it is intended to permit addressing in a manner similar to that of the postal service. It should be possible to send messages to Juan Gómez, Calle Iturrigorriaga 117, Santander, Spain; or to The Personnel Officer, Apex Process Industries, South Loop, Hamilton, Ontario, Canada. Name-servers within the network should translate these addresses to network addresses for those UAs which are permanently connected, or to UA identifiers for others; plus the network addresses of their owning MTAs. The RTS will route a message from its originating MTA to its destination MTA(s); and if we assume full connectivity of MTAs, this routing involves no transit MTAs. The destination MTA will use the RTS to route the message to a permanently connected destination UA, or hold it until a not permanently connected destination UA 'logs in' and identifies itself to the MTA. In principle, several users could share a UA, with the separation of messages for them done within the UA. Again, several UAs could share a network address, such as that of a computer in which different UAs were implemented. Such situations would be reflected in the entries in the name-server. Finally, many users not registered in MHS could share a UA, in the manner of a shared Telex terminal. In this case the message text is used to identify the intended recipient within the UA.

For both administrative and addressing reasons the MHS is divided into Management Domains (MDs). An MD is responsible for the handling of subscribers within it: their connections, passwords, entries in the name-server, billing, etc. Although much remains to be defined in this area, in principle an MTA receiving a message for a UA in another MD (as identified by a country name or other suitable word in the address), will not search its name-server for the UA (where it will not be found), but will forward it to a designated MTA in the destination MD, which will use its name-server to find the destination UA. There should be no requirement for transit MDs, no more than there is for transit MTAs. MDs may be public or private, but must always contain at least one MTA. (see Fig. 6.30).

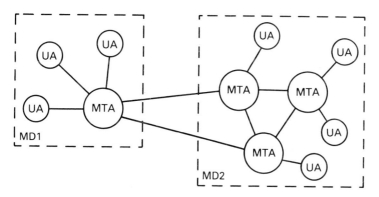

Fig. 6.30 X.400 MHS management domains.
MD = management domain.

6.4.2.2 *MHS Service Elements*

An MHS offers various 'service elements' to its users. By 'service elements' are meant individual facilities which may always apply, or may be invoked when required, or which are optional—that is the service element may be selected as being available or not, independently of its being invoked. Some of the more important service elements are

(i) Access management or the control of access by UAs to the MHS, using passwords, etc.

(ii) Message identification. Used for later reference to the message, in particular for delivery confirmation.

(iii) Delivery time-stamp indication. Self-explanatory.

(iv) Non-delivery notification. A destination MTA can use this service element to advise a sending UA that the destination UA has not received a message.

(v) Registered encoded information types. A UA can register with the MTS what types of coded information it can receive, e.g. Teletex only.

(vi) Alternative recipient allowed. An originator of a message may specify that, if the selected destination UA is unavailable, then an alternative recipient UA may get the message. Such an alternative recipient must, of course, be properly designated as such by destination UAs which wish to use this service element.

(vii) Deferred delivery. The MTS holds the message until a specified time expires, before delivering it.

(viii) Delivery notification or explicit notification of delivery.

(ix) Multi-destination delivery. A sender may send his message to multiple UAs.

(x) Disclosure of other recipients. If a message goes to multiple destinations, this facility allows each recipient to be informed as to the identities of the others.

(xi) Explicit conversion. A sender may request the MTS to perform explicit conversion of the message coding.

(xii) Probe. Using this service element, a sender may test the availability of a destination UA *before* sending a message.

(xiii) Hold for delivery. A UA may request the MTS to hold incoming messages for it, and not to deliver them until authorized.

There are more service elements than those listed above. Additionally, the Inter-Personal Message Service has its own long list of service elements, covering such aspects as the importance, sensitivity, expiry date, subject indication and encryption of messages—and also other topics.

Finally, an MHS is supposed to support a directory service, with the appropriate service elements for its use. The name-server is of course a directory itself, which is used not by people but by computer software. An output from the name-server is inserted directly into message headers for routing purposes. By contrast, a directory service is a service for users, supporting interactive searches by the public and insertions and modifications by the persons authorized to maintain the directory. Such on-line user-oriented directories are familiar in other fields, e.g. in the French telephone network, and it is natural that an MHS would also provide this service.

6.4.2.3 MHS Problem Areas

The X.400 Recommendations cover many of the aspects that must be addressed by the designers and implementors of the MHS. However, some topics, such as the addressing of destinations and message identification (particularly when foreign MDs are considered) require considerable clarification. Moreover, there are other topics of immediate relevance to any MHS designer, which are scarcely mentioned in X.400; partly because they have been overlooked, perhaps; partly because they do not require standardization. Some of these topics are discussed in the following paragraphs.

The MTA 'Network'. Should an MTA act as transit switch between two other MTAs, or should a network of MTAs be regarded as fully connected by lower layer network services? In the previous discussion we assumed a fully connected MTA network, so that no message passes through more than two MTAs, at least within a single MD. This approach is logical, since it avoids duplicating lower layer switching functions. It may not always be economical. For example, a privately owned MHS might be more cheaply implemented using leased circuits between certain chosen MTAs, with transit-switching functions being provided in MTAs where necessary; rather than relying on point-to-point dial-up (e.g. an X.25 call) between the source and destination MTAs. See Fig. 6.31.

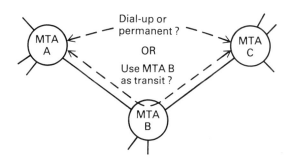

Fig. 6.31 Fully connected MTAs, or transit-switching?

The answer to the question 'Which approach is best?' depends on the tariffs for leased circuits and for calls; the additional cost of the software to support transit-switching in an MTA and the volumes of traffic handled.

Dimensioning, Response Times and Storage Capacity. How many MTAs should there be in an MD? How long should a message take to reach its destination? What capacity should be provided for holding undelivered messages?

A single MTA in an MD provides a simple structure in which all files are held in one place. There are three broad categories of files: Files holding user messages; files holding name-server and directory information; files holding administrative data, including records of usage per customer for billing purposes. However, the existence of only one MTA makes the whole MD more susceptible to failure. Additionally, should traffic grow beyond the capacity of this MTA the design of the MTS will have to be changed to support multiple MTAs. In all but the simplest cases, it is probably wiser to employ a design based on multiple MTAs from the start. However, an MTS based on multiple MTAs implies distributed files, with all the well-known problems of ensuring their coherence.

With regard to response times and transnetwork delays, the application is fortunately not very demanding. A sender of a message in a typical MHS is more concerned about its guaranteed delivery rather than when it is delivered, provided the delay (assuming the destination is available) does not exceed a few seconds—or even minutes. Of course the longer a typical message remains in the MHS the more storage and work space must be provided for messages in transit, but the real problem here will be presented by undelivered messages. Assuming the MHS infrastructure is based on a packet-switched network, and that there are three 'hops' at most per message transfer within an MD (UA-to-MTA, MTA-to-MTA, MTA-to-UA), we could reasonably assume that each hop takes less than 0.5 seconds and processing within an MTA takes less than 1 second. This would give a maximum transfer delay of 3.5 seconds, which is almost certainly acceptable.

An example may help to clarify the situation further (Fig. 6.32). A public telecommunications administration handling some 1 million telephone subscribers plans to support 100 000 MHS subscribers, who are estimated to generate 50 000 messages per day. The busy hour message-rate is estimated at 5 per second. The MTA network consists of 5 fully connected MTAs; and assuming traffic is evenly distributed, each MTA will handle 1.8 messages per second peak load. If the average message length is under 1000 octets (in practice 600 octets are assumed), the character rate is obviously perfectly manageable. Spread over a multiplicity of X.25 channels and circuits it is indeed trivial, representing at most 15 packets per second. More significant is the message processing load which will involve file accesses to the name-server, accounting files, temporary files for messages and back-up of messages (see below), etc. It has been estimated that perhaps 10 to 20 disk accesses per message

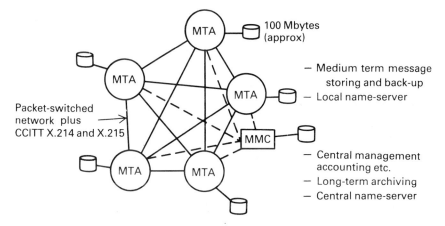

100 Mbytes (approx)

— Medium term message storing and back-up
— Local name-server

Packet-switched network plus CCITT X.214 and X.215

— Central management accounting etc.
— Long-term archiving
— Central name-server

Fig. 6.32 An X.400 MHS to serve 100000 subscribers. MMC = message management centre.

per MTA are required, giving 18 to 36 disk accesses per second per MTA. This is more serious. It is clear that a key consideration in establishing the capacity of an MTA, and therefore the number of subscribers it should handle, is the speed and efficiency of the filing system.

How long do messages remain in the MHS? In the above example, it is the policy of the administration that all messages delivered to the MHS should be held in two separate locations until safely delivered, as a protection against equipment failures. If an average hold time of one day is assumed for a message (because a user is expected to log in and extract his backlog of undelivered messages once every two days) then storage in the MHS is required for twice 50000, i.e. 10^5 messages. This implies that message buffering requires some 100 Moctets. This is to be divided over the (five) MTAs; and then the storage capacity must be increased to handle the other files such as the name-server, and statistical and billing data.

In the system discussed it is a design aim that the MTAs should be microprocessor-based systems, using conventional Winchester disk technology. Both the peak disk access rates and the storage requirements point to the multiple MTA configuration that has been chosen. It remains to be seen how accurate are the assumptions on which these conclusions are based.

Backing-up Messages. A message-switching service is expected to be reliable (see Section 3.3). It should not lose messages. One approach to designing an MHS is to make no explicit provision for duplicating messages against loss, but simply advise subscribers that, if they are concerned, they should use the Delivery Notification service element (see Section 6.4.2.2). This is not regarded as sufficient in many systems, so other approaches are required, for example

(i) Assume the RTS will not lose messages in transit between MTAs, and between MTAs and UAs. Provided sessions are only cleared when a message has been safely delivered to disk, then the problem reduces to one of the security of disks. This can be handled conveniently by duplicating disk storage at each point and holding two identical copies of the one message on two independent disks. Failure of an MTA or a communication link can be repaired and the user will only perceive a delay in the service, but not a loss of messages—provided that both disks do not fail at once. This approach to back-up is simple, but requires more hardware.

(ii) An alternative is to hold duplicate copies of a message at different sites, e.g. one at one MTA, one at another MTA. If the source and destination MTAs are distinct, they should be the MTAs in question; but they could be the same. Additionally there is the problem of ensuring that two copies of the message in the MHS are established before releasing the session with the source MTA. The activity concept of the session layer could be useful here; but we may be considering concatenated sessions, e.g. UA-to-MTA (source), MTA (source)-to-MTA (Destination).

(iii) Another approach is to back up messages at a central site, a Message Management Centre (MMC). This, however, is going to load the MMC with all the traffic—precisely what we tried to avoid by building a multiple-MTA system.

(iv) A fourth approach is to compromise. Duplicate copies of a message will be held in the MTAs, unless a message remains undelivered for a long time, when the back-up copy will be sent to and held in the MMC. For example, a source MTA could hold two copies of a message until one was safely delivered to a destination MTA, when it would delete one copy. When the message is delivered, the copies at the source and destination MTAs will be deleted. If the message remains undelivered for a long time, the source MTA will transfer its copy to the MMC. If source and destination MTAs are one and the same, then the MMC is given a duplicate copy as soon as the message enters the system. This procedure is complicated, but is likely to prove the most efficient for a large MHS. It has the merit that the MMC, which would also keep statistical and billing records of messages, is in a position to know the state and whereabouts of undelivered messages, and is the natural archive for really long-term cases.

Other schemes for the back-up of messages can be drawn up, but it is unlikely that any will prove simple to implement. It is only necessary to consider what happens when an MTA fails and later re-enters service, to see that there are many complications.

MHS Administration. In section 5.1 the question of network management was considered; and in the previous section the concept of a Message Management Centre (MMC) was introduced. Although the MMC is concerned with the management of the MHS and not that of the infrastructure, there are sufficient similarities between them to justify not discussing the details of handling new and lapsed subscribers, gathering statistics, etc. again. However, an MMC will have some unique functions and problems of its own, for example

(i) There is the problem of the long-term handling of undelivered messages. Are they archived? If so, how are they recovered?

(ii) There is the name-server problem. A name-server could grow to be very large and cumbersome and it could become difficult to maintain identical copies of it on all MTAs. One approach is to have a local name-server, handling only those UAs which belong to a given MTA, at that MTA; and a master name-server at the MMC, available for remote referencing.

(iii) Although an MMC is clearly necessary in some form or other, the X.400 protocols only cover a very few of the functions which it might need to use. New protocols for MTA-MMC communication need to be devised.

(iv) It would be natural to have an MMC per MD, although for a very small MD the MMC could be implemented in an MTA rather than in a separate computer. But an MHS can cover several MDs, possibly over many countries. Do MMCs communicate directly, e.g. for billing purposes, or are such functions handled off-line?

(v) How are users of an MHS billed? Two principles would appear to be desirable

—Senders of messages should be charged, not receivers (apart from a standing charge). It is not reasonable that receivers be made to pay for 'junk mail' which will certainly proliferate on an MHS. It should be noted that many mailbox systems charge persons for receiving mail they do not want—including telecommunication charges and mailbox usage charges.

—The network charges, i.e. the charges for using the RTS, should be built into the MHS charges. A message, in passing through an MHS may use several network and session-connections, e.g. between MTAs. Again it is unreasonable that a subscriber should pay for several concatenated calls, where he could in principle use one call, for example if he used Teletex. The implication is that the RTS should bill the MHS, and the MHS bill the subscriber; probably without explicit reference to the subscriber's use of the RTS, but rather incorporating implicit average RTS charges.

6.5 CONCLUSION

In this chapter the OSI Reference Model and protocols and systems based on it, have been discussed at some length. It will be appreciated that the architecture does indeed provide a framework for discussing a variety of networking services and applications. It will also be appreciated that, even within the confines of CCITT, there exists a formidable range of Recommendations in this area. There seems little doubt that the edifice of services and protocols will continue to grow in the years ahead. It is to be hoped that the structure does not become top-heavy. There are already plenty of indications that the development costs of OSI-compatible software and the run-time overheads, are acting as deterrents to the adoption of OSI standards.

REFERENCES

1 *Open Systems Interconnection—Basic Reference Model* IS 7498, International Standards Organisation. Other related standards are *Transport Layer* IS 8072/8073; *Session Layer* IS 8326/8327; *Presentation Layer* DIS 8822/8823 and *File Transfer* DP 8571.
2 *OSI System Description Techniques, Recommendations X.200–X.250* CCITT Red Book **VIII. 5,** Geneva, 1985.
3 *Terminal equipment and protocols for telematic services. Series T Recommendations* CCITT Red Book **VII. 3,** Geneva, 1985.
4 A solution to the problem is provided by the Bankers' Algorithm, described by E.W. Dijkstra (1969) in *Cooperating Sequential Processes* Ed. F. Genuys Academic Press, London.
5 A good report and bibliography of the European Informatics Network (EIN) is to be found in *EIN-COST PROJECT 11* EIN/80/001, National Physical Laboratory, UK.

6 An overview of Cyclades plus bibliography is to be found in *Cyclades—Un Reseau Informatique General* IRIA, B.P.-5, 78150 Le Chesnay, France.

7 Purser M. (1982) The Euronet Diane network for information retrieval. *Information Technology: Research and Development* **1,** 197–216.

8 *Centernet. Virtual Terminal Protocol* (VTP) Regnecentralen (af 1979) RCSL No. 43-GL11428, 1981, Copenhagen, Denmark.

9 The 'Coloured Books' are issued by the Joint Network Team, National Physical Laboratory, UK, and include the *Yellow Book (Transport Protocol)*; *Green Book (PAD)*; *Blue Book (File Transfer)*; *Red Book (Remote Job Entry)* and *Grey Book (JNT Mail)*.

10 The Performance of a File Transfer Protocol across Packet-Switched Networks N. Fitzpatrick *et al.* (1984) in *Performance of Computer-Communication Systems* Ed. W. Bux, H. Rudin, North-Holland.

11 *Telematic Services. Recommendations F.160–F.350* CCITT Red Book, **II. 5,** Geneva, 1985.

12 Other document architectures are to be found in IBM's *Document Content Architecture (DCA)* and *Document Interchange Architecture (DIA)* and in ISO's *Office Document Architecture (ODA)* and *Office Document Interchange Format (ODIF),* ISO DP 8613/1–10.

13 *Message Handling Systems. Recommendations X.400–X.430* CCITT Red Book **VIII. 7,** Geneva, 1985.

Chapter 7
More Bandwidth, more Flexibility, more Services

In the preceding six chapters various aspects of computers in telecommunications networks have been considered. The discussion has ranged over the use of computers for the control of, nodes and switches; the interfacing of computers to networks; and the procedures for transnetwork communication. The technology reviewed either already exists, or is reasonably firmly specified; as, for example, in the case of ISDN interfaces, or higher level applications such as X.400 Message Handling.

In this chapter we try to look a bit further into the future, beyond ISDNs. In any such attempt there is of course a risk of identifying 'important' developments which in fact never take place; and an even greater risk of failing to mention or even foresee developments which turn out to be fundamental in hindsight. That risk must be accepted. Therefore the material in this chapter, which attempts to identify the key elements in future developments, must be read remembering always that the author may, like many a better man before him, be mistaken.

7.1 FUTURE DEVELOPMENTS—AN OVERVIEW

Two current developments are seen as fundamental to all future developments in telecommunication networks
(1) The rapidly increasing bandwidth available on cable-based circuits due to the advances in the technology of optical fibres.
(2) The possibility of increasing the intelligence of networks, due to the universal introduction of stored programme control (SPC) in nodes.

Optical fibres can carry digital information at rates of hundreds of Megabits per second (Mbps), and indeed at Gigabit per second (Gbps) rates. Network operators naturally, and unashamedly, look for traffic to fill this capacity. The obvious candidate is video information of all sorts, from videophones, to TV entertainment (currently carried in most countries by private dedicated 'networks', or rather, star distribution systems); and including video conferencing, security monitoring, high

266

quality graphical and pictorial information, and digitized documents. Such high volume traffic is not readily handled on an ISDN based on 64 Kbps, and there is clearly a need for an Integrated Broadband Communications Network (IBCN) [1].

Since users will rarely want permanent access to any particular high bandwidth source of video data, future networks must be able to allocate bandwidth on demand, and switch bandwidth channels. This clearly has profound implications for network technology at the transmission and switching level, where currently most switches are designed to handle only the equivalent of 64 Kbps channels. Additionally, the real-time nature of much video traffic points towards circuit-switching as the basic technique, since it introduces negligible variations in transnetwork delays. A question therefore arises as to the future of packet-switching and its relationship with basically circuit-switching networks.

Moreover, many of the services likely to use the high bandwidth channels are inherently multipoint. For example, this is true of entertainment sources broadcasting to many users and of video-conferencing.

This then brings us to the second fundamental development: The need for greater intelligence in the network, and the possibility of providing it via SPC nodes. The concept is that of the 'soft' or 'user-defined' network, in which the SPC capability is used not merely to handle internal network signalling, accounting, etc., but also to provide very extensive facilities and functions directly to the user. At the very least the user should be able to allocate his high bandwidth access channels at will to videophone communications or to selected TV entertainment sources. Projects of this sort already exist in some countries. In multipoint applications, such as multiparty video conferencing, users will require the ability to identify, and attach themselves to existing video conferences—and the organizers will wish to specify to the network who is entitled to do so. Moreover, the providers of broadcast services on a public network will also probably require this type of managerial control over receivers.

Additionally users will expect to find on public networks all those facilities available on PBXs (see Chapter 5), such as redirection of incoming calls to another destination, blocking or priority handling of calls from named sources, etc. In general calls should be 'personalized', by which is meant routed between persons rather than between 'terminals', to permit the serving of mobile users. This at once raises the problem of authenticating users when they 'connect' to the network—not merely authenticating users in a service provider which they access across a network. In short, the greater flexibility that can be offered on SPC-based networks implies a greater responsibility on the part of all parties, in particular the provider of the network services, to ensure the security of the services both by authenticating users and protecting traffic against 'attack' of all sorts, e.g. by using encryption.

In the following sections some of the points raised above are discussed in a little more detail.

7.2 FLEXIBLE HIGH-SPEED SWITCHING

To understand some of the problems involved in handling higher bandwidth digital channels, where there is a requirement to be able to set up (i.e. route and switch) channels of, for example, 2 Mbps for high speed data, or 34 Mbps (or higher) for TV, we return to the digital circuit switch of Chapter 2 which handles 64 Kbps channels.

This narrow-band switch, like most IBCN switches, is a time-space-time (TST) switch, with 512 slots forming the basic frame which repeats 8000 times per second. On input, one (out of up to 128) 512-slot stream, which could represent 16 PCM 32-channel links, is buffered in 512 'speech stores', whence it is extracted in a different, more-or-less random order to feed to the space switch, under control of the control stores. This 'time-slot-interchange' is between the slot allocations in the incoming 512-slot frame and the slot allocations in the internal frame. The space switch is driven 4 million times per second to make cross-connections between the 128 streams, and the switched information ends up in output 'speech stores'. Thence a further time-slot-interchange maps the information from internal slots to the slots to be used in the output 512-slot stream.

It is important to note that there is no reason why two slots in an incoming frame should end up in the same relative positions in an outgoing frame, see Fig. 7.1. Their relative positions can be altered at both the input time-slot-interchange and the output time-slot-interchange. Far from this being a disadvantage it is the principal mechanism for avoiding internal blocking. It permits the avoidance, on input, of internal slots aleady occupied by other cross-connections; on output, of already occupied slots in the output frame.

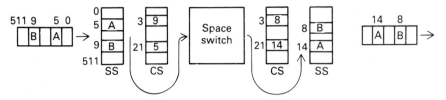

Fig. 7.1   Reversal of a time-slot sequence in a TST switch. SS = speech (i.e. data) store; CS = control store.

7.2.1 Handling Calls Requiring Different Bandwidth

Suppose now we use this system to switch a complete 2 Mbps 32-channel PCM link, which we assume, for simplicity, occupies the first 32 slots of the 512-slot input frame. It is required on output that the first 32 slots of the output frame hold the same information and in the same order as the input frame. This requirement may not be possible to satisfy when the 2 Mbps call arises, since some of the first 32 output slots may already be occupied. There is a significant probability of blocking. However, let us suppose the requirement can be satisfied, and that the output of the output time-slot-interchanger is not randomly ordered, but that the input time-slot-interchanger is still random, see Fig. 7.2. In this case it is clear that samples from different frames can be muddled together, as illustrated in the figure where contiguous slots ABC in an input frame end up with slots B,C adjoined to slot A from the *subsequent* input frame.

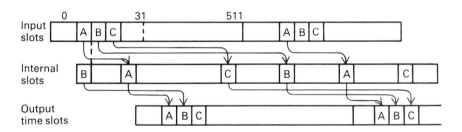

Fig. 7.2   Muddling of samples from different input frames in a TST switch.

There are various approaches to solving this problem. The obvious solution, of forcing the input time-slot-interchanger to allocate ordered contiguous internal slots, usually introduces too high a probability of internal blocking to be feasible. However, if synchronism between all three frames (input, internal and output) can be maintained by suitable delays, and with suitable buffering, then the random use of internal slots may be maintained, see Fig. 7.3. Moreover, the probability of blocking at the output frame, and the overheads in switching a group of channels as coordinated rather than independent individuals, can be reduced by basing the system on a permanent grouping scheme. For example, slots in internal and input/output frames could be grouped four-at-a-time, two-at-a-time or singly. A request for a 384 Kbps channel could then be met by allocating one four-at-a-time and one two-at-a-time groups, made up of basic 64 Kbps slots, see Fig. 7.4. Studies have shown that such an approach reduces blocking probabilities, compared with trying

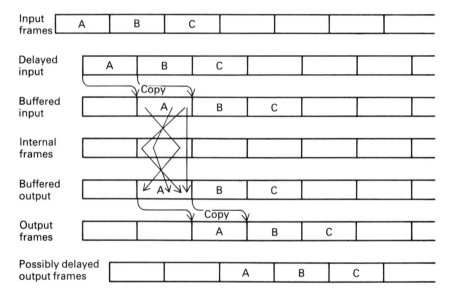

Fig. 7.3 Random internal time-slot switching achieved by synchronizing all frames and buffering.

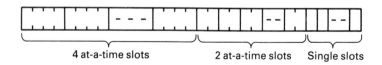

Fig. 7.4 Grouping of time-slots.

to allocate all the required slots contiguously, while reducing the over-heads involved in switching all the slots independently [2].

Rather than try to build up wide-band channels by amalgamating narrow-band (e.g. 64 Kbps) channels, an alternative approach is to begin with wide-band switching and break down the wide-band channels to narrow-band where required, using multiframing techniques. By way of an example, consider a network in which each subscriber has access to eight 34 Mbps channels, adequate for video-entertainment given efficient coder/decoders (codecs), and one more 34 Mbps channel on which voice, data etc. are multiplexed [3]. Four subscriber lines are handled by each time-slot-interchanger of the experimental switch, so that there are thirty-six 16-bit slots in the basic frame which repeats 2.168 million times per second (see Fig. 7.5). The space switch operates at $36 \times 2.168 = 78$ MHz, and supports 256 time-slot-interchangers or 1024 subscribers, plus trunks; and switches 16 bits in parallel at each crosspoint.

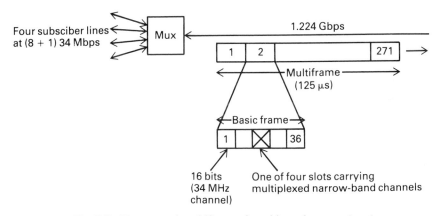

Fig. 7.5 Frames and multiframes for wide and narrow-band.

The narrow-band channels in this experimental system are handled by embedding 271 basic frames into a normal 125 μs multiframe. Suppose one slot in a basic frame carries n narrow-band channels. Then n times in the 125 μs multiframe the values in the control stores of the time-slot-interchangers and the space switch must be changed to route the narrow-band channels through the space switch at the appropriate internal slot-time. In effect, there must be fast control stores with 36 slots, four of which are cyclically refilled from four slow control stores with 271 slots. Similarly, there must be slow data stores, to hold narrow-band data until the appropriate internal frame within the multiframe arrives; because the space division switching between input and output of narrow-band channels requires not only a common internal time-slot but also a common internal frame.

It will be appreciated that the control of internal blocking in such a system is complex and in the particular case examined the designers have opted to give different Grades of Service to different types of traffic. One approach to reducing the blocking problem could be to fix permanently the internal time-slots to be used for the multiplexed narrow-band channels, and to effectuate the time-slot-interchange by moving channels between the frames in the multiframes, rather than between time-slots in the frames, see Fig. 7.6. (Of course, in the par-

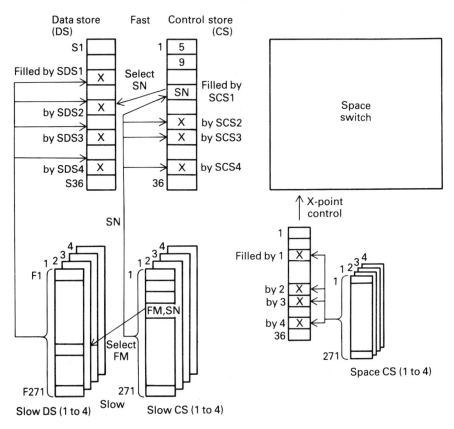

Fig. 7.6 Switching and multiframes with slow and fast stores. SN = slot N identifier in frame; FM = frame M identifier in multiframe.

ticular example, interchanges between the four time-slots carrying multiplexed traffic in the frame will also be required.)

7.2.2 Packetizing Circuit-Switching

It could be extremely complex to build a large switch handling mixes of channels of different bandwidths, as might be required, for example, for switching between local switches which in turn directly serve subscribers. But the need for such 'hub' switches (see Fig. 7.7) is likely to be accentuated, in future networks based on optical fibres. This is because, although optical fibre technology is competitive in terms of the cost per bps of capacity provided, its large capacity must be used if its advantages are not to be outweighed by the high installation and termination costs being spread over insufficient user traffic.

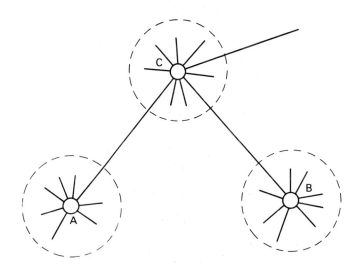

Fig. 7.7 A 'hub' network.

In short, high bandwidth networks naturally tend to have 'star' or 'tree' topologies rather than a mesh, for economic reasons. In Fig. 7.7 the most economical way of handling traffic between A and B is very likely to be through C, rather than directly between A and B; since spare capacity is very probably available on the links AC and BC at marginal cost, whereas the link AB involves new cable and terminations to handle the probably small direct traffic. Of course, in any particular case the sums must be done, but the results based on optical fibre technology are more likely to favour switching A to B traffic through C, than if conventional technology were used.

A further reason for preferring tree topologies is that distribution networks, such as those of TV entertainment, are naturally tree-structured, with the source (or 'head-end') at the root of the tree—and these services are probably the dominant users of bandwidth in future networks.

Based on the above reasoning, one possible approach to designing a wide-band circuit-switching network is the following
(i) Local nodes handle local subscribers, performing switching between them.
(ii) All traffic between a local and other nodes is handled via a hub node.
(iii) The hub only switches high bandwidth channels. For example, the minimum switching unit at the hub could be 2 Mbps. Such channels could themselves be carriers of multiple subchannels at lower bit rates, which are switched in the local nodes.
(iv) Hubs are interconnected via higher-level hubs, also providing interfaces to external networks.

Such a tree network apparently does not provide alternative routes between nodes. It does, however, provide a logically fully connected network, in which the internodal links are dynamically reconfigurable (see Fig. 7.8). Thus, low volume overflow traffic can indeed be offered alternative routing by providing a 'tandem' switching function in a local node, i.e. switching traffic between two local nodes in a third (see Fig. 7.9). A similar approach can be used to handle low volume external traffic, which might not justify the establishment of a special high-bandwidth channel to carry it.

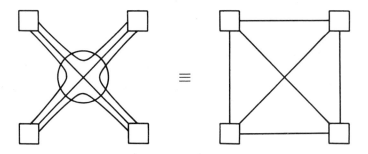

Fig. 7.8 A hub network equivalent to a fully connected one.

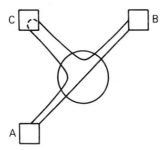

Fig. 7.9 An alternative route from A to B in a hub network is provided by 'tandem' switching at C.

Turning to the hub switch itself, the aim would be to provide a single high capacity switch, leaving the complex 'intelligent' operations distributed over the local switches. For example, the individual optical fibres could carry information at the H4 rate (34 Mbps), representing sixteen 2 Mbps channels, or some mix with higher bandwidths, or a single 34 Mbps channel. The switch need only operate at $16 \times 8000 = 128$ KHz, compared with the MHz rates of previous examples, because the basic repeating frame has fewer, but larger, slots. In fact a slot holds 256 bits, a 'packet' rather than 8 bits.

To simplify the amalgamating of 2 Mbps channels into higher bandwidth switching units, the hub switch can be designed to be non-blocking. At the time-slot-interchange stage this is achieved by having $2n-1$ internal slots to handle the n external slots in a frame. In the example $n = 16$, so there are 31 internal slots, and the switch operates at 248 KHz, not the 128 KHz mentioned above. This number of internal slots ensures that if there is a free slot in an input frame on one H4 link and a free slot in an output frame on another H4 link, a common internal slot can always be found for cross-connecting them (see Fig. 7.10). The reasoning applies *a fortiori* if it is required to cross-connect more than one 2 Mbps slot, for example four making up an 8 Mbps channel. The handling of amalgamated slots is much more easily done with a hub switch of this design, than was the case in our previous examples, because of the slower switch operation rate and the non-blocking nature of the time-slot-interchange.

Moreover, the space switch, which may have to handle relatively large numbers of lines (e.g. 512×512), could be designed to be not only non-blocking but also self-routing [4]. To achieve this, each 256-bit

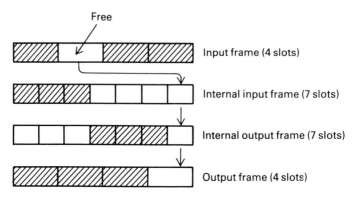

Free

Input frame (4 slots)

Internal input frame (7 slots)

Internal output frame (7 slots)

Output frame (4 slots)

Fig. 7.10 Avoidance of internal blocking by having $(2n-1)$ internal slots for n input or output time-slots.

packet is supplemented with a 'header' identifying its destination output line on the far side of the space switch. The space switch then consists of a 'sorter' network followed by an ordinary fully connected distribution network, of the type considered in Chapter 2. It is the function of the sorter network to ensure that no blocking occurs in the distribution network, by sorting the packets which are presented to it synchronously, in parallel. The basic switching units are all (2×2), so the decision to be taken by each unit, on the basis of the headers of two input packets, is: Do they 'crossover' or not? The important point about such a design is that reallocation of internal time-slots, for example to handle new calls or possibly to accommodate a high bandwidth 'amalgamated' channel, does not require any modification of the space switch or its control. The space switch adapts itself automatically (see Fig. 7.11).

It is worth noting that such a space switch could be 'pipelined'. Provided that the transit delay for the space switch is the same for all packets they need not cross the switch 'instantaneously', since a constant phase shift between input and output will not upset the synchronism. If

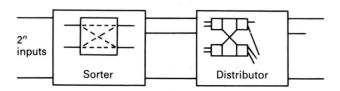

2^n inputs

Sorter

Distributor

Fig. 7.11 A non-blocking switch built from (2×2) components.

a packet passes through N nodes in traversing an $(M \times M)$ space switch, N space-switching operations (each of which handles up to M connections) can be overlapped. Such an approach allows transputer-like devices [5] using, say, 10 Mbps serial input/output, to be considered for the elementary nodes in the space switch. Without this pipelining a transputer would probably be too slow.

In the above example 2 Mbps slots of (256+) bits are handled as packets of data to be routed through the hub switch synchronously. We have already come across some of the problems which arise by attempting to build a synchronous network. They range from the overall low-level clocking problem, to the danger of muddling data from different frames when time-slot-interchanging due to phase differences. A more radical approach to designing an Integrated Broadband Communications Network (IBCN) is to make the whole network asynchronous (see Fig. 7.12).

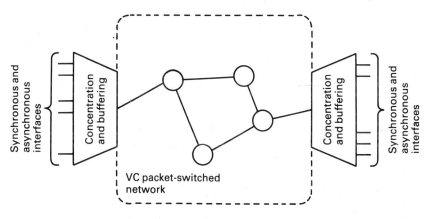

Fig. 7.12 An ATD network supporting all traffic on a VC packet-switched subnetwork.

In this Asynchronous Time-Division switching (ATD) [6], the network internally is nothing but a VC packet-switching network in which
(i) All packets are of the same size (e.g. 16 octets).
(ii) Once established, a VC has a fixed route through the network.
(iii) Capacity is allocated to a VC, on establishment, in accordance with its required bit rate.
(iv) A continuous, even, stream of packets is maintained on the circuits carrying multiplexed traffic by the insertion of synchronizing packets.

At the user's interface to the network his isochronous (e.g. digitized voice or video) or anisochronous bit stream is built into packets and sent off through the network asynchronously towards the destination. At the destination user's interface the packets are reassembled and their contents delivered in the form in which they originally entered the network (this information being conveyed when the call is set up). To make such a scheme function two things are required

(1) That the network can maintain a steady performance; i.e. deliver the capacity requested when a call is set up, with a reasonably constant transnetwork delay. (Buffering at source and destination interfaces takes care of minor fluctuations in delay.) This can be achieved with packet-switching technology provided the error rates are negligible, so retransmissions are not required. Using all digital circuits of, for example, 140 Mbps, this may be taken to be the case.

(2) That the user does not exceed the bit rate he requested on setting up the call. This can be enforced by a local flow control mechanism, such as the so-called 'leaky bucket'. The bucket is the buffers available on input to the network; the leak is the steady removal of packets at the contracted rate for sending across the network. When the bucket becomes full the user's input is thrown away. Flow control is of course only necessary for anisochronous traffic whose actual intput rate is normally less than its maximum possible input rate.

7.2.3 Fast Packet-Switching

In the previous section it was discussed how both continuous (isochronous) and bursty (anisochronous) information could be carried on an asychronous packet-switched network. But such a network has to operate at very high bit rates. Can the software which performs packet-switching cope with the load? Packet-switching software is of two categories

(1) The software which obeys the protocol(s).

(2) The switching software.

The first software is 'per line'. In principle, one or more microprocessors can be dedicated to each line connected to the switch; so that obeying the protocol is performed in parallel by different processors on different lines. Indeed VLSI chips are under development for parallel processing of the three lower OSI levels on the same line. A Level 3 packet, corresponding to one Level 2 frame, can be processed in parallel with the processing of the next Level 2 frame; or even with that of the *same* Level 2 frame provided that Level 3 processing is aborted if the Level 2 frame check sequence (FCS) fails.

Thus the loading problem is essentially in the switching which is centralized, not in the protocol-handling which is naturally distributed. The difficulty resides in the fact that packets to be switched must be accessible, in principle, to *all* the protocol modules so that they may be carried between them, depending on how the calls are routed. In traditional packet-switches this accessibility is achieved by using shared memory—perhaps a single unit, or perhaps some hierarchy of memories based on groupings of lines connected to the switch. These shared memories readily become a bottleneck, since they are accessed frequently by many other modules, and imply mutual exclusion and similar software lockout mechanisms to prevent destructive interference between their users.

Rather than use a shared memory (time-division multiplexed in a complex manner by its accessing modules), physical movement of traffic switched between modules can be used. For example a LAN could interconnect the processors handling the protocols (Fig. 7.13), although this is unlikely to achieve the desired switching rates of some Gbps to handle many wide-band channels. Another approach is to use a space switch. If packets are all the same size, as in the ATD example, they can be buffered to ensure they all have the same phase and the switch can operate at a regular clock rate. The switch should be non-blocking.

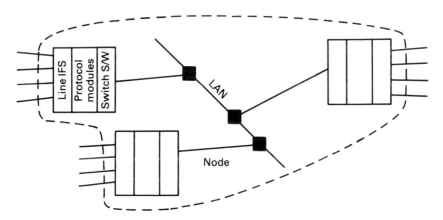

Fig. 7.13   A packet-switching node built from microprocessors interconnected via a LAN.

Alternatively, the switch could be made to operate much faster than its feeding lines. By providing each node within such a switch with buffering

[7], it is possible to serialize packets which are looking for the same outlet from a node, without the queue reaching back to the feeding source (see Fig. 7.14). The switch is also effectively non-blocking. Again, transputers could be considered for the elementary nodes, provided that they are fast enough.

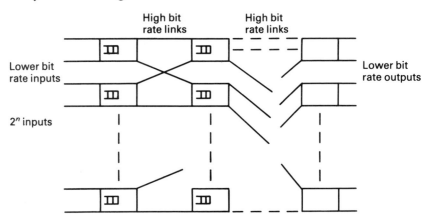

Fig. 7.14 A non-blocking switch which queues packets. □□□ = queue of packets awaiting output if more than one requires the same output link.

These remarks may be concluded by observing that, when wide-band traffic is considered, the distinction between packet-switching and circuit-switching becomes less clear. On the one hand packet-switching, asynchronous by nature, can be used to avoid the tyrannies of high-frequency, network-wide synchronism and data can be switched in packet units rather than in octets; on the other hand, at the heart of the switch cross-connections must still be made, and this can often be performed most efficiently by a non-blocking space switch operating on (ideally) fixed-length packets of the same phase, i.e. synchronized by local buffering.

Finally, it must be emphasized that all the switching techniques discussed above are electronic. Optical technology is assumed to provide the high bandwidth channels between switches, but the optical signals are converted to electronic on the entry to a switch, and vice versa on output. However, optical space-switching is an available technology, capable of switching optical channels carrying data at Gbps rates [8]. These switches are still electronically controlled and a central problem is how to make the *control* operate fast enough, and sufficiently well synchronized, to split, for example, time-division multiplexed channels on an optical carrier. Optical-switching is the subject of much research and maybe the technology will advance sufficiently to permit fully optical switches to be built in the not too remote future.

7.3 MULTIPOINT COMMUNICATION

By 'multipoint communication' we mean communication between more than two persons, terminals or computers. Although in daily life multipoint communication is perhaps even more commonplace than point-to-point communication, only one aspect of it, namely broadcasting, is properly served by telecommunication networks. The telecommunications equivalent of the 'meeting', or the structured meeting complete with chairman, agenda, secretary, voting procedures and minutes, exists only in embryonic form.

Before considering how multipoint applications are, or could be, supported on telecommunication networks, the two broad categories of such applications will be examined in more detail.

7.3.1 Broadcasting

We use the term broadcasting to signify point-to-multipoint communication in its widest sense. There is a single source, and many destinations, which may vary dynamically.

In the broadcasting of entertainment, such as TV, the source is more or less permanent and the channels it uses are known publicly. Would-be receivers can tune in readily, or connect themselves to those channels. Generally, all the information available to a receiver is present all the time, each information stream on its own channel being immediately accessible by a receiver (see Fig. 7.15). However, it may be that there are fewer channels than potential information streams, so that a user must first select the information stream by sending a command to the source in the reverse direction, which then allocates a forward channel on which to transmit to the receiver (see Fig. 7.16). This is the situation with various pay-TV schemes. In general, in such broadcasting systems, no attempt is made to check the quality of reception—or indeed if a receiver receives anything at all.

Another form of broadcasting is 'distribution', in which a single source sends information to several named recipients. This is the typical

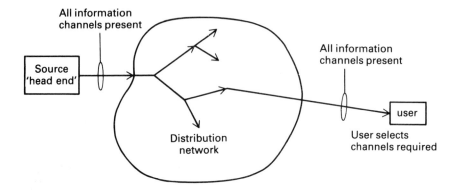

Fig. 7.15 Normal broadcasting.

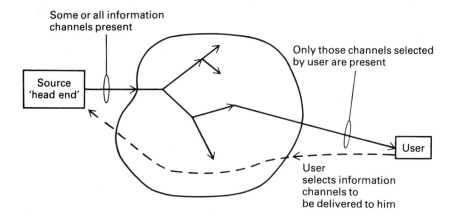

Fig. 7.16 Broadcasting on demand.

situation of document distribution. Particular examples have been discussed under the heading 'Message-Switching', both in Chapter 3 and
when considering X.400 MHS in Chapter 6. Such systems are based on
intelligent distribution centres (such as X.400 MTAs) *above* the telecommunications infrastructure. The broadcasting is an application, but the
network connections are point-to-point. A source sending to *N* destinations effectively sets up *N* point-to-point links, if not from itself,
then from some remote relaying distribution centre to which the source
has a point-to-point link (Fig. 7.17). In these distribution systems there

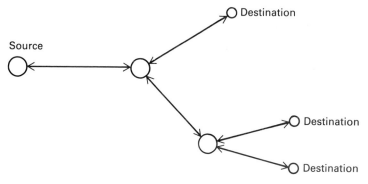

Fig. 7.17 Broadcasting by copying between point-to-point links ⟷ = point-to-point link.

is sometimes, but rarely, explicit confirmation to the source that a receiver has received his information correctly. More commonly the distribution service is taken to be secure and to guarantee delivery of anything entrusted to it. This avoids the problem: What does a source do if it receives positive confirmation of reception from some destinations, negative confirmation from others and no response at all from the rest?

7.3.2 Teleconferencing

Teleconferencing is a loosely defined term covering any service which allows many users to communicate over a network as members of the teleconference. All users have the right to be sources of messages as well as destinations, although this right may not necessarily be given simultaneously to all participants.

One well-known, non real-time, teleconferencing service is provided by 'Porta-Com', a program package developed by the University of Stockholm, Sweden [9]. It may be regarded as providing communal 'mailboxes' on a host computer. To each defined teleconference (and there may be many in the system) there corresponds such a communal mailbox, into which members of the teleconference may place messages. Other members may later read the messages, comment on them, etc. The system maintains, for each member, a record of which messages he has or has not seen.

Users of Porta-Com may, of course, belong to several teleconferences and the system allows them to move between them at will. Facilities exist for establishing new teleconferences, restricting membership if so desired, etc. The system may be accessed over (for example) packet-switched networks; and one version, Eurokom, based at University College, Dublin, is heavily used by the EEC-sponsored Esprit program.

However, teleconferencing systems such as Porta-Com are essentially non-real-time, although if more than one member of a teleconference is logged in at the same time, the messages input by one member do become available to all the other members almost at once. By contrast, a very simple, but not to be despised, *real-time* teleconferencing facility may be built on a central computer, accessible via a network, by simply echoing all input as it is made, to all connected participants (Fig. 7.18).

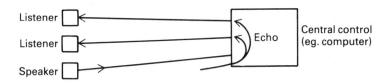

Fig. 7.18 A simple real-time teleconference. (The central control can reallocate the turn to speak.)

For example, an organizer could create a teleconference for a specified date and time, advising would-be participants by, for example, electronic mail. At the designated time they call the central computer and log in to the teleconference, which has now been activated. Using simple scroll-mode terminals over a packet-switched network, the participants may request the turn to 'speak' by depressing some special character key. The system allocates the turn to those requesting, using a cyclic algorithm. A 'speaker's' typed input is echoed to all active participants until he relinquishes the turn. A chairman may be designated (special log in) with the right to interrupt the current speaker or reallocate the turn, etc. Voting procedures may be added. Users may easily record the entire teleconference, e.g. on a printer or a diskette attached to their terminal.

Such a (memory-less) teleconference facility can readily be extended to support voice or indeed video, given adequate channels. The echoing procedure can be performed by simple switching at the central site. The centralized control, supervising logging in to the teleconference (including notifying already present participants), logging out and managing the turn to speak, is almost trivial.

Nevertheless, if N users are to be supported, the central site will require access to N low-speed control channels and N voice or video channels (probably only half-duplex), simultaneously. If these channels are wide-band, the centralized approach gives rise to a potential problem caused by the total bandwidth required at the central site, which is likely to exceed what is available at most subscribers' terminations. However, if the teleconferencing service is not based on a subscriber's site and equipment, but is made a centralized network service, the number N is likely to be much larger, since many teleconferences may be required to be supported simultaneously.

Thus one is led to question the idea of centralized teleconferencing. Why not base the wide-band interconnection of users on a multipoint connection?

7.3.3 Interconnecting Many Users

Various solutions are possible to the problem: How are many users interconnected via a network simultaneously? For simplicity only one general approach will be discussed here, which is designed to address the broadcasting and teleconferencing services of the sort that have just been discussed. The broad principles of the approach are

(i) Control and 'data' (i.e. conventional data, text, voice or video) traffic are handled separately.

(ii) Data traffic is carried on non-centralized branching multipoint connections, so as to make the most efficient use of wide-band channels.

(iii) Control traffic is to/from a control point which is in principle centralized, although it could be distributed in large systems. This approach is taken because broadcasting and teleconferencing both typically require central control at the application level (e.g. a 'turn-to-speak' allocator or chairman of a teleconference).

(iv) The control point is co-located with a data source/sink on one of the branches of the multipoint connection (see Fig. 7.19).

Suppose it is required that a new participant be added to the multipoint connection, either as a receiver of broadcast information or as a member of some sort of teleconference. If the decision comes from the participant himself, he calls the control point (using a conventional point-to-point narrow-band channel) and, after suitable checking of his

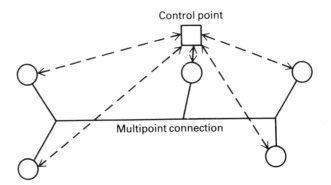

Fig. 7.19 A possible multipoint configuration. ○ = participant in multipoint connection; ←--→ = control signalling independent of data traffic.

credentials, the control point starts to establish a wide-band data channel for him. Alternatively, the decision to add the new participant could arise at the control point itself, in which case it would proceed to establish the data channel directly.

To establish the data channel, the control point simply makes a data call, with the same call identification as the existing multipoint connection, but to the new participant. At each switching node along the route, an outgoing physical path towards the new participant is selected by a routing algorithm. If this path already carries a channel used by the multipoint connection, this is incorporated into the new data channel being established. If no such channel is available, a new one is reserved. For each internodal channel forming a link in the multipoint connection, a record of participants using it should be held. Thus, when a particular participant's data channel is cleared, the internodal links used by it are cleared only if he was the only user (and the multipoint connection is not permanent, as might be the case with all but the local node to end-user links of a broadcast entertainment distribution system).

The actual switching of multipoint connections falls into two categories—half-duplex and full-duplex.

(1) *Half-duplex switching* means that at any time there is only *one* transmitter, or input to the switch, although there may be many receivers, or outputs from the switch. The identity of the transmitter may change with time (see Fig. 7.20), allowing an output to become an input, and the former input to become an output. Such half-duplex operation covers all forms of broadcasting and the one-speaker-at-a-time form of telecon-

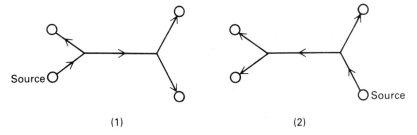

Fig. 7.20 (1) becomes (2)—a 'half-duplex' turnaround on a multipoint connection.

ferencing previously discussed. (Note that any control signals, which might appear to imply a need for full-duplex operation, are carried on control not data channels.)

If the network is based on packet-switching, the generation of multiple outputs from a single input to a node is done simply by copying. The half-duplex traffic flow can be enforced by discarding any input from all but the currently active 'sending' participant at the nodes local to the other participants.

Of more interest perhaps is the implementation of multi-output circuit-switching. For example, if the switch is a digital TST switch, the easiest way to provide the multiple outputs is by choosing a single common *internal* time-slot, for access to the space switch by all participants, and making the multipoint connection in the space switch. The time-slot interchange, in the time switches, will be between a time-slot in an incoming frame and the internal slot, on input; and between the internal slot and a time-slot in an outgoing frame, on output. It is assumed that the *links* between switches are full-duplex, with a slot in a frame in both directions reserved for the multipoint connection, permitting ready reversal of the half-duplex traffic.

To see how such a switch might work a modified version of the TST switch of Chapter 2 is presented in Fig. 7.21. Multiple outputs to the *same* link are handled by an additional control store (ACS) on the output side of each time-slot-interchange. This specifies which data (speech) stores are to be used to fill which slots in the link. Normally, for example, data store 8 on line 12 corresponds to slot 8 on the link, but multipoint output can be achieved by placing a pointer to data store 8 in several places in the ACS (e.g. 8 and 23 as illustrated). The space switch also performs multipoint output but to *different* links, using control stores

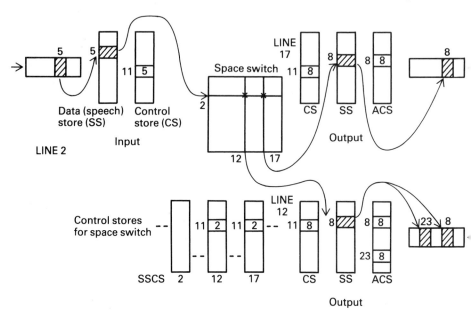

Fig. 7.21 A TST switch handling multipoint output (line 2, slot 5 input) ACS = additional control store; SS = speech (data) store; CS = control store; SSCS = space switch control store.

(SSCS) which refer to space switch outputs, not inputs as previously. For example, SSCS 12 and 17 in Fig. 7.21 both have 2 in internal time-slot 11, to signify that both links 12 and 17 take their input from link 2 at internal time-slot 11. (This space switch could also be used to echo the input traffic back to link 2, by putting 2 in slot 11 of SSCS 2.)

If multiple outputs from the space switch are unacceptable, a separate internal time-slot can be allocated for space switch output to each link participating in the multipoint connection, the input to the space switch coming from the same entry in the data store corresponding to the current 'sender's' link, but at different internal time-slots. This, of course, requires more internal time-slots.

Figure 7.22 shows the same multipoint connection, but with time-slot 23 on link 12 the input and the other three participants outputs. The SSCS entries for internal time-slot 11 have all changed to reflect that input is from link 12, not link 2 as previously. Also, the input side of link 12 has been brought into play to send slot 23 to the space switch. It is worth noting that the output time-slot-interchangers need no modification (if echo of input is acceptable) when a change of sender takes

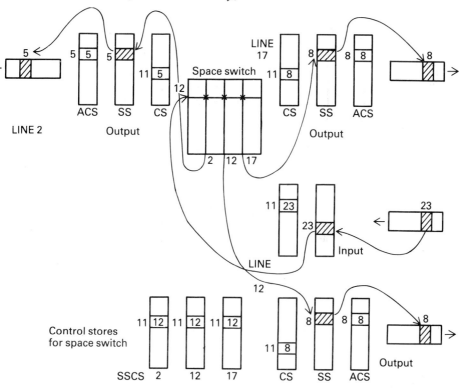

Fig. 7.22 The TST switch of Fig. 7.21 with line 12, slot 23 input but some multipoint connection.

place; and the input time-slot-interchangers require modification only if the change is to another sender on the same *link* as the previous one. The change of sender is essentially handled by changing the SSCS entries.

A non-blocking ($n \times n$) space switch has been drawn, but other designs, such as those mentioned in Section 7.2, could be used. However, there is a definite blocking probability in the time-switching. A new participant wishing to join the multipoint connection may find that the internal time-slot being used by the connection (11 in our example) is already occupied by some other call on his link. To a certain extent, however, this is mitigated by the fact that if many users share a single internal time-slot, there are fewer remaining users to occupy other slots; the total number of channels supported by the switch is finite.

A half-duplex switch does, of course, suppose that it is directed when to change input (sender), if it is used for teleconferencing. This command is assumed to emanate from the control point and to be sent to every switch on the path of the multipoint connection.

(2) *Full-duplex switching* supposes that all channels between all participants in a multipoint connection are full-duplex, and are always available. That is, a participant may transmit at any time, although if two do so simultaneously there will be interference.

If packet-switching is used, the interference will (presumably) consist of the interleaving of packets from different sources into the one virtual circuit, thereby causing confusion at the destinations—not to mention probably overloading the channels.

If circuit-switching applies, the different inputs will be 'added' together, e.g. using an Exclusive OR (XOR). Provided that silent inputs deliver all-zero digital information no interference will occur when there is only one sender. Figure 7.23 shows how this could be done by adding an input ACS to the TST switch of Figs. 7.21 and 7.22 which XORs the multiple inputs from a single link into the data store, and which supposes that the space switch also XORs multiple inputs from different links. The space switch is now of some complexity, since its control must ensure that all the crosspoints shown on Fig. 7.23 are made simultaneously at internal time-slot 11.

An easier way to handle the full-duplex multipoint switching in the space switch, maintaining the normal procedure of making only one crosspoint on any input and output link at a time, is illustrated in Fig. 7.24. Here XORing into the output data stores is performed (serially), but the input time-slot-interchangers and the space switch are unchanged from the original example of Chapter 2. This is achieved by treating the multipoint inputs to the switch, N say, as independent. Unfortunately this results in the need to make $N(N-1)$ crosspoints per cycle of the switch, as seen from the space switch control stores of Fig. 7.24. In this example the switch handles four inputs, giving twelve crosspoints.

7.3.4 Summary on Multipoint Communications

It should be clear from the foregoing discussion that, whereas it is intuitively obvious that the connections involved in multipoint communications should be made in a distributed fashion over the switches of a network rather than centrally, the complexities involved are considerable. These complexities are dependent on the nature of the service to be provided. If switching is what we have called 'half-duplex', appro-

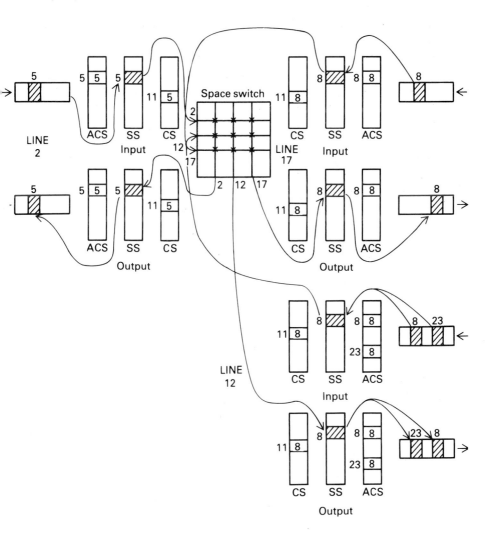

Fig. 7.23 The multipoint connection of Figs 7.21 and 7.22, but supporting 'full-duplex' traffic.

priate control signals must pass between switches to inform them when the 'sender', the current single speaker, changes so that they may reconfigure their internal connections. If 'full-duplex' switching is used, there is no need for such control signals, since no reconfiguration is necessary; but the operation of the switch is internally considerably more compli-

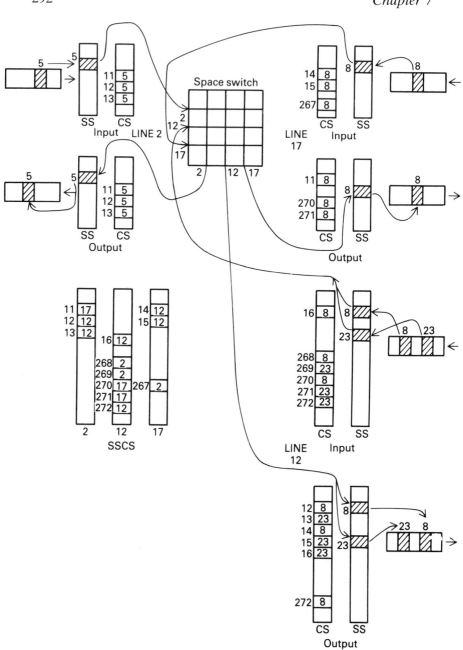

Fig. 7.24 The same 'full-duplex' multipoint connection of Fig. 7.23, but using separate internal time-slots per direction.

cated and internal blocking (circuit-switching) or channel overloading (packet-switching) can become serious problems, difficult to analyse let alone to resolve.

7.4 EXTENDING THE SCOPE OF THE OSI REFERENCE MODEL

The OSI/RM, discussed in Chapter 6, is usually viewed as being implemented by layers of protocols, with their corresponding 'peer entities', or protocol modules, which obey them. A given layer combines both control and data transfer functions. For example, the transport layer protocol provides commands to establish and clear transport connections, and to effect flow control on them, as well as transferring user data end-to-end.

It may be reasonably stated that *the protocols* are based on in-band signalling, i.e. the one channel is used to carry both signalling and data information. *The services*, however, defined in the OSI/RM, are provided at the interfaces between the $N-$ and $(N+1)$-layers *locally*, i.e. within some computer, and there is no need for any stipulation within the service specification itself as to how those services must be implemented. Out-of-band signalling, e.g. CCS, could in principle be used with no effect visible to the user.

In the ISDN Recommendations, such as I.430/431, I.440/441 and I.450/451, the application of layered protocols to CCS channels, as well as to user channels, has already been introduced (see Chapter 5). This separation of control traffic from user traffic, while at the same time maintaining the OSI/RM structure on both of them, goes some way to resolve the problem posed when originally discussing X.25 (Chapter 3). The problem is: When a user sends an X.25 packet into a network, to whom is he talking? Nominally, he is addressing a DCE. Actually, he is sending data information to a remote user; flow control information to an (often unknown) entity anywhere between himself and the remote user; and resets and call request and clear commands to all network nodes involved in the call, as well as to the remote user. Would it not be simpler to separate these distinct types of commands into different channels, directly linking the sender to the required destination; rather than pushing them down the same channel addressed, effectively, 'to whom it may concern'?

But maybe the problem is still deeper. The OSI/RM does not

explicitly support multipoint communications. As discussed in the previous section (7.3) multipoint *applications* exist, but it is quite valid to produce an OSI point-to-point subset which does not yet support them. But at the user-to-network interface perhaps it is *not* valid. A case could be made that talking to a network is a multipoint conversation by definition, if the network has more than one node. The relaying of control signals from node to node along a route may be sensible when considering traditional in-band circuit-switched networks; but when signalling is carried on an almost independent network, the multipoint nature of signalling traffic becomes obvious. Would it not be better to recognize it as such, and tackle the problem accordingly? (See Fig. 7.25.)

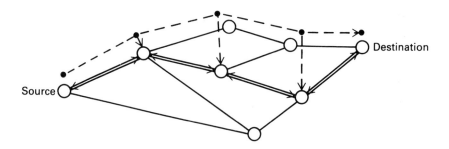

Fig. 7.25   The multipoint nature of control signalling. $\Longleftrightarrow$ = route of 'data' traffic; $\leftarrow\!-\!\rightarrow$ = multipoint connection for control signals.

There are indeed many complex and unresolved problems in this area of network 'architecture'. Taking the existence of parallel data (or voice or video) and control networks as a fact, the problems may perhaps be summarized by the following questions: Should one or both of the control and data networks be capable of handling multipoint connections? Does the OSI/RM apply to both networks and if so what are the relationships between them? How is the control network controlled; does it in turn require another control network to set up its control channels? (If the answer to the last question is 'Yes' one may well add another: Does every network require another control network *ad infinitum?*)

In the ISDN Recommendation I.320 the CCITT has tentatively addressed the problem of applying the OSI/RM to 'data' networks with parallel control networks, and it is in accordance with the general architecture outlined in I.320 that the I.400-series Recommendations for interfacing have been developed. I.320 recognizes distinct user and control 'perspectives', leading for example to a view of an (I.450) ISDN interface as illustrated in Fig. 7.26. The Recommendation also recognizes distinct 'contexts', referring to the use of a particular set of protocols across a particular interface and includes a collection of complicated three-dimensional pictures intended to elucidate the concepts involved. However, the least that can be said is that considerably more work will have to be done in this area before the full extent of the role of the OSI/RM can be agreed.

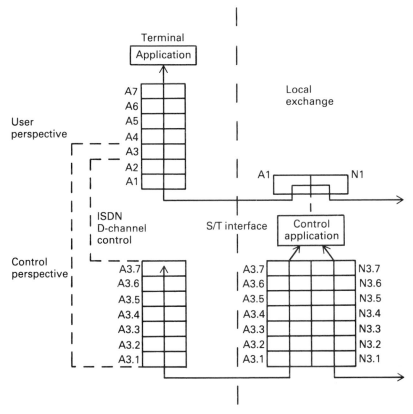

Fig. 7.26 ISDN Layer 3 in the 'user perspective' seen as an application in the 'control perspective'.

One example of the kind of situation to be addressed by the OSI/RM in the future may be taken from the 'soft' network mentioned at the beginning of this chapter. Consider a user who is temporarily moving location. He wishes calls from person A to follow him to his new location; calls from B or C to be redirected to his colleague at another location; calls from D to be recorded for later playback; and all other calls to be rejected (with an explanatory message). Such a requirement could apply to voice or data traffic. To fulfill it the network must be able to

(i) Support calls from users instructing the network what to do with incoming calls which may arise in the future (i.e. commands unrelated to any existing call).

(ii) Route and generally handle calls according to their *source* as well as their destination. This is a radical change to most routing policies, see Chapter 4.

(iii) Recognize sources and destinations by *names*, which are then mapped into physical addresses reflecting their current locations. This implies name-servers on the network with all the consequent induced traffic; e.g. consider an incoming call from an external network to a named destination for which the external network cannot provide the physical address.

(iv) Provide storage or recording facilities in the network, together with all the necessary dialogues to enable the intended recipient to identify and access his recorded messages.

(v) Allow a user to define the messages to be sent to incoming calls to him, which are rejected by the network on his instructions.

It is clear that, at least, the OSI/RM must be able to handle a wide range of user-to-network interchanges which are quite unrelated to an existing call or to one being set up.

A second example of a situation that the OSI/RM should be able to handle in the future is that of a user joining, as a recipient, an existing broadcasting (or possibly a teleconference) service. For simplicity, earlier in this chapter, this was considered as a two-stage process: The user calls the broadcaster asking for connection; then the broadcaster establishes a (different) channel to him for the broadcast traffic. In this case two, related, end-to-end connections are made. There may or may not be a need to standardize the procedures associated with these connections; but there is a need to relate them one to another, so that the user only accepts a broadcast call (for which he will no doubt have to pay) if he really ordered it earlier.

To avoid the difficulties of maintaining references between quite separate sessions, one might envisage a scheme in which the user calls the network and attaches himself directly to the broadcast service at the node nearest to him on its route. This supposes that the service has an identity known in advance by both network and user (e.g. TV channel 13); that the 'nearest node' can be found by the network; that the network can authorize this connection, i.e. recognize that the user who is connecting has authority or credit to do so; and that, later, the supplier of the broadcast service can interrogate the network as to users and their connection times, both for statistical and charging purposes.

In both approaches we see, once again, that the user-to-network or user-to-user dialogues, whose nature is beyond the current scope of the OSI/RM, are needed.

A major part of this problem of extending the scope of the OSI/RM resides in the fact that the networks, to which it is to be applied, are still only at the design or experimental stage and future IBCNs may be even less like existing networks. It may be necessary to change the OSI/RM to reflect reality in retrospect rather than to attempt to bend reality (i.e. the network designs) to fit the OSI/RM.

7.5 THE PROVISION OF SECURITY IN NETWORKS [10]

A network allows, deliberately, the interconnection of many subscribers. The possibility of one subscriber overhearing another's conversation due to malfunction of a switch, or to intentional wire-tapping, exists. Perhaps more seriously, the possibility of one subscriber impersonating another to deceive a third; or of a subscriber connecting to a destination to which he is not authorized to connect, also exists. The ability to interconnect users—the very purpose of the network—is a security risk.

Moreover, in the preceding section (7.4), the need for extensive user-to-network, as well as user-to-user, communication has been suggested. Clearly the network itself must be protected from malicious actions; such as subscriber A commanding the redirection of subscriber B's incoming calls by impersonating subscriber B. The possibilities of misuse of a network increase as the network's functions extend, and future 'soft' networks could be soft targets, unless proper security procedures are built into the design.

The International Standards Organisation (ISO) has addressed this topic of security in relation to the OSI/RM in an addendum to the ISO 7498 standard (ISO's version of OSI/RM) [11]. This addendum considers (i) Security services (e.g. access control, confidentiality of data, traffic flow security, non-repudiable information exchange).

(ii) Security mechanisms (e.g. encipherment, digital signatures) for implementing the services.

(iii) The relationship between services, mechanisms and layers of the OSI/RM.

(iv) Security management (e.g. distribution of keys for encipherment, introduction of new subscribers).

The addendum does not consider algorithms, procedures or protocols, but rather reviews 'architectural' aspects of security. It provides a useful starting point for the present brief discussion.

The ISO 7498 addendum lists more than a dozen security services which may be usefully grouped under three main headings

(1) Confidentiality. This is the range of services which ensure that users' conversations cannot be understood by unauthorized third parties. It is generally implemented by encrypting the conversation. We use 'encipherment' and 'encryption' indifferently to signify the transformation of intelligible information (plaintext) to concealed form (ciphertext), usually by means of an algorithm controlled by one or more keys. The reverse process is 'decipherment' or 'decryption'. (See Fig. 7.27.)

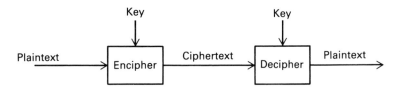

Fig. 7.27 Encipherment (encryption) and decipherment (decryption).

(2) Authentication. This term is used loosely to cover all those security services whose objective is to ensure that a message transferred between users is genuine and unaltered (data integrity); that the users are whom they purport to be (source or destination authentication); and that the users cannot subsequently disown the message, denying having sent or received it (non-repudiation). Included in the concept of a 'genuine, unaltered message' is the *uniqueness* of every message, so that it is not possible to record a valid message and retransmit it later (replay) and have it accepted as valid a second time. (The danger of replay is particularly obvious in the case of transferring money by messages over a network.) A particular case of authentication is that of authenticating

a user's logging in procedure, whether to another user's system or to the network itself (access control).

Many methods can be used to implement the authentication of messages. For example, data integrity could be ensured by a check sequence (e.g. a cyclic redundancy check, or CRC) as used to detect errors in normal data communications. However, anyone could maliciously alter a message so protected, recalculate and append the CRC; and the fraud would be undetected. This is because the CRC procedure is public knowledge. If the check-generating procedure were a secret between sender and receiver the data integrity would be more secure; but one user could still fraudulently generate messages to himself and claim they came from the other. Because of this possibility, a receiver cannot *prove* that a valid message which he received did in fact come from the sender. Thus, if the full authenticity of messages is to be assured, a mechanism is required which binds together the text, the sender's identity and a uniqueness code such as a sequence number (as a protection against replay), into a single unit—an authentic message.

The mechanism for realizing this full authenticity of messages is that of the digital signature (Fig. 7.28). The signature relies on two keys: a secret or private one known only to the sender and a public one known to the recipient(s). The sender transforms the message and the uniqueness code using an algorithm controlled by the secret key and sends the resulting signed message

$$S = T_{SK}(M, U)$$

where T_{SK} is the transform controlled by the secret key (SK); M is the message text and U is the uniqueness code.

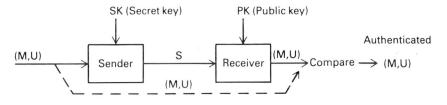

Fig. 7.28   Authentication of a message and its sender by means of a digital signature. M = message; U = unique identifier; S = signed version of (M,U); $\leftarrow\!\!-\!\!\rightarrow$ = optional sending of (M,U) in clear (plaintext).

The receiver performs some reverse transform R_{PK}, controlled by the public key to recover the message and uniqueness code

$$M, U = R_{PK}(S).$$

The receiver normally gauges the authenticity of the received message and uniqueness code by seeing if they 'make sense'. In most cases the chances that the application of R_{PK} to S will result in sense, if S was generated with a key other than SK, are infinitesimally small. However, if the message is not secret, there is no reason why M (and U) should not be sent with S, the signed message, as an additional check. This is also illustrated in Fig. 7.28.

(3) Traffic Flow Security. This service is concerned with concealing the *existence* of communication between users over a network. It may be thought desirable, for example, to conceal the mere fact that A is in communication with B, not just the substance of their communication. It is typically implemented by inserting 'padding' traffic into the genuine traffic and then enciphering (i.e. scrambling) all the resultant traffic, so that sense cannot be distinguished from nonsense by an eavesdropper.

Another implementation technique involves altering the routing of traffic, dynamically, to conceal its characteristics.

The ISO 7498 addendum recommends in which layers of the OSI/RM the various security services should be provided, optionally. Both confidentiality and authentication (as defined above) are recommended as belonging to the presentation layer (6), although certain aspects of these services could be provided at the network (3) and transport (4) layers— and possibly other layers. Traffic flow security, on the other hand is recommended as belonging to Layers 1, 3 and 7. The justification for these allocations, which could be disputed, is to be found in the addendum.

7.5.1 Public Key Systems

It is not the purpose of this section to discuss in detail the algorithms which can be used to encipher or authenticate messages, which can be found in the literature. However, some general principles should be explained.

Most modern techniques are based on the concept of the public algorithm, controlled by keys which may be secret or public. Of course, the algorithm, that is the procedure used to transform data, could be a secret, but in an 'open system' this would be a positive disadvantage.

It would mean that users would have to develop or install software or hardware to perform as many algorithms as there were distinct communities with whom they wished to communicate, assuming each community used its own secret algorithm. Moreover, the divulgence of the secret algorithm to authorized persons only could be a very difficult business to manage. It is simpler to have a standard algorithm which, for example, translates plaintext to ciphertext under the control of a key—which is the 'key' item.

Of course, the algorithm must be such that, knowing the plaintext and the ciphertext (and the algorithm) it should not be feasible to deduce the key. This ensures that an 'attacker' cannot break the system by discovering by chance or design a plaintext-ciphertext pair—the so-called 'known plaintext' attack. However, if decipherment is to be possible, there must be a reverse process capable of delivering plaintext from ciphertext using the same or another key. Usually this is performed using the *same* algorithm, identical to that used for encipherment or possibly slightly modified, so that only one basic version of it is required both for encipherment and decipherment. Thus the algorithm is a function with two inputs, (encipherment key plus plaintext) or (decipherment key plus ciphertext) and one output (ciphertext) or (plaintext), respectively; but which given the text input and output cannot reveal the other input, the key.

If the encipherment and decipherment keys are the same, the procedure, though apparently simple, suffers from two defects
(1) Firstly, consider N users wishing to communicate separately and secretly with each other. Each user must hold $(N-1)$ secret keys and there are $N(N-1)/2$ secret keys altogether. The problem of managing these keys is obviously non-trivial.
(2) Secondly, a common encipherment and decipherment key does not permit the use of the digital signature mechanism, as discussed earlier, since recipients can forge messages to themselves.

By contrast, the use of two distinct keys, a secret and a public one, allows the digital signature mechanism to be used; and reduces the number of secret keys to N (one per user) [12]. Encipherment (as opposed to generating signed messages) may now be performed by using the public key to encipher the plaintext message P, and using the secret key to decipher the ciphertext message C. Using our former notation

$$C = R_{PK}(P)$$
$$P = T_{SK}(C).$$

But if, as discussed, a single algorithm A is used for both T and R we have the following

Signing Messages: $\quad\quad\quad S = A(SK; M, U)$
$$M, U = A(PK; S)$$

Enciphering Messages: $\quad C = A(PK; P)$
$$P = A(SK; C).$$

In short, authentication and confidentiality can be handled with the same algorithm and the same pairs of keys. Each user requires only a single secret key, SK, for signing or deciphering; and one copy of each other user's public key, PK, for authenticating signed messages or enciphering.

Of course, there is a severe restriction on the functions involved. It may be assumed that an enemy knows, in certain circumstances, A the algorithm, PK the public key, and both plaintext P and ciphertext C, or signed message S and raw message M, U—but he must not be able to deduce the secret key SK from all these. Put more precisely, the computational complexity of deducing SK from knowledge of the other items must be such that, using known techniques, centuries of computer time are needed to do it.

Fortunately an algorithm, based on exponentiation, has been discovered which meets these stringent requirements. It is the famous RSA technique [13], and works as follows

(i) Represent the message to be transformed (P or M, U) as a number X, say, e.g. using ordinary ISO-7 code and treating the bit stream as a number.

(ii) Raise X to the power of one key $K1$, say, and evaluate it Modulo N, where N, is a large number, specially chosen (see below). The result is the transformed version of X, Y say

$$Y = X^{K1} \text{ (Modulo } N\text{)}.$$

(iii) To reverse the transform raise Y to the power of the other key $K2$, say, and evaluate it Modulo N. With suitable choice of $K1$, $K2$ and N we have

$$X = Y^{K2} \text{ (Modulo } N\text{)} = (X^{K1})^{K2} \text{ (Modulo } N\text{)}$$
$$= X^{K1 \cdot K2} \text{ (Modulo } N\text{)}.$$
$$= X.$$

Because the operations of exponentiation by $K1$ and $K2$ commute ($X^{K1.K2} = X^{K2.K1}$) we can use the same pair of keys for authentication and encipherment. The choice of N, $K1$, $K2$ is as follows

$N = p.q^*$ where p and q are large primes (and are kept secret)

$K2.K1 = 1$ (Modulo $(p-1).(q-1)$). This is easily arranged if one key is chosen to be prime relative to $(p-1).(q-1)$. The other key is then its unique inverse.

The essence of the security rests in the unfeasibility of calculating p and q given N, if N is very large.

In summary we now have

Signing Messages:
$$S = (M, U)^{SK} \text{ (Modulo } N)$$
$$M, U = S^{PK} \text{ (Modulo } N)$$

Enciphering Messages:
$$C = P^{PK} \text{ (Modulo } N)$$
$$P = C^{SK} \text{ (Modulo } N).$$

The RSA procedure has so far been proof against attempts to break it and the calculations involved in exponentiation using numbers 100 to 200 digits long have been found to be not so time-consuming as to make them unusable in practical situations.

The public-key approach in general, and the RSA algorithm in particular, is now a well-established technique whose use is illustrated in the following two examples.

7.5.2 The OSIS Approach [14]

The first example of the use of the RSA procedure to provide security on a network is that of the Open Shop for Information Systems (OSIS) project. OSIS starts from the observation that, while an OSI network allows any user or computer to contact any other, this universal connectivity is limited by the fact that one cannot *use* the services provided by the remote system without previously becoming a subscriber to them. One must log in to the service supplier—which means that one must previously have been issued with a password, account number, etc.

*In the RSA system there are further restrictions on p and q to hinder an attacker finding X by repeatedly re-encrypting the encrypted version of X, Y until Y reappears. The *previous* value in the re-encryption sequence is then X.

OSIS proposes to remove this restriction by allowing open shopping for information, i.e. immediate access to all information systems (computers) members of the scheme, by means of a 'token'—a sort of intelligent credit card. Each user owns his own token which can be interfaced to a terminal by means of a token reader. The token is used to engage in a secure dialogue (with the remote service supplier) whose essential purpose is to authenticate the user, so that the service supplier can accept or reject him; and if he is accepted, can recover the charges for use of the service from the user's bank.

A user is identified by his public key, which is in turn 'certified' (i.e. signed) by his bank as genuine. The bank's signature is of course generated by means of the bank's secret key; and the service supplier is given the bank's public key to be able to authenticate it. Thus the service supplier accepts the user, effectively identified by user's public key (UPK), authenticated by a bank identified by bank's public key (BPK). The invoice for the service may be sent to the bank to debit the user's account. Note that the service supplier must know who the bank is, to be able to trust its authentication of the user and to know whither to send the invoice. (Provision is made in OSIS to inhibit the invention of imaginary banks by fraudulent users, see below.) However, the service supplier need not know who the user is. All the supplier knows is UPK, which only means something to the user's bank. The user can remain *anonymous*, which can be a very desirable feature of an information service.

The authentication procedure in OSIS is slightly more complicated than indicated up to now. Firstly, all messages of any sort (including public keys) which are signed are transmitted in plaintext also. The signing is done on a *hashed* version of the message, so

$$\text{Signature} = (\text{Hash (sent message)})^{SK} \text{ Modulo } N.$$

Authentication on reception consists in hashing the plaintext message and comparing it with the inverted signature

$$\text{Hash (received message)} \overset{?}{=} (\text{Signature})^{PK} \text{ Modulo } N.$$

This hashing serves three purposes
(1) The reduction of message length to less than that of N.
(2) The avoidance of a user discovering his own secret key (which he must not know—only his token knows it) by submitting trivial or special numbers to be signed and analysing the result.

(3) The avoidance of the invention of bogus signatures from random numbers. For example, without hashing, a user could invent a bank's signature (of his public key) and by applying the bank's known public key, 'create' a public key for himself. He would then of course have to find a corresponding secret key, but maybe repeated attempts could turn up a trivial public key which would make this task easy. With hashing, this approach would deliver only a bogus hashed public key, not a bogus public key.

The hashing is a one-way function, i.e. the input cannot be derived from the output.

Secondly, the authentication is three-layered, with a central bank (C) being added to the user's bank (B) and the user (U). Essentially, on accessing a service supplier for the first time a user sends to the supplier

(i) UPK, his public key, to be used to authenticate any signed messages he sends (and to encrypt messages to him if required).

(ii) $A(BSK; UPK)$, his public key signed by his bank using its secret key BSK. A is the exponentiation algorithm, including hashing and the Modulo N operation. $A(BSK; UPK)$ is, as are all the other quantities in this list which are sent, held in his token in a secure form. It is *not* calculated in the token, which must not know BSK; it is stored as it is when the token is issued.

(iii) BPK, his bank's public key, to authenticate UPK from $A(BSK; UPK)$.

(iv) $A(CSK; BPK)$, his bank's public key signed by the central bank using its secret key CSK.

The central bank's public key, CPK, will be held by the service supplier, enabling him to authenticate BPK. However, rather than rely solely on such a simple access control procedure (which could be easily recorded and played back by an enemy), the OSIS system follows it by a second stage in which the service supplier sends a random number, R, in response to the user's initial service request and the user must append to this number a date and time stamp, D, sign the result and send it back to the service supplier

$$\text{User's reply} = A(USK; R, D)$$

where USK = User's Secret Key.

The service supplier authenticates the reply using PSK. R and D then become session identifiers used in all subsequent signing and authentication during the session. (In fact even this method is not proof against a wire-tapper stealing the communicants' public keys and replacing them with his own and a still more secure 'interlock protocol' exists to inhibit this.)

Thirdly, in order to speed up the RSA algorithm, OSIS uses a fixed public key exponent of 65 537 and varies only the Modulus N; so that UN is in fact the user's public key, BN the bank's public key, etc.

The user's token holds the numbers (i) to (iv) above plus CPK, USK and the Personal Identity Number (PIN) of the user. All these items are unmanipulatable and USK and PIN are unexplorable. The token (Fig. 7.29) contains a microprocessor, memory, touch-keyboard and a display. It is activated by entering the correct PIN, three false entries

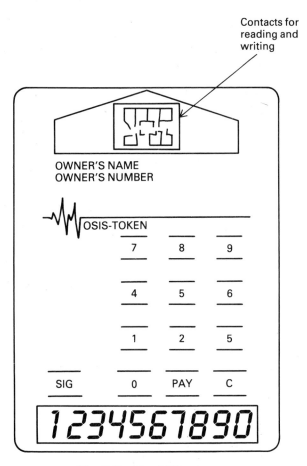

Fig. 7.29 The OSIS token.

serving to disable it to prevent exploration. Once activated, it can be used to sign messages submitted to it by the terminal, under control of a 'Sign' key. It can also, obviously, authenticate, encipher and decipher messages submitted to it.

Finally, the token can be used to authorize payments in response to payment demands sent to it from the service supplier, in accordance with a payment protocol, again under control of a special key.

It will be appreciated that the range of applications to which the OSIS concept and procedures can be put is large. It will also be appreciated that there are many questions which can be asked about the security of the system, which cannot be answered in the space available here. In particular there is the question of key generation and token creation. The reader is referred to the relevant publications.

7.5.3 Security and Message Handling Systems

A second example of the need for security mechanisms in network services may be presented by considering Message Handling Systems (MHS), such as those conforming to the X.400 Recommendations as discussed in Chapter 6. The requirement may be stated briefly thus
(i) The MHS must be able to authenticate the sender and receiver(s) of a message, and they must be able to authenticate the MHS, so that all parties know to whom and from whom they are (directly) sending or receiving messages. This is authentication between MTAs and UAs.
(ii) The MHS must also certify the identity of the sender of a message to the receiver(s). This certification by the MHS is necessary since a valid UA, duly authenticated by the MHS at the UA-MTA interface, could still send a message to another UA purporting to come from a third UA. This could be done by simply replaying some old message from the third UA, and since in an MHS there is no real-time exchange of information between sending and receiving UA, there is no possibility of end-to-end authentication to inhibit this. The MHS itself must be used as a sort of public notary to certify the genuineness of the sender.
(iii) Messages between UAs must be encrypted to provide confidentiality in transit.

In considering how these requirements may be met, we consider only the simple case of a *single* receiver for a message from a sender.

Access to the MHS. The X.400 Recommendations control access by means of passwords. A more thorough approach is

(i) The UA sends UPK, $R1+A$(USK; UPK, $R1$) to the MTA, where the symbols are as in Section 3.5.2, and $R1$ is a random number generated by the UA. In short, the UA sends its public key and $R1$, signed, to the MHS.

(ii) The MTA replies by sending $R2$, $R1+A$(MDSK; $R2$, $R1$). 'MD' signifies Management Domain which we take, for simplicity, to be equivalent to the MHS. $R2$ is a random number generated by the MTA. Thus the MTA, having authenticated the UA's message (which could be a replay), returns $R1$ with a new $R2$, signed.

(iii) The UA authenticates the MHS using MDPK, the MD's public key, which we suppose is known to it. Due to the presence of the echoed $R1$ this authentication is secure; it cannot be a replay. The UA then sends $R2$, $R1+A$(USK; $R2$, $R1$) to the MTA.

(iv) The MTA authenticates the UA conclusively, since a replayed message is impossible due to the presence of $R2$.

Thereafter $(R2, R1)$ can be used as a session identifier for all exchanges between UA and MTA. Indeed one could suppose that in a very secure system all commands, X, belonging to the P3 protocol between the UA and MTA would be signed and encrypted (ensuring, among other things, a degree of traffic flow security). For example

UA to MTA A^*(MDPK; $(X, R2, R1+A$(USK; $X, R2, R1$)))
MTA to UA A^*(UPK; $(X, R2, R1+A$(MDSK; $X, R2, R1$)))

(note A^* means the encryption function, i.e. without any prior hashing of the data).

Sending A Message. To send a message to a remote UA, $\overline{U}$, the sending UA requests from the MHS the public key $\overline{UPK}$ so that the message may be enciphered. Then the sending UA can form an encrypted message

$$M' = A^*(\overline{UPK}; (M, I+A(USK; M, I)))$$

where M is the message and I is an identifier for the message, such as a sequence number. M' contains the message M, signed by the sender, and end-to-end encrypted. The MHS must now certify the sender which it can do by appending UPK to M', assuming the MHS is using local authentication of commands from the sender on the UA-MTA interface.

Delivering A Message. We assume that the $M'+$UPK combination can be transferred securely across the MHS using signatures and encryption (to conceal UPK and so provide traffic flow security) as required.

It can finally be delivered to the destination as a P3 incoming message command, $M'+$UPK being signed by the MHS using the local session identifiers $\overline{R2}, \overline{R1}$.

$$\text{Incoming Message} = A^*(\overline{\text{UPK}}; (M'+\text{UPK}, \overline{R2}, \overline{R1}$$
$$+A(\text{MDSK}; M'+\text{UPK}, \overline{R2}, \overline{R1}))).$$

The receiver can decrypt the command using $\overline{\text{USK}}$; authenticate the command's provenance and UPK, using MDPK; decrypt the message (M' to M) using $\overline{\text{USK}}$; authenticate the original sender using UPK, which it has just received.

A final point is that, in the absence of an intelligent token, the system may be made to work with a read-only card, or a diskette. A UA would require on its diskette USK, UPK, MDPK. These could all be held in encrypted form—and possibly scattered about the diskette—with the PIN being used to find and decrypt them. The PIN would not be recorded anywhere. It would be memorized by the owner of the diskette. When operational the UA would have decrypted values of, e.g. USK inside it, and the program would need to contain self-destructive features to minimize the risks involved.

As with all such security systems for networks, there are management aspects which are non-trivial, but which are not discussed here.

7.6 CONCLUSION

In this final chapter future trends in the development of networks have been guessed at and reviewed. Starting from the assumption that wide-band transmission facilities and stored program control of nodes must lead to higher-speed traffic and a more flexible range of network services—the concept of the 'soft' network—the need for and the techniques of high-speed switching have been explored. The support of multipoint connections is also seen as a requirement in future networks.

Given a 'soft' network whose service functions are to a certain extent under the control of users, the role of the OSI/RM becomes further stretched, in particular due to the need to include features allowing more extensive user-to-network conversations. At the same time, the flexibility and openness of these future networks gives rise to a whole range of security problems, which have been considered briefly in the last section.

REFERENCES

1 Plans for a European Integrated Broadband Communications Network (IBCN) come under the RACE programme of the Commission of the European Communities, Brussels, from whom publications may be obtained.

2 Saito Y *et al.* (1986) *A study on Broadband Time-Division Switch.* Proceedings of International Zurich Seminar on Digital Communications.

3 van Baardewijk. J (1986) *An Experimental All-in-One Broadband Switch.* Proceedings of International Zurich Seminar on Digital Communications.

4 A useful overview of switching is in A Survey of Interconnection Networks Feng, T-Y *Computer* **16,** 12–30.

5 *Transputer Reference Manual* INMOS Ltd, Bristol, UK.

6 Thomas A *et al.* (1984) *Asynchronous time-division techniques.* Proceedings of the International Switching Symposium, Florence.

7 *Performance Analysis of a Packet Switch Band on a Single-Buffered Banyan Network.* IEEE Journal on Selected Areas in Communications, 1983.

8 *High speed Wide-band Digital Switching and Communication Utilizing Guided Wave Optics* L. Thylen. Proceedings of 1986 International Zurich Seminar on Digital Communications.

9 *Porta-Cam* QZ, Stockholm University Computing Centre, Stockholm, Sweden.

10 A standard work on security is *Security for Computer Networks* by D.W. Davies and W.L. Price. John Wiley, New York 1984.

11 *Addendum to ISO 7498 on Security Architecture.* International Standards Organization.

12 Public key systems were introduced in *New Directions in Cryptography* by Diffie W. and Hellman M (1976). IEEE Transactions on Information Theory, IT-22.

13 Rivert R, Shamir A, Adleman L (1977) *A method for obtaining Digital Signatures and Public-Key Cryptosystems.* Massachusetts Institute of Technology Press, Cambridge, MA.

14 A good overview of OSIS is in *Der GMD-Spiegel 1/86.* Gesellschaft für Mathematik und Datenverarbeitung MBH, Sankt Augustin D-5205, West Germany.

Glossary

This glossary attempts to explain in simple terms expressions and phrases used in the text. A more official list of definitions of some of the terms may be found in Fascicle X.1 of the CCITT Red Book (1985).

Alternative routing The provision of alternative routes through a network, between calling and called terminals, to be used when the normal route is unavailable or overloaded.

Anisochronous transmission A transmission process such that between any two significant instants (e.g. bits) in the same group (e.g. a character) there is always an integral number of unit time intervals. Between two significant instants located in different groups there is not always an integral number of unit intervals.

Asynchronous transmission A loose term usually employed to refer to stop-start transmission, which is a form of anisochronous (q.v.) transmission in which coded characters in an envelope of stop and start bits are sent at irregular intervals.

Attributes When used to refer to fields on a display, such as the screen of a terminal, an attribute specifies how the contents of the field should be displayed. For example, the contents could be suppressed (e.g. a password), or highlighted (e.g. using reverse-video), or protected from manual alteration.

Authentication A procedure for ensuring that the recipient of a message can be assured that the message has been sent by the purported sender and has not been (maliciously) altered. See also 'Digital signature'.

Baud rate The rate at which symbols are sent over a channel. The baud rate is not necessarily equal to the bit rate since one symbol (e.g. a waveform) may be used to encode more than one bit.

Bearer circuit A physical circuit and its basic signalling procedure for conveying symbols, which could be analogue or digital. For example, a digital bearer circuit could possibly carry unrestricted binary information (bits). More frequently, the bit stream carried is restricted by the requirement that it must comply with certain formats or include special bit patterns for synchronization or similar purposes. A *bearer service* is provided by a bearer circuit and includes whatever restrictions may apply to the information which may be carried by it.

Bit Error Rate (BER) The average number of bits which are received in error after transmission across a channel. A BER of 10^{-5} implies that, on average, the channel corrupts 1 bit in 10^5.

Bit-stuffing A procedure for inserting extra bits (usually zeros) into a data stream so as to ensure that the data are not mistaken for special bit sequences which trigger control actions on reception. The extra bits, so inserted, are extracted on reception by *bit-stripping*. Bit-stuffing is a technique which permits *transparent* transmission of user data, i.e. the sending of arbitrary user data across a channel which reacts to special bit-sequences.

Broadband A loose term, generally used to refer to channels which can carry information at rates in excess of 64000 bps (64 Kbps). In practice, a *broadband network* would usually be supposed to carry data at rates of several million bps (Mbps).

Broadcasting The sending of information from a single source to multiple destinations simultaneously. More precisely this would be called *point-to-multipoint* communication.

Buffering The temporary holding of information in transit. Buffering is employed extensively in store-and-forward networks (q.v.) and is the principal technique employed to ensure that short-term bursts of transmitted information do not overload the capacity of the channels used.

Capacity In information theory, the term *capacity* has a precise meaning related to the raw information rate of a channel and its bit error rate (q.v.). The capacity is essentially the maximum rate at which information may be transmitted error-free through the channel. More generally, the capacity of a circuit is the amount of traffic it can carry. This might mean the maximum effective bit rate, or, for example, the maximum number of simultaneous calls which can be supported on the circuit.

Call-collision Call-collision occurs when two stations, at opposing ends of a (free) channel, both select it simultaneously for establishing a new call to the other end.

Call-switching Call-switching in a network implies that the network recognizes the existence of calls between users, e.g. for charging purposes. A call is formally established, used and cleared.

Carrier Sense Multiple Access with Collision Detection (CSMA-CD) A technique, used particularly in Local Area Networks (q.v.), for sharing a common physical circuit. A would-be user senses if 'carrier', i.e. a signal, is present on the circuit, and, if not, seizes the circuit for itself. If two or more would-be users do this more or less simultaneously a collision results. They must be able to detect such a collision and take appropriate recovery action.

CCITT The International Telegraph and Telephone Consultative Committee of the International Telecommunication Union, with headquarters in Geneva. CCITT produces recommendations every four years for facilitating the interconnection of telecommunication networks and equipment throughout the world.

Checksum A numerical value calculated from the contents of a message and appended to it on transmission. On reception, the same calculation is performed on the *received* message and a comparison made between the result and the *received* checksum. If the two are the same, the message is assumed to have been received correctly.

Circuit-switching In a circuit-switched network, a circuit of the required capacity is established between users for the duration of a call. It can be regarded as a continuous physical path, without buffering (q.v.). Circuit-switching nearly always implies call-switching (q.v.), but the reverse does not necessarily apply.

Closed user group A facility whereby certain users, in agreement with a network administration, may constitute themselves into a group in which they are only allowed to communicate with each other. The agreement may be relaxed, for example to allow them to call (but not be called by) non-members of the group.

Compression The techniques (of which there are many) whereby the volume of information in a message or communication may be reduced without affecting its essential contents. Compression presupposes that the original message contained redundant information.

Common Channel Signalling (CCS) The use of a common channel for the *control* of many communication channels. A CCS channel is usually faster and more reliable than the channels which it controls.

Concentration The merging of many channels into fewer channels whose total capacity is less than the total capacity of the source channels. Concentration presupposes that all source channels are not active simultaneously so economies can be achieved by the merging.

Contingency analysis Applied to networks, contingency analysis is a range of techniques for analysing what the consequences would be if, for example, a circuit or a switch failed, or if traffic patterns changed significantly.

Credits In data networks credit mechanisms exist to regulate the flow of data and to ensure that each user does not take more capacity than he should. The mechanisms issue *credits* to users, for example the right to send two or more blocks of data, which they must not exceed until given new credits.

Crosspoints In a switch, a *crosspoint* is made at the point where an input circuit may be connected to an output one. If many cross-connections are to exist simultaneously many crosspoints must be available. It is usually a fundamental objective of the design of a switch to minimize (subject to constraints) the number of crosspoints, since the number is equal to the product of the number of inputs and the number of outputs, unless restricted. The term has its origins in space-division switches (q.v.), but can be generalized to other types of switches.

Data Circuit-Terminating Equipment (DCE) The piece of equipment which terminates the line to a subscriber from a data network and which provides a connection point and interface for his data terminal equipment (q.v.).

Datagram In a packet-switched data network (q.v.) a datagram is a self-contained packet of information, which can be routed by the network to its destination independently of any other packets in transit. A datagram is like a letter in the post.

Data Terminal Equipment (DTE) The user's data equipment, such as a computer or terminal, which he connects to a data circuit-terminating equipment (q.v.) to access a network.

Data Switching Exchange (DSE) A switch, node or exchange in a data network.

Decipherment See Encipherment.

Decryption See Encryption.

Digital signature A digital code attached to a message, and generated from the message by means of the sender's *secret* key. Using a different but related technique, e.g. a public key, a recipient can check the validity of the message and its accompanying signature and thereby be assured that no one else could have sent the message. (See Authentication.)

Direct Inward Dialling (DID) A facility whereby an external caller from a public network can access an internal line on a private network, e.g. on a private branch exchange (PBX), directly. The term Direct Dial-In (DDI) is also used.

Document architecture A term used for the formal description of a document in terms of paragraphs, headings, footnotes, etc.

Dual-Tone Multiple Frequency (DTMF) The technique used by push-button telephones for transmitting selected numbers, e.g. the number of the called subscriber. Two frequencies (tones), from a selection of discrete frequencies, are transmitted when a button is depressed.

Electronic mail A general term for messages of the sort normally sent on paper (text, drawings, etc.) when sent in electronic form (usually digitally encoded) over a network.

Encipherment Taken to be synonymous with Encryption (q.v.).

Encryption The process whereby intelligible information ('plaintext' or 'clear text') is transformed to a form which cannot be understood ('ciphertext') by the general public and, in particular, unauthorized meddlers. The reverse process of transforming ciphertext to plaintext is called *decryption* (or *decipherment*).

End-to-end communication Communication across a network between users. End-to-end messages are passed across, but not read or acted on, by the network.

Exchange As in 'telephone exchange'. An exchange is a 'node' in a network, comprising the switch which switches traffic and all the additional functions for controlling the switching, signalling to users and to other exchanges, etc.

Facsimile A technique for encoding and transmitting information held on paper. A scanner scans the paper in a series of parallel lines, and records what it reads at each point or 'pixel', e.g. as a binary bit (1 = Black, 0 = White) or as an octet to allow various shades of grey. The interval between pixels in a scan line, and between successive lines, is usually of the order of 0.1 mm. The information read can be reproduced by a suitable printer.

Flow control The control of the flow of blocks of data in any store-and-forward network to prevent data sources overloading channels, switches or data sinks. Many flow control techniques exist. (See, for example, Credit and Window.)

Full-duplex or two-way simultaneous transmission When traffic flows simultaneously in both directions over a communication link. (See Half-Duplex.)

Gateway A connection between two (or more) networks. A gateway is usually an intelligent (i.e. programmed) piece of equipment, which maps commands and responses used in the protocols of one network into those used on the other. In general, gateways are complex, non-standard and built to resolve a particular interconnection problem.

Grade of Service (GOS) In traditional telephony the GOS is the probability of not being able to establish a call to a given destination, due to the required circuits and switching connections being already occupied by other calls. Typically, a user should experience a GOS of 5% or less, implying that the GOS for individual components (trunks, switches) along the route should be considerably smaller. In modern networks GOS is often taken to refer to any measure of the quality of the service, e.g. the time taken to set up a call on a store-and-forward network.

Half-duplex or two-way alternate transmission When traffic can flow in both directions over a communication link, but not simultaneously.

Hunting A procedure for systematically finding a free port on the destination equipment to service an incoming call from a network. The call would normally be addressed to one port and the hunting procedure would hunt for another, if the addressed one were already occupied. Hunting is a familiar technique for handling calls from the public telephone network to a PBX with more than one exchange line.

In-band signalling Occurs when the channel used to carry information between users of a network is also used to carry signalling between users and network components, and between network components themselves. The presence of in-band signalling obviously restricts the full exploitation of his channel by a user. (See out-of-band signalling and common channel signalling.)

Integrated Broadband Communications Network (IBCN) A network capable of providing switched broadband (q.v.) channels to users. The channels may be used indifferently to carry voice, data, TV, etc. IBCNs are still in the research and development stage.

Integrated Services Digital Network (ISDN) A network providing switched digital 64 Kbps channels (with some variants) to users, suitable for carrying voice, data, electronic documents, etc. ISDNs provide a *single* physical interface to a user for all these services. ISDNS are the subject of CCITT's I-Series Recommendations.

Internal blocking Occurs when the output line, desired by an input line to a switch, is free; but when no path can be established between the two through the switch due to the presence of other calls. An increased probability of internal blocking is usually the consequence of minimizing the number of crosspoints (q.v.) in a switch.

Isochronous transmission A transmission process such that between any two significant instants there is always an integral number of unit intervals. In isochronous transmission there is a real or imaginary continuous and regular clock with which all significant events are synchronized.

Local Area Network (LAN) A network extending over a distance of up to a few kilometres for interconnecting computing and similar equipment. LANs normally transmit at relatively high bit rates, e.g. 10 Mbps.

Mailbox (electronic) A file on a computer belonging to one (or possibly several) users, into which other users may place text messages for the owner of the mailbox to read. A mailbox service is supplemented with many facilities for copying, deleting, replying to and performing other operations on messages.

Message Handling Systems (MHS) Computer-based systems for exchanging text messages between users. The term MHS often refers implicitly to the CCITT X.400 Recommendations.

Message-switching The sending of messages between users by relaying them from computer to computer, normally using the store-and-forward technique. Message-switching networks usually provide high guarantees against loss or incorrect delivery of messages. (See also Message Handling Systems.)

Modem pool A collection of modems, usually attached to a PBX (q.v.) which may, on demand, be attached to and used with analogue voice circuits when those circuits are being used for digital data.

Name-server A computer-based service on a network which, using a database of subscribers, returns a subscriber's network address (or equivalent) when given his name or similar identification.

Network User Identifier (NUI) The identifier (e.g. a string of characters) for a user of a network, which he should transmit to the network prior to requesting service, so that the network knows that he is an authorized user. In addition to an NUI, the user will probably have a password. NUIs apply, in particular, to public packet-switched networks.

Octet Eight bits.

Open Systems Interconnection (OSI)/Reference Model (RM) A model for describing data communication systems and procedures, in which different functions are allocated to different layers in a hierarchy of layers. The OSI/RM has its origins with the International Standards Organization.

Out-of-band signalling The sending of control signals between user and network equipment, and between network components, on channels other than those used for the real user traffic. (See also in-band signalling and common channel signalling.)

Packet Assembler/Disassembler (PAD) A device for building packets (for transmission on a packet-switched network) from an asynchronous character stream from a simple terminal, and for performing the reverse operation for data leaving the network for the terminal.

Packet-switching A particular case of store-and-forward switching (q.v.) in which the packets (data blocks) sent through the network are always less than some maximum size (e.g. 128 octets). This ensures short transit delays.

Peer entity The corresponding (software) module in a remote piece of equipment, on the same layer of the OSI/RM (q.v.), with which a given module exchanges information and commands according to a protocol (q.v.).

Primitive In the OSI/RM (q.v.) a primitive is one of the basic set of commands available *locally* (e.g. within the same computer) to a user of a module on a given layer.

Private Branch Exchange (PBX) In telephony a PBX is a private exchange allowing telephones on extension lines to call each other and also to access, and be accessed by, the public telephone network. Modern PBXs usually have facilities for supporting data as well as voice traffic.

Protocol A set of rules and procedures for communicating between two or more (remote) software modules, usually on the same layer of the OSI/RM (q.v.), where applicable.

PTT A general term for the administrations operating the public telecommunications services of a country.

Pulse Code Modulation (PCM) A technique for encoding, transmitting and decoding voice signals in digital form. Typically, the analogue voice signal is sampled 8000 times per second and encoded as an 8-bit digital number.

Quaranting The holding of data on reception until it is in a fit state (complete, error-free) to be delivered to a user.

Rate adaption The technique(s) for enabling data at a given bit rate to be carried on bearer channels of a higher bit rate.

Routing The technique(s) for selecting a path through a network on which to send traffic between a given set of users.

Slippage In synchronous networks, where all transmission is supposed to be in synchronism with a given clock, slippage occurs if more than one clock is used and the resulting transmission rates on interconnecting links are not identical.

Space-division switching The interconnection of input and output circuits to/from a switch by making a physical cross-connection between them. See Time-Division Switching.

Start-stop transmission See Asynchronous Transmission.

Store-and-forward switching A technique for sending data through a network, in which the data are divided into blocks and each block is completely received (stored) at any node or exchange in the network before being forwarded onwards.

Stored Program Control (SPC) The control of exchanges, particularly telephone exchanges, by programmed computers.

Synchronous transmission Transmission in which devices work in synchronism under control of common clocking. This usually implies isochronous (q.v.) transmission.

Telematic service In CCITT parlance a telematic service is a service for transferring text (in its widest sense) between users over a telecommunications network. The users will normally be supplied by the PTT with special terminal devices for sending and receiving. Examples of telematic services are Facsimile, Teletex and Videotex (q.v.).

Teletex A service for sending and receiving text messages between specialized terminals over (in principle) any suitable network. The Teletex terminals conform to certain character sets, allowing the support of most common languages, and provide extensive format control for laying out the text on a page of paper. The Teletex service has its own protocols (q.v.) and standards.

Telex A public circuit-switched international telegraph network for interconnecting 50 baud terminals, consisting of keyboards and printers, for sending text messages.

Time congestion The proportion of time during which a resource such as a switch, or all the circuits on a trunk line, is fully occupied by traffic.

Time-Division Multiplexing (TDM) The technique(s) of sharing a resource (e.g. a circuit) between several users, apparently simultaneously, by allocating access to that resource in interleaved short periods of time.

Time-Division Switching In the most general case, time-division switching is the time-division multiplexing (q.v.) of a switch. That is, the switch takes a sample from an input line and transfers it to an output line; then addresses another input line, and so on; and repeats the cycle when all lines have been served. The switch must obviously be fast compared with the speed of the lines. A particular case of time-division switching is time-slot-interchanging, in which the switch transfers samples between different time slots in circuits carrying time-division multiplexed channels.

Time-Space-Time (TST) Switching A switching technique in which input traffic passes sequentially through a time-division switch (a time-slot-interchanger) then a space-division switch then another time-division switch, before output.

Token A token is generally a term used to describe a 'right', e.g. the right to transmit, which is exchanged between users of a telecommunications facility to ensure orderly use of the facility and to control the dialogue.

Toll-free (Number) A destination address on a network which may be called without incurring network charges. A toll-free number effectively always accepts reverse-charging, without the need for a request. (The term is from the USA.)

Topology The topology of a network is the pattern of interconnections of links and nodes, without reference to the lengths of the links or the locations of the nodes.

Traffic Strictly, the traffic in a network over a given period is the total holding time of all the calls in that period. The *traffic flow* is the traffic divided by the length of the period and is thus the average holding time multiplied by the call rate. More generally, the term 'traffic' is used as a shorthand for 'information in transit'.

Traffic matrix A square array in which the entry in the ith row jth column gives (typically) the traffic flow from node i to node j in a network.

Trunk (circuit) Trunk circuits are internal links between nodes in a network, but do not connect to user's equipment.

TST-switching See Time-Space-Time Switching.

Videotex A service for providing cheap access by the public to computer-based data banks. The user, typically, has a simple keyboard for the input of commands, coupled to a domestic TV set for displayed output, and accesses the data bank via the telephone network using a basic modem.

Virtual Call, Virtual Circuit (VC) In packet-switched networks, a VC is a 'call', recognized by the network, but which is not circuit-switched. It represents a temporary association between a pair of users, for the purpose of exchanging packets using the store-and-forward technique. The term 'virtual circuit' is perhaps better than 'virtual call', since the call is real enough; it is the circuit which is virtual or imaginary.

Virtual Terminal (VT) A virtual or ideal terminal for which control procedures and protocols (q.v.), such as the *Virtual Terminal Protocol* (VTP) can be defined, so that any computer obeying these procedures may use the VT remotely over a network. In practice a *real* terminal will then have to emulate the VT, if the system is to work.

Window Window mechanisms are flow control mechanisms (q.v.) in which a would-be sender has a 'window', or range of sequential numbers to be attached to his transmitted blocks of data, which he may use. When he has sent sufficient blocks to exhaust his window he may send no more, until some control procedure advances his 'lower window-edge'.

Index